D1278352

5 STEPS TO A 5™

AP English Literature

2020

5 STEPS TO A 5

AP English Literature

2020

Barbara L. Murphy
Estelle M. Rankin

McGraw Hill

New York   Chicago   San Francisco   Athens   London   Madrid
Mexico City   Milan   New Delhi   Singapore   Sydney   Toronto

Copyright © 2020, 2018 by McGraw-Hill Education. All rights reserved. Printed in the United States of America. Except as permitted under the United States Copyright Act of 1976, no part of this publication may be reproduced or distributed in any form or by any means, or stored in a database or retrieval system, without the prior written permission of the publisher.

1 2 3 4 5 6 7 8 9   LHS   24 23 22 21 20 19   (Cross-Platform Prep Course only)
1 2 3 4 5 6 7 8 9   LHS   24 23 22 21 20 19   (Elite Student Edition)

ISBN   978-1-260-45566-3   (Cross-Platform Prep Course only)
MHID   1-260-45566-1

e-ISBN   978-1-260-45567-0   (Cross-Platform Prep Course only)
e-MHID   1-260-45567-X

ISBN   978-1-260-45568-7   (Elite Student Edition)
MHID   1-260-45568-8

e-ISBN   978-1-260-45569-4   (Elite Student Edition)
e-MHID   1-260-45569-6

Trademarks: McGraw-Hill Education, the McGraw-Hill Education logo, *5 Steps to a 5,* and related trade dress are trademarks or registered trademarks of McGraw-Hill Education and/or its affiliates in the United States and other countries and may not be used without written permission. All other trademarks are the property of their respective owners. McGraw-Hill Education is not associated with any product or vendor mentioned in this book.

AP, Advanced Placement Program, and *College Board* are registered trademarks of the College Board, which was not involved in the production of, and does not endorse, this product.

McGraw-Hill Education products are available at special quantity discounts to use as premiums and sales promotions or for use in corporate training programs. To contact a representative, please visit the Contact Us pages at www.mhprofessional.com.

Cross-Platform Prep Course
Single User License Terms and Conditions

Access to the digital content included with this book is governed by the McGraw-Hill Education License Agreement outlined below. By using this digital content you agree to the terms of that license.

DURATION OF LICENSE. Access to the Cross-Platform Prep Course will expire one year from your initial login.

Your purchase of this McGraw-Hill Education product, including its access code through a retail store is subject to the refund policy of that store.

The Content is a copyrighted work of McGraw-Hill Education and McGraw-Hill Education reserves all rights in and to the Content. The Work is © 2020 by McGraw-Hill Education, LLC.

RESTRICTIONS ON TRANSFER. The user is receiving only a limited right to use the Content for user's own internal and personal use, dependent on purchase and continued ownership of this Cross-Platform product. The user may not reproduce, forward, modify, create derivative works based upon, transmit, distribute, disseminate, sell, publish, or sublicense the Content or in any way commingle the Content with other third party content, without McGraw-Hill Education's consent.

LIMITED WARRANTY. The McGraw-Hill Education Content is provided on an "as is" basis. Neither McGraw-Hill Education nor its licensors make any guarantees or warranties of any kind, either express or implied, including, but not limited to, implied warranties of merchantability or fitness for a particular purpose or use as to any McGraw-Hill Education Content or the information therein or any warranties as to the accuracy, completeness, currentness, or results to be obtained from, accessing or suing the McGraw-Hill Education content, or any material referenced in such content or any information entered into licensee's product by users or other persons and/or any material available on or that can be accessed through the licensee's product (including via any hyperlink or otherwise) or as to non-infringement of third party rights. Any warranties of any kind, whether express or implied, are disclaimed. Any material or data obtained through use of the McGraw-Hill Education content is at your own discretion and risk and user understands that it will be solely responsible for any resulting damage to its computer system or loss of data.

Neither McGraw-Hill Education nor its licensors shall be liable to any subscriber or to any user or anyone else for any inaccuracy, delay, interruption in service, error or omission, regardless of cause, or for any damage resulting therefrom.

In no event will McGraw-Hill Education or its licensors be liable for any indirect, special or consequential damages, including but not limited to, lost time, lost money, lost profits or good will, whether in contract, tort, strict liability or otherwise, and whether or not such damages are foreseen or unforeseen with respect to any use of the McGraw-Hill Education content.

CONTENTS

Preface   ix
Acknowledgments   xi
Credits   xii
About the Authors   xiii
Introduction: The Five-Step Program   xv

STEP 1   Set Up Your Study Program

1 **What You Should Know About the AP Literature Exam   3**
Background on the Advanced Placement Exam   4
Reasons for Taking the Advanced Placement Exam   5
What You Need to Know About the AP Lit Exam   5

2 **How to Plan Your Time   9**
Three Approaches to Preparing for the AP Literature Exam   9
Calendars for Preparing for the AP Literature Exam   11

STEP 2   Determine Your Test Readiness

3 **The Diagnostic/Master Exam   17**
A Walk Through the Diagnostic/Master Exam   17
Diagnostic/Master Exam   19
Afterword   28

STEP 3   Develop Strategies for Success

4 **Section I of the Exam: The Multiple-Choice Questions   31**
Introduction to the Multiple-Choice Section of the Exam   31
Types of Multiple-Choice Questions   34
Scoring the Multiple-Choice Section   36
Strategies for Answering the Multiple-Choice Questions   37
Answer Sheet for Diagnostic Multiple-Choice Questions   45
The Multiple-Choice Section of the Diagnostic/Master Exam   47
Answers and Explanations   55

5 **The Prose Passage Essay   59**
Introduction to the Prose Passage Essay   59
Types of Prose Passage Essay Questions   60
Rating the Prose Passage Essay   61
Timing the Essay   61
Working the Prompt   62
Reading and Notating the Prose Passage   63
Writing the Opening Paragraph   67
Writing the Body   69
Sample Student Essays   71
Rating the Student Essays   73
Rapid Review   76

6 The Poetry Essay 77
Introduction to the Poetry Essay 77
Types of Prompts Used for the Poetry Essay 78
Timing and Planning the Poetry Essay 78
Working the Prompt 79
Reading and Notating the Poetry Selection 80
Writing the Opening Paragraph 85
Writing the Body of the Poetry Essay 86
Sample Student Essays 88
Rating the Student Essays 90
Rapid Review 91

7 The Free-Response Essay 93
Introduction to the Free-Response Essay 93
Types of Free-Response Prompts 96
General Rubrics for the Free-Response Essay 97
Timing and Planning the Free-Response Essay 97
Working the Prompt from the Diagnostic/Master Exam 98
Developing the Opening Paragraph 102
Developing the Body of the Essay 103
Sample Student Essays 104
Rating the Student Essays 106
Final Comments 107
Rapid Review 107

STEP 4   Review the Knowledge You Need to Score High

Introduction to Review Section 111

8 Comprehensive Review—Prose 113
Introduction to Prose 113
Five Aspects of Every Narrative 114
Types of Novels 119
Literary Terminology 120
Prose Analysis 122
Final Comments 124
Rapid Review 125

9 Comprehensive Review—Poetry 127
Introduction to Poetry 127
The Structure of Poetry 128
Types of Poetry 130
Interpretation of Poetry 143
Poems for Comparison and Contrast 149
Rapid Review 151

STEP 5   Build Your Test-Taking Confidence

Practice Exam 1 155
Section I 157
Section II 167
Answers to Multiple-Choice Questions 170
Answers and Explanations 171
Rating the Essay Section 173

Sample Student Essays   174
Sample Student Essays   177
Sample Student Essays   179

Practice Exam 2   183
Section I   185
Section II   195
Answers to Multiple-Choice Questions   199
Answers and Explanations   200
Rating the Essay Section   202
Sample Student Essays   209

Appendixes

Suggested Reading Guide   215
Classicism   215
Realism   216
Romanticism   217
Impressionism   218
Expressionism   218
Naturalism   219

General Bibliography   221
Recommended Poets   221
Recommended Authors   221

Glossary   225

Websites   229

Welcome to our latest revised AP Literature class. As we said in the earlier versions of this book, we are first and foremost teachers who have taught Advanced Placement to literally thousands of students who successfully took the AP exam. With this guide, we hope to share with you what we know as well as what we have learned from our own students.

We see you as a student in our class—only quieter! Our philosophy has always been NOT to teach only for the AP test. Instead, our goal has always been to develop those insights, appreciations, and skills that lead to advanced levels of facility with literature and composition. These are the very same skills which will enable you to do well on the AP Literature exam. Our aim is to remove your anxiety and to improve your comfort level with the test. We believe that you are already motivated to succeed; otherwise, you would not have come this far. And, obviously, you would not have purchased this prep book.

Since you are already in an English class, this book is going to supplement your literature course readings, analysis, and writing. We are going to give you the opportunity to practice processes and techniques that we know from experience REALLY WORK! If you apply the techniques and processes presented in this book, we are confident you can succeed in both the course and on the exam.

We have listened to comments and suggestions from both instructors and students of AP English Literature, and keeping their thoughts in mind, this revised text has more interactive activities and practice to help hone those skills needed to do well in class and on the AP Literature exam. In addition, there are special review questions and activities related to specific chapters that McGraw-Hill has available on its website devoted to the *5 Steps* series. There you can test how well you have internalized the material in the chapter.

Let's begin.

ACKNOWLEDGMENTS

Our love and appreciation to Allan and to Leah for their constant support and encouragement. Our very special thanks to our professional mentors who have guided us throughout our careers: Steven Piorkowski and Howard Damon. To the following for their support and suggestions: Diane Antonucci, Richard Andres, Mary Moran, Mike Thier, Mark Misthal, Dave Martin, Edward Stern, and Michael Hartnett—thank you.

The authors wish to acknowledge the participation, insights, and feedback provided us by the following colleagues and students:

Islip High School:
  Teacher: Marge Grossgold
  Students: Caitlin Rizzo and Katelyn Zawyrucha

Jericho High School:
  Teachers: Diane Antonucci, Michael Hartnett
  Students: Tara Arschin, Samantha Brody, Jenna Butner, Julie Ivans, Grace Kwak, Ari Weiss, Erica Ross, David Swidler, and Sherli Yeroushalmi

Massapequa High School:
  Teachers: Sue Bruno and Rosemary Verade
  Student: Margaretta Dimos

Solomon Schechter School:
  Teachers: Dennis Young and Miriam Fischer
  Students: Yadin Duckstein, Ari Lucas, and Jonathan Kotter

Wantagh High School:
  Teachers: Sherry Skolnick and Pat Castellano
  Student: Lauren Manning

Also, our thanks to Danielle Tumminio and Andrew Brotman.

CREDITS

From AS I LAY DYING by William Faulkner, copyright © 1930 and renewed 1958 by William Faulkner. Used by permission of Random House, Inc.

"To David, About His Education," by Howard Nemerov, from VOICES: THE 6th BOOK edited by Geoffrey Summerfield, published by Rand McNally and Company, Chicago, 1969. Used by permission of Margaret Nemerov.

"The Flowers" from IN LOVE & TROUBLE: STORIES OF BLACK WOMEN, copyright © 1973 by Alice Walker. Reprinted by permission of Harcourt, Inc.

"To a Friend Estranged from Me" by Edna St. Vincent Millay. From COLLECTED POEMS, HarperCollins. Copyright © 1928, 1955 by Edna St. Vincent Millay and Norma Millay Ellis. All rights reserved. Reprinted by permission of Elizabeth Barnett, literary executor.

From THE GOLD CELL by Sharon Olds, copyright © 1987 by Sharon Olds. Used by permission of Alfred A. Knopf, a division of Random House, Inc.

"Love Poem" by John Frederick Nims. From SELECTED POEMS BY JOHN F. NIMS, University of Chicago Press. Copyright © 1982 by John F. Nims. Reprinted by permission of Bonnie Larkin Nims.

"The Naked and the Nude," by Robert Graves, from COMPLETE POEMS by Robert Graves. Used by permission of Carcanet Press Limited, Manchester, England. On behalf of the Trustees of the Robert Graves Copyright Trust.

"Snake," from THE COMPLETE POEMS OF D. H. LAWRENCE by D. H. Lawrence, Viking Press, 1964. Used by permission of Laurence Pollinger Limited and the Estate of Frieda Lawrence Ravagli.

"The Writer" from THE MIND-HEALER, copyright © 1971 by Richard Wilbur. Reprinted by permission of Harcourt, Inc.

ABOUT THE AUTHORS

Barbara L. Murphy taught AP Language and other college-level courses at Jericho High School for over 26 years. She has been a reader of the AP Language and Composition exam since 1993 and is a consultant for the College Board's AP Language and Composition and Building for Success divisions, for which she has conducted workshops, conferences, and Summer Institutes. She is currently on the faculty of Syracuse University's Project Advance in English.

After earning her B.A. from Duquesne University and her M.A. from the University of Pittsburgh, Ms. Murphy did her doctoral course work at Columbia University. She also holds professional certifications in still photography and motion picture production and is one of the founding members of the women's film company Ishtar Films.

Estelle M. Rankin taught AP Literature at Jericho High School for over 25 years. She was honored with the AP Literature Teacher of the Year award by the College Board in 1996. She also received the Long Island Teacher of the Year award in 1990. She was the recipient of the Cornell University Presidential Scholars' Award and has been recognized by the C.W. Post Master Teachers Program.

Ms. Rankin earned her B.A. from Adelphi University and her M.A. from Hofstra University. She has pursued further graduate work in the field of creative studies at Queens College and Brooklyn College.

She has done extensive work in the research and development of the film, drama, and creative writing curriculum, SAT prep, and the new NYS Regents benchmarks for English, and has participated in numerous AP Literature conferences and workshops. Ms. Rankin is currently a College Board consultant for pre-AP and AP English. Her finest teachers were her parents, Edward and Sylvia Stern.

Ms. Murphy and Ms. Rankin are also the coauthors of McGraw-Hill's *5 Steps to a 5: AP English Language, Writing the AP English Essay,* and *Writing an Outstanding College Application Essay.*

INTRODUCTION: THE FIVE-STEP PROGRAM

Some Basics

Consider this section as a map of the new territory you are going to explore. We will provide the general directions, and you can decide when, where, and how you will follow this map.

Reading

We believe that reading should be an exciting interaction between you and the writer. You have to bring your own context to the experience, and you must feel comfortable reaching for and exploring ideas. You are an adventurer on a journey of exploration, and we will act as your guides. We will set the itinerary, but you will set your own pace. You can feel free to "stop and smell the roses" or to explore new territory.

The Journey

On any journey, each traveler sees something different on new horizons. So, too, each student is free to personalize his or her own literary experience, provided he or she tries at all times to strive for excellence and accuracy.

Critical Thinking

There are no tricks to critical thinking. Those who claim to guarantee you a score of 5 with gimmicks are doing you a disservice. No one can guarantee a 5; however, the reading and writing skills you will review, practice, and master will give you the very best chance to do your very best. You will have the opportunity to learn, to practice, and to master the critical thinking processes that can empower you to achieve your highest score.

The Beginning

It is our belief that if you focus on the beginning, the rest will fall into place. Once you purchase this book and decide to work your way through it, you are beginning your journey to the AP Literature exam. We will be with you every step of the way.

Why This Book?

We believe we have something unique to offer you. For over 25 years we have addressed the needs of AP students just like you. And we've been fortunate to learn from these students. Therefore, the content of this book reflects genuine student concerns and needs. **This is a student-oriented book**. We will not overwhelm you with pompous language, mislead you with inaccurate information and tasks, or lull you into a false sense of confidence with easy shortcuts. We stand behind every suggestion, process, and question we present. There is no "busywork" in this book.

We know you will not do every activity. Therefore, think of this book as a resource and guide to accompany you on your AP Literature journey to the exam. This book is designed to serve many purposes. It will:

- Clarify requirements for the AP English Literature exam.
- Provide you with test practice.
- Show you rubrics (grading standards) on which you can model and evaluate your own work.
- Anticipate and answer your questions.
- Enrich your understanding and appreciation of literature.
- Help you pace yourself.
- Make you aware of the Five Steps to Mastering the AP English Literature exam.

Organization of the Book

We know that your primary concern is to obtain information about the AP Literature exam. So, we begin at the beginning with an overview of the AP exam in general. We then introduce you to our Diagnostic/Master exam, which we use throughout the book to show you the ins and outs of an AP Literature test. In separate chapters you will become familiar with both sections of the exam. We will lead you through the multiple-choice questions and explain how you should answer them. Then we will take you through the essay questions and discuss approaches to writing these essays.

Because you must be fluent in the language and processes of literary analysis and composition, we provide a Comprehensive Review section in both prose and poetry. This review is not a mere listing of terms and concepts. Rather, it is a series of practices that will hone your analytical and writing skills. But, do not fear. You will find terms and concepts clearly delineated within their contexts. We also provide annotated suggestions for high-interest prose and poetry readings.

A separate section of the book contains practice exams. Here is where you will test your skills and knowledge. You may be sure that the prose and poetry selections included in each exam are on the AP level. The multiple-choice questions provide you with practice in responding to typical types of questions asked in past AP exams. The essay questions are designed to cover the techniques and terms required by the AP exam. The free-response essays are both challenging and specific, yet they are broad enough to suit all curricula. After taking each test, you can check yourself against the explanations of every multiple-choice question and the ratings of the sample student essays.

The final section is one that you should not pass over. It presents a Suggested Reading Guide, a General Bibliography, a Glossary of Terms that may be of importance to you, and a list of websites related to the AP Literature exam.

Introduction to the Five-Step Preparation Program

The **Five-Step Program** is a powerful program designed to provide you with the best possible skills, strategies, and practice to help lead you to that perfect 5 on the Advanced Placement English Literature exam that is administered each May to more than 350,000 high school students. Each of the five steps will provide you with the opportunity to get closer and closer to the 5, which is the gold medal to all AP students.

Step 1: Set Up Your Study Program

- Useful information about the Advanced Placement program and exams
- Three alternative study schedules and advice for determining which is best for you

Step 2: Determine Your Test Readiness

- A first look at the overall exam, to be repeated in greater detail later

Step 3: Develop Strategies for Success

- Learn about the test itself
- Learn to read multiple-choice questions
- Learn how to answer multiple-choice questions, including whether or not to guess
- Learn how to deconstruct the essay prompts
- Learn how to plan the essay

Step 4: Review the Knowledge You Need to Score High

- Practice activities that will hone your skills in close reading
- Practice activities in critical thinking
- Practice activities in critical/analytical writing

Step 5: Build Your Test-Taking Confidence

- Two practice exams that test how well honed your skills are
- Rubrics for self-evaluation

Finally, at the back of the book you'll find additional resources to aid your preparation. These include:

- A comprehensive review of literary analysis
- A glossary of terms
- A bibliography for further reading
- A list of websites related to the AP English Literature exam

The Graphics Used in This Book

To emphasize particular skills and strategies, we use several icons throughout this book. An icon in the margin will alert you that you should pay particular attention to the accompanying text. We use three icons:

 This icon points out a very important concept or fact that you should not pass over.

 This icon calls your attention to a problem-solving strategy that you may want to try.

 This icon indicates a tip that you might find useful.

Boldfaced and *italicized* words indicate important terms as well as those that are included in the Glossary at the back of the book.

Throughout the book you will find margin notes and boxes. We want you to pay close attention to these areas because they can provide tips, hints, strategies, and explanations that will help you reach your full potential.

5 STEPS TO A 5™

AP English Literature

2020

STEP **1**

Set Up Your Study Program

CHAPTER **1**   What You Should Know About the AP Literature Exam
CHAPTER **2**   How to Plan Your Time

CHAPTER 1

What You Should Know About the AP Literature Exam

IN THIS CHAPTER

Summary: Information about the AP English Literature and Composition exam and its scoring

Key Ideas

✪ Learn answers to frequently asked questions
✪ Learn how your final score is calculated
✪ Learn tips for successfully taking the exam

The College Board has introduced changes to the AP English Literature exam that will be reflected in the next exam.

You should be aware of the following:

    The rating of the exam will remain 1, 2, 3, 4, 5.

    Multiple choice will comprise 45% of the final score, with the essay section of the exam comprising 55%.

- There are <u>**no changes**</u> to MC questions.
- There are <u>**no changes**</u> to the types of prompts (FRQ): poetry + prose + free response
- There is <u>**renewed emphasis**</u> on skills development in consideration of prose + poetry + longer works

> - **The <u>MAJOR CHANGE</u> is in the method of rating essays**
>   - From holistic to analytic
>   - **From 9 points to 6 points**
>   - 6 points
>   - ✓ 1 point for thesis/claim
>   - ✓ 4 points for appropriate evidence and commentary
>   - ✓ 1 point for syntax and complexity

Background on the Advanced Placement Exam

"AP" does not stand for "Always Puzzling." The following should help lift the veil of mystery associated with the AP exam.

What Is the Advanced Placement Program?

The Advanced Placement program was begun by the College Board in 1955 to construct standard achievement exams that would allow highly motivated high school students the opportunity to be awarded advanced placement as freshmen in colleges and universities in the United States. Today, there are more than 39 courses and exams with over 2.7 million students from every state in the nation, and from foreign countries, taking the annual exams in May.

As is obvious, the AP programs are designed for high school students who wish to take college-level courses. The AP Literature course and exam are designed to involve high school students in college-level English studies in both literature and composition.

Who Writes the AP Literature Exam?

According to the folks at the College Board, the AP Literature exam is created by college and high school English instructors called the AP Development Committee. The committee's job is to ensure that the annual AP Literature exam reflects what is being taught and studied in college-level English classes in high schools.

This committee writes a large number of multiple-choice questions that are pretested and evaluated for clarity, appropriateness, and a range of possible answers. The committee also generates a pool of essay questions, pretests them, and chooses those questions that best represent the full range of the scoring scale to allow the AP readers to evaluate the essays fairly.

It is important to remember that the AP Literature exam is thoroughly evaluated after it is administered each year. This way, the College Board can use the results to make course suggestions and to plan future tests.

What Are the Advanced Placement Scores, and Who Receives Them?

Once you have taken the exam and it has been scored, your test will be assigned one of five numbers by the College Board:

- 5 indicates you are extremely well qualified.
- 4 indicates you are well qualified.
- 3 indicates you are qualified.
- 2 indicates you are possibly qualified.
- 1 indicates you are not qualified to receive college credit.

A score of 5, 4, 3, 2, or 1 will be reported to your college or university first, to your high school second, and to you third. All this reporting is usually completed by the middle to end of July.

Reasons for Taking the Advanced Placement Exam

At some point during the year, every AP student asks the ultimate question: Why am I taking this exam?

Good question. Why put yourself through a year of intensive study, pressure, stress, and preparation? To be honest, only you can answer that question. Over the years, our students have indicated to us that there are several prime reasons why they were willing to take the risk and to put in the effort:

- For personal satisfaction
- To compare themselves with other students across the nation
- Because colleges look favorably on the applications of students who elect to enroll in AP courses
- To receive college credit or advanced standing at their colleges or universities
- Because they love the subject
- So that their families will really be proud of them

There are plenty of other reasons, but no matter what the other reasons might be, the top reason for your enrolling in the AP Lit course and taking the exam in May should be to feel good about yourself and the challenges you have met.

What You Need to Know About the AP Lit Exam

Let's answer a few of the nitty-gritty questions about the exam and its scoring.

If I Don't Take an AP Lit Course, Can I Still Take the AP Lit Exam?

Yes. Even though the AP Lit exam is designed for the student who has had a year's course in AP Literature, there are high schools that do not offer this type of course, yet there are students in these high schools who have also done well on the exam. However, if your high school does offer an AP Lit course, by all means take advantage of it and the structured background it will provide you.

How Is the Advanced Placement Literature Exam Organized?

The exam has two parts and is scheduled to last 3 hours. The first section is a set of multiple-choice questions based on a series of prose passages and poems. You will have 1 hour to complete this part of the test. The second section of the exam is a 2-hour essay-writing segment consisting of three different essays: one on prose, one on poetry, and one free-response based on a major work of literary complexity.

After you complete the multiple-choice section and hand in your test booklet and scan sheet, you will be given a brief break. Note that you will not be able to return to the multiple-choice questions when you return to the examination room.

Must I Check the Box at the End of the Essay Booklet That Allows the AP People to Use My Essays as Samples for Research?

No. This is simply a way for the College Board to make certain that it has your permission if it decides to use one or more of your essays as a model. Checking the box will not affect your grade.

How Is My AP Lit Exam Scored?

Let's look at the basics first. The multiple-choice section counts for 45 percent of your total score, and the essay section counts for 55 percent. Next comes a four-part calculation: the raw scoring of the multiple-choice section, the raw scoring of the essay section, the calculation of the composite score, and the conversion of the composite score into the AP grade of 5, 4, 3, 2, or 1.

How Is the Multiple-Choice Section Scored?

The scan sheet with your answers is run through a computer that counts the number of correct answers. Questions left blank and questions answered incorrectly are treated the same and get no points. There is no longer a "guessing penalty," which formerly involved the deduction of a fraction of a point for answering a question but getting it wrong.

How Is My Essay Section Scored?

Each of your essays is read by a different, trained AP reader. The AP/College Board people have developed a highly successful training program for these readers. This factor, together with many opportunities for checks and double checks of essays, ensures a fair and equitable reading of each essay.

The scoring guides are carefully developed by a chief faculty consultant, a question leader, table leaders, and content experts. All faculty consultants are then trained to read and score just *one* essay question on the exam. They actually become experts in that one essay question. No one knows the identity of any writer. The identification numbers and names are covered, and the exam booklets are randomly distributed to the readers in packets of 25 randomly chosen essays. Table leaders and the question leader review samples of each reader's scores to ensure that quality standards are consistent.

Each essay is scored as 6, 5, 4, 3, 2, 1, plus 0, with 6 the highest possible score. Once your essay is given a number from 6 to 1, the next set of calculations is completed using a formula developed to account for the score of each essay. This is the raw score for the essay section of the exam.

$$(\text{pts.} \times 3.055) + (\text{pts.} \times 3.055) + (\text{pts.} \times 3.055) = \text{essay raw score}$$
$$\text{Essay 1} \qquad\qquad \text{Essay 2} \qquad\qquad \text{Essay 3}$$

How Is My Composite Score Calculated?

The total composite score for the AP Lit test is 150. Of this score, 55 percent is the essay section; that equals 82.5 points. The multiple-choice section is 45 percent of the composite score, which equals 67.5 points. Each of your three essays is graded on a 6-point scale; therefore, each point is worth 4.58. Divide the number of multiple-choice questions by 67.5.

If you add together the raw scores of each of the two sections, you will have a composite score.

"Over the years, in comparison to students who fight the material, I've found students who receive the 4s and 5s are those who truly allow themselves to relate to the literature covered in the class."
—Pat K.
   AP teacher

How Is My Composite Data Turned into the Score That Is Reported to My College?

Keep in mind that the total composite scores needed to earn a 5, 4, 3, 2, or 1 are different each year. This is determined by a committee of AP/College Board/Educational Testing Service directors, experts, and statisticians. The score is based on items such as:

- AP distribution over the past three years
- Comparability studies
- Observations of the chief faculty consultant
- Frequency distributions of scores on each section and the essays
- Average scores on each exam section and essays

However, over the years a trend is apparent which indicates the number of points required to achieve a specific score:

- 150–100 points = 5
- 99–86 = 4
- 85–67 = 3

Scores of 2 and 1 fall below this range. You do not want to go there.

What Should I Bring to the Exam?

You should bring:

- Several pencils with erasers
- Several *black* pens (black ink is easier to read than other colors)
- A watch
- Something to drink—water is best
- A quiet snack
- Tissues

Is There Anything Else I Should Be Aware Of?

You should be aware of the following:

- Allow plenty of time to get to the test site.
- Wear comfortable clothing.
- Eat a light breakfast or lunch.
- Remind yourself that you are well prepared and that the test is an enjoyable challenge and a chance to share your knowledge. Be proud of yourself! You worked hard all year. Now is your time to shine.

Is There Anything Special I Should Do the Night Before the Exam?

We certainly don't advocate last-minute cramming. If you've been following the guidelines, you won't have to cram. But there may be a slight value to some last-minute review. Spend the night before the exam relaxing with family or friends. Watch a movie; play a game; gab on the phone, blog, or Twitter. Then find a quiet spot. While you're unwinding, flip through your own notebook and review sheets. Recall some details from the full-length works you've prepared and think of your favorite scenes. By now, you're bound to be ready to drift off. Pleasant dreams.

CHAPTER 2

How to Plan Your Time

IN THIS CHAPTER

Summary: Assess your own study patterns and preparation plans.

Key Ideas
- ✪ Explore three approaches
- ✪ Choose a calendar that works for you

Three Approaches to Preparing for the AP Literature Exam

No one knows your study habits, likes, and dislikes better than you do. So you are the only one who can decide which approach you want and/or need to adopt to prepare for the Advanced Placement Literature exam. Look at the brief profiles below. These may help you to place yourself in a particular prep mode.

You're a full-year prep student (Approach A) **if:**

1. You're the kind of person who likes to plan for a vacation or the prom a year in advance.

2. You'd never think of missing a practice session, whether it's your favorite sport, musical instrument, or activity.

3. You like detailed planning and everything in its place.

4. You feel you must be thoroughly prepared.

5. You hate surprises.

6. You're always early for appointments.

You're a one-semester prep student (Approach B) **if:**

1. You begin to plan for your vacation or the prom 4–5 months before the event.

2. You are willing to plan ahead so that you will feel comfortable in stressful situations, but you are okay with skipping some details.

3. You feel more comfortable when you know what to expect, but a surprise or two does not floor you.

4. You're always on time for appointments.

You're a 4–6 week prep student (Approach C) **if:**

1. You accept or find a date for the prom a week before the big day.

2. You work best under pressure and tight deadlines.

3. You feel very confident with the skills and background you've gained in your AP Literature class.

4. You decided late in the year to take the exam.

5. You like surprises.

6. You feel okay if you arrive 10–15 minutes late for an appointment.

CALENDARS FOR PREPARING FOR THE AP LITERATURE EXAM

This is a personal journey, and each of you will have particular time constraints. Choose the calendar that will work best for you.

Calendar for Approach A: Yearlong Preparation for the AP Literature Exam

Although its primary purpose is to prepare you for the AP Literature exam you will take in May, this book can enrich your study of literature, your analytical skills, and your writing skills.

SEPTEMBER–OCTOBER (Check off the activities as you complete them.)

_____ Determine the student mode into which you place yourself.

_____ Carefully read Chapters 1 and 2.

_____ Pay close attention to the walk through the Diagnostic/Master exam.

_____ Take a close look at the AP Central website(s).

_____ Skim the Comprehensive Review section.

_____ Buy a highlighter.

_____ Flip through the entire book. Break in the book. Write in it. Highlight it.

_____ Get a clear picture of what your own school's AP Literature curriculum is.

_____ Review the Bibliography and establish a pattern of outside reading in the literary genres (pp. 221–223).

_____ Begin to use the book as a resource.

NOVEMBER (The first 10 weeks have elapsed.)

_____ Write the free-response essay in the Diagnostic/Master exam.

_____ Compare your essay with the sample student essays.

_____ Refer to the section on the free-response essay.

_____ Take five of our prompts and write solid opening paragraphs.

DECEMBER

_____ Maintain notes on literary works you studied in and out of class.

_____ Refine your analytical skills.

_____ Write the prose passage or poetry essay in the Diagnostic/Master exam. (This will depend on the organization of your own curriculum.)

_____ Compare your essay with sample student essays.

JANUARY (20 weeks have elapsed.)

_____ Write the third essay in the Diagnostic/Master exam. (This will depend on the one you did previously.)

_____ Compare your essay with sample student essays.

FEBRUARY

_____ Take the multiple-choice section of the Diagnostic/Master exam.

_____ Carefully go over the explanations of the answers to the questions.

_____ Score yourself honestly.

_____ Make a note of terms, concepts, and types of questions that give you difficulty.

_____ Review troublesome terms in the Glossary.

MARCH (30 weeks have elapsed.)

_____ Form a study group.

_____ Outline or create a chart for full-length works that would be appropriate for the free-response essay.

_____ Choose a favorite poem and create an essay question to go with it, or use one of our suggested prompts.

_____ Choose a prose passage or essay and create an essay question to go with it, or choose one of our suggested prompts.

_____ Write the poetry essay.

_____ Write the prose essay.

_____ Compare essays and rate them with your study group. (Use our rubrics.)

APRIL

_____ Take Practice Test 1 in the first week of April.

_____ Evaluate your strengths and weaknesses.

_____ Study appropriate chapters to correct your weaknesses.

_____ Practice creating multiple-choice questions of different types with your study group.

_____ Develop and review worksheets for and with your study group.

MAY—First 2 Weeks (THIS IS IT!)

_____ Highlight only those things in the Glossary you are still unsure of. Ask your teacher for clarification. Study!

_____ Thoroughly prepare three to five complete, full-length works; include several quotations that you can work into various responses.

_____ Write at least three times a week under timed conditions.

_____ Take Practice Test 2.

_____ Score yourself.

_____ Give yourself a pat on the back for how much you have learned and improved over the past 9 months.

_____ Go to the movies. Call a friend.

_____ Get a good night's sleep. Fall asleep knowing you are well prepared.

GOOD LUCK ON THE TEST.

Calendar for Approach B:
Semester-Long Preparation for the AP Literature Exam

Working under the assumption that you've completed one semester of literature studies, apply those skills you've learned to prepare for the May exam.

You have plenty of time to supplement your course work by taking our study recommendations, maintaining literary notations, doing outside readings, and so on.

We divide the next 16 weeks into a workable program of preparation for you.

JANUARY–FEBRUARY (Check off the activities as you complete them.)

_____ Carefully read Chapters 1 and 2.

_____ Write the three essays in the Diagnostic/Master exam.

_____ Compare your essays with the sample student essays.

_____ Complete the multiple-choice section of the Diagnostic/Master exam.

_____ Carefully go over the answers and explanations of the answers.

_____ Take a close look at the Bibliography for suggestions on possible outside readings.

MARCH (10 weeks to go.)

_____ Form a study group.

_____ Outline or create a chart for full-length works that would be appropriate for the free-response essay.

_____ Choose a favorite poem and create an essay question to go with it, or use one of our suggested prompts.

_____ Choose a prose passage or essay and create an essay question to go with it, or choose one of our suggested prompts.

_____ Write the poetry essay.

_____ Write the prose essay.

_____ Compare essays and rate them with your study group. (Use our rubrics.)

APRIL

_____ Take Practice Test 1 in the first week of April.

_____ Evaluate your strengths and weaknesses.

_____ Study appropriate chapters to correct your weaknesses.

_____ Practice creating multiple-choice questions of different types with your study group.

_____ Develop and review worksheets for and with your study group.

MAY First 2 Weeks (THIS IS IT!)

_____ Highlight only those things in the Glossary you are still unsure of. Ask your teacher for clarification. Study!

_____ Thoroughly prepare at least three to five complete, full-length works; include several quotations that you can work into various questions.

_____ Write at least three times a week under timed conditions.

_____ Take Practice Test 2.

_____ Score yourself.

_____ Give yourself a pat on the back for how much you have learned and improved over the past 9 months.

_____ Go to the movies. Call a friend.

_____ Get a good night's sleep. Fall asleep knowing you are well prepared.

GOOD LUCK ON THE TEST.

"One of the first steps to success on the AP exam is knowing your own study habits."
—Margaret R.
  AP English
  teacher

Calendar for Approach C:
4–6 Week Preparation for the AP Literature Exam

At this point, we are going to assume that you have been developing your literary, analytical, and writing skills in your English class for more than 6 months. You will, therefore, use this book primarily as a specific guide to the AP Literature exam.

Remember, there is a solid review section in this text to which you should refer.

Given the time constraints, now is not the time to try to expand your AP Literature background. Rather, it is the time to limit and refine what you already know.

APRIL

_____ Skim through Chapters 1 and 2.

_____ Carefully go over the "rapid reviews."

_____ Strengthen, clarify, and correct areas you are weak in after taking the Diagnostic/Master exam.

_____ Write a minimum of three sample opening paragraphs for each of the three types of essays.

_____ Write a minimum of two timed essays for each type of essay on the exam.

_____ Complete Practice Test 1.

_____ Score yourself and analyze your errors.

_____ Refer to appropriate chapters to correct your weaknesses.

_____ Refer to the Bibliography.

_____ If you feel unfamiliar with specific poetic forms, refer to the list of suggested, appropriate works.

_____ Create review sheets for three to five solid, full-length works.

_____ Skim and highlight the Glossary.

_____ Develop a weekly study group to hear each other's essays and to discuss literature.

MAY—First 2 Weeks (THIS IS IT!)

_____ Complete Practice Test 2.

_____ Score yourself and analyze your errors.

_____ Refer to appropriate chapters to correct your weaknesses.

_____ Go to the movies. Call a friend.

_____ Get a good night's sleep. Fall asleep knowing you are well prepared.

GOOD LUCK ON THE TEST.

STEP 2

Determine Your Test Readiness

CHAPTER **3** The Diagnostic/Master Exam

CHAPTER 3

The Diagnostic/Master Exam

IN THIS CHAPTER

Summary: Put yourself to the test with the diagnostic exam.

Key Ideas
- ❂ Peruse the multiple-choice section in Section I of the exam
- ❂ Familiarize yourself with the essays in Section II

KEY IDEA

A Walk Through the Diagnostic/Master Exam

"You know, from my experience with AP exams, I've learned never to assume anything."
—Jeremy G.
  AP student

This chapter presents our version of an Advanced Placement Literature and Composition exam which we use throughout this book to demonstrate processes, examples, terms, and so on. We call this the Diagnostic/Master exam. You will not be taking this exam at this point, but we would like you to "walk through" the exam with us now.

The first part of this 3-hour exam is always the multiple-choice section, which lasts 1 hour. It is related to both prose passages and poetry. The multiple-choice section of the Diagnostic/Master exam contains two prose passages from different time periods and of different styles. It also has two poems from different time periods and of different forms. The multiple-choice questions for each selection were developed to provide you with a wide range of question types and terminology that have been used in the actual AP Lit exams over the years.

To begin to know what the exam looks like, take some time to look through the multiple-choice section of the Diagnostic/Master exam. Do not try to answer the questions; just peruse the types of passages and questions.

- Take a turn through all of the pages of the test and familiarize yourself with the format.
- See where the longer and shorter readings are.
- See how many prose and poetry passages there are.

- Check the total number of questions and know what you are facing.
- Check out the essay prompts.

A Word About Our Sample Student Essays

We field-tested each of the essay questions in a variety of high schools, both public and private. We could have chosen to present essays that would have "knocked your socks off," but we chose to present samples that are truly representative of the essays usually written within the time constraints of the exam.

These essays are indicative of a wide range of styles and levels of acceptability. We want you to recognize that there is not one model to which all essays must conform.

"To Thine Own Self Be True" (Polonius—*Hamlet*)

"Be true to yourself" is always the best advice and is especially appropriate for a writer. Listen to your teacher's advice; listen to our advice; **listen to your own voice**. Yours is the voice we want to "hear" in your writing. Use natural vocabulary and present honest observations. It is wonderful to read professional criticism, but you cannot adopt someone else's ideas and remain true to your own thoughts. Trust your brain—if you've prepared well, you'll do well.

DIAGNOSTIC/MASTER EXAM

Advanced Placement Literature and Composition

Section I

Total time—1 hour

Carefully read the following passages and answer the questions that come after them.
Questions 1–10 are based on the next passage.

Now Goes Under . . .
by Edna St. Vincent Millay

Now goes under, and I watch it go under, the sun
    That will not rise again.
Today has seen the setting, in your eyes cold
    and senseless as the sea,
Of friendship better than bread, and of bright charity   5
That lifts a man a little above the beasts that run.

That this could be!
That I should live to see
Most vulgar Pride, that stale obstreperous clown,
So fitted out with purple robe and crown   10
To stand among his betters! Face to face
With outraged me in this once holy place,
Where Wisdom was a favoured guest and hunted
Truth was harboured out of danger,
He bulks enthroned, a lewd, and insupportable stranger!   15

I would have sworn, indeed I swore it:
The hills may shift, the waters may decline,
Winter may twist the stem from the twig that bore it,
But never your love from me, your hand from mine.

Now goes under the sun, and I watch it go under.   20
Farewell, sweet light, great wonder!
You, too, farewell—but fare not well enough to dream
You have done wisely to invite the night before the darkness came.

1. The poem is an example of a(n)
  A. sonnet
  B. lyric
  C. ode
  D. ballad
  E. dramatic monologue

2. The setting of the sun is a symbol for
  A. the beginning of winter
  B. encountering danger
  C. the end of a relationship
  D. facing death
  E. the onset of night

3. The second stanza is developed primarily by
   A. metaphor
   B. simile
   C. personification
   D. hyperbole
   E. allusion

4. "He" in line 15 refers to
   A. Wisdom
   B. Truth
   C. I
   D. Pride
   E. charity

5. According to the speaker, what separates man from beast?
   A. love
   B. friendship
   C. charity
   D. truth
   E. wisdom

6. For the speaker, the relationship has been all of the following *except*
   A. honest
   B. dangerous
   C. spiritual
   D. ephemeral
   E. nourishing

7. The reader can infer from the play on words in the last stanza that the speaker is
   A. dying
   B. frantic
   C. wistful
   D. bitter
   E. capricious

8. "This once holy place" (line 12) refers to
   A. the sunset
   B. the relationship
   C. the sea
   D. the circus
   E. the Church

9. The cause of the relationship's situation is
   A. a stranger coming between them
   B. the lover not taking the relationship seriously
   C. the lover feeling intellectually superior
   D. the lover's pride coming between them
   E. the lover being insensitive

10. The speaker acknowledges the finality of the relationship in line(s)
   A. 1–2
   B. 7
   C. 8
   D. 16
   E. 18–19

Questions 11–23 are based on the following passage.

The sea-reach of the Thames stretched before us like the beginning of an
interminable waterway. The air was dark above Gravesend, and farther back still
seemed condensed into a mournful gloom, brooding motionless over the biggest and
the greatest town on earth.

   "I was thinking of very old times, when the Romans first came here, nineteen   5
hundred years ago—the other day . . . Light came out of this river since—you say knights?
Yes; but it is like a running blaze on a plain, like a flash of lightning in the clouds. We live
in the flicker—may it last as long as the old earth keeps rolling! But darkness was here
yesterday. Imagine the feelings of a commander of a fine—what d'ye call 'em?—trireme
in the Mediterranean, ordered suddenly to the north; run overland across the Gauls in a   10
hurry; put in charge of one of these craft the legionnaires—a wonderful lot of handy men
they must have been, too—used to build, apparently by the hundred, in a month or two, if
we may believe what we read. Imagine him here—the very end of the world, a sea the color
of lead, a sky the color of smoke, a kind of ship about as rigid as a concertina—and going
up this river with stores, or orders, or what you like. Sandbanks, marshes, forests, savages—   15
precious little to eat for a civilized man, nothing but Thames water to drink. No Falernian

wine here, no going ashore. Here and there a military camp lost in a wilderness, like a needle in a bundle of hay—cold, fog, tempests, disease, exile, and death—death skulking in the air, in the water, in the bush. They must have been dying like flies here. Oh yes—he did it. Did it very well, too, no doubt, and without thinking much about it either, except afterwards to brag of what he had gone through in his time, perhaps. They were men enough to face darkness. And perhaps he was cheered by keeping his eye on a chance of promotion to the fleet at Ravenna by and by, if he had good friends in Rome and survived the awful climate. Or think of a decent young citizen in a toga—perhaps too much dice, you know— coming out here in the train of some prefect, or tax-gatherer, or trader even, to mend his fortunes. Land in a swamp, march through the woods, and in some inland post feel the savagery, the utter savagery, had closed round him—all that mysterious life of the wilderness that stirs in the forest, in the jungles, in the hearts of wild men. There's no initiation either into such mysteries. He has to live in the midst of the incomprehensible, which is also detestable. And it has a fascination, too, that goes to work upon him. The fascination of the abomination—you know, imagine the growing regrets, the longing to escape, the powerless disgust, the surrender, the hate."

    He paused.

    "Mind," he began again, lifting one arm from the elbow, the palm of the hand outwards, so that, with his legs folded before him, he had the pose of a Buddha preaching in European clothes and without a lotus flower—"Mind, none of us would feel exactly like this. What saves us is efficiency—the devotion to efficiency. But these chaps were not much account, really. They were no colonists; their administration was merely a squeeze, and nothing more, I suspect. They were conquerors, and for that you want only brute force— nothing to boast of, when you have it, since your strength is just an accident arising from the weakness of others. They grabbed what they could get for the sake of what was to be got. It was just robbery with violence, aggravated murder on a great scale, and men going at it blind— as is very proper for those who tackle a darkness. The conquest of the earth, which mostly means taking it away from those who have a different complexion or slightly flatter noses than ourselves, is not a pretty thing when you look at it too much. What redeems it is the idea only. An idea at the back of it; not a sentimental pretense but an idea; and an unselfish belief in the idea—something you can set up, and bow down before, and offer a sacrifice to . . . "

11. In the passage, *darkness* implies all of the following *except*
    A. the unknown
    B. savagery
    C. ignorance
    D. death
    E. exploration

12. The setting of the passage is
    A. Africa
    B. Ancient Rome
    C. the Thames River
    D. the Mediterranean
    E. Italy

13. The tone of the passage is
    A. condescending
    B. indignant
    C. scornful
    D. pensive
    E. laudatory

14. Later events may be foreshadowed by all of the following phrases *except*
    A. "Imagine the feelings of a commander . . . "
    B. ". . . live in the midst of the incomprehensible . . . "
    C. ". . . in some inland post feel the savagery . . . "
    D. "They must have been dying like flies here."
    E. ". . . the very end of the world . . . "

15. The narrator draws a parallel between
   A. light and dark
   B. past and present
   C. life and death
   D. fascination and abomination
   E. decency and savagery

16. In this passage, "We live in the flicker . . ." (lines 7–8) may be interpreted to mean *ALL* of the following *EXCEPT*
   A. In the history of the world, humanity's span on earth is brief.
   B. Future civilizations will learn from only a portion of the past.
   C. Periods of enlightenment and vision appear only briefly.
   D. The river has been the source of life throughout the ages.
   E. A moment of present-day insight about conquest.

17. One may conclude from the passage that the speaker
   A. admires adventurers
   B. longs to be a crusader
   C. is a former military officer
   D. recognizes and accepts the presence of evil in human experience
   E. is prejudiced

18. In the context of the passage, which of the following phrases presents a paradox?
   A. "The fascination of the abomination . . ."
   B. ". . . in the hearts of wild men"
   C. "There's no initiation . . . into such mysteries"
   D. ". . . a flash of lightning in the clouds"
   E. ". . . death skulking in the air . . ."

19. The lines "Imagine him here . . . concertina . . ." (lines 13–14) contain examples of
   A. hyperbole and personification
   B. irony and metaphor
   C. alliteration and personification
   D. parallel structure and simile
   E. allusion and simile

20. According to the speaker, the one trait which saves Europeans from savagery is
   A. sentiment
   B. a sense of mystery
   C. brute force
   D. religious zeal
   E. efficiency

21. According to the speaker, the only justification for conquest is
   A. the "weakness of others"
   B. it's being "proper for those who tackle a darkness . . ."
   C. their grabbing "what they could get for the sake of what was to be got"
   D. ". . . an unselfish belief in the idea . . ."
   E. "The fascination of the abomination"

22. In the statement by the speaker, "Mind, none of us would feel exactly like this" (line 36), "this" refers to
   A. ". . . a Buddha preaching in European clothes . . ." (lines 35–36)
   B. ". . . imagine the growing regrets . . . the hate." (lines 31–32)
   C. "What redeems it is the idea only." (lines 45–46)
   D. ". . . think of a decent young citizen in a toga . . ." (line 24)
   E. "I was thinking of very old times . . ." (line 5)

23. The speaker presents all of the following reasons for exploration and conquest *except*
   A. military expeditions
   B. ". . . a chance of promotion"
   C. ". . . to mend his fortunes . . ."
   D. religious commitment
   E. punishment for a crime

Questions 24–35 are based on the following poem.

>That time of year thou mayst in me behold
>When yellow leaves, or none, or few, do hang
>Upon those boughs which shake against the cold,
>Bare ruin'd choirs, where late the sweet birds sang.
>In me thou see'st the twilight of such day   5
>As after sunset fadeth in the west;
>Which by and by black night doth take away,
>Death's second self, that seals up all in rest.
>In me thou see'st the glowing of such fire,
>That on the ashes of his youth doth lie,   10
>As the deathbed whereon it must expire,
>Consum'd with that which it was nourish'd by.
>This thou perceiv'st, which makes thy love more strong,
>To love that well which thou must leave ere long.

24. "That time of year" (line 1) refers to
A. youth
B. old age
C. childhood
D. senility
E. maturity

25. "Death's second self" (line 8) refers to
A. "That time of year"
B. "sunset fadeth"
C. "the west"
D. "ruin'd choirs"
E. "black night"

26. Line 12 is an example of
A. paradox
B. caesura
C. parable
D. hyperbole
E. metonymy

27. "Twilight of such day" (line 5) is supported by all of the following images *except*
A. "sunset fadeth"
B. "the glowing of such fire"
C. "west"
D. "Death's second self"
E. "ashes of his youth"

28. "This thou perceiv'st" (line 13) refers to
A. the beloved's deathbed
B. the sorrow of unrequited love
C. the passion of youth expiring
D. the beloved's acknowledgment of the speaker's mortality
E. the speaker sending the lover away

29. The poem is an example of a(n)
A. elegy
B. Spenserian sonnet
C. Petrarchan sonnet
D. Shakespearean sonnet
E. sestina

30. The poem is primarily developed by means of
A. metaphor
B. argument
C. synecdoche
D. alternative choices
E. contradiction

31. The irony of the poem is best expressed in line
A. 5
B. 7
C. 10
D. 11
E. 12

32. "It" in line 12 can best be interpreted to mean
   A. a funeral pyre
   B. spent youth
   C. the intensity of the speaker's love
   D. the impending departure of his beloved
   E. the immortality of the relationship

33. An apt title for the poem could be
   A. Love Me or Leave Me
   B. Death Be Not Proud
   C. The End Justifies the Means
   D. Love's Fall
   E. Grow Old Along with Me

34. The tone of the poem can best be described as
   A. contemplative
   B. defiant
   C. submissive
   D. arbitrary
   E. complaining

35. The speaker most likely is
   A. jealous of the beloved's youth
   B. pleased that the lover will leave
   C. unable to keep up with the young lover
   D. unwilling to face his own mortality
   E. responsive to the beloved's constancy

Questions 36–47 are based on the following passage.

Poets and Language
by Percy Bysshe Shelley

Poets, according to the circumstances of the age and nation in which they appeared, were called, in the earlier epochs of the world, legislators, or prophets: a poet essentially comprises and unites both these characters. For he not only beholds intensely the present as it is, and discovers those laws according to which present things ought to be ordered, but he beholds the future in the present, and his thoughts are the germs of the flower and the fruit of latest time. Not that I assert poets to be prophets in the gross sense of the word, or that they can foretell the form as surely as they foreknow the spirit of events; such is the pretense of superstition, which would make poetry an attribute of prophecy, rather than prophecy an attribute of poetry. A poet participates in the eternal, the infinite, and the one; as far as relates to his conceptions, time and place and number are not. The grammatical forms which express the moods of time, and the difference of persons, and the distinction of place, are convertible with respect to the highest poetry without injuring it as poetry; and the choruses of Aeschylus, and the book of Job, and Dante's Paradise, would afford, more than any other writings, examples of this fact, if the limits of this essay did not forbid citation. The creations of sculpture, painting, and music, are illustrations still more decisive.

Language, colour, form, and religious and civil habits of action, are all the instruments and materials of poetry; they may be called poetry by that figure of speech which considers the effect as a synonym for a cause. But poetry in a more restricted sense expresses those arrangements of language, and especially metrical language, which are created by that imperial faculty, whose throne is curtained within the invisible nature of man. And this springs from the nature itself of language, which is a more direct representation of the actions and passions of our internal being, and is susceptible of more various and delicate combinations, than colour, form, or motion, and is more plastic and obedient to the control of that faculty of which it is the creation. For Language is arbitrarily produced by the imagination, and has relation to thoughts alone; but all other materials, instruments, and conditions of art, have relations among each other, which limit and interpose between conception and expression. The former is a mirror which reflects the latter as a cloud which enfeebles, the light of which both are mediums of communication . . .

Poets are the hierophants* of an unapprehended inspiration; the mirrors of the gigantic shadows which futurity casts upon the present, the words which express what they understand not; the trumpets which sing to battle, and feel not what they inspire; the influence which is moved not, but moves. Poets are the unacknowledged legislators of the world.

*Hierophants: chief priests, advocates.

36. The passage is an example of
    A. the opening of a novel
    B. the opening of an autobiography
    C. an essay
    D. an ode
    E. a dramatic monologue

37. According to Shelley, a poet is a combination of
    A. historical figure and patriot
    B. artist and priest
    C. grammarian and poet
    D. sculptor and musician
    E. lawmaker and seer

38. In lines 5 and 6, "the germs of the flower and the fruit of latest time" can best be interpreted to mean
    A. the guardian of the future
    B. that the poet's thoughts destroy conventional thinking
    C. that the poet is clairvoyant
    D. that the poet is the gardener of thought
    E. that the current thoughts of the poet presage the future

39. According to Shelley, "the pretense of superstition" (lines 7–8) is
    A. the ability to "foreknow" events
    B. the ability to control the future
    C. to grant immortality to the poet
    D. to be a legislator
    E. the ability to change the future

40. Shelley asserts that grammatical forms (lines 10–15) serve all the following purposes *except*
    A. to indicate verb tense
    B. to clarify pronoun agreement
    C. to solidify relative pronouns
    D. to forbid citation
    E. to enhance poetry

41. The reader may infer that the book of Job and the works of Aeschylus and Dante
    A. are too far in the past to be of value today
    B. are examples of Shelley's theories
    C. have injured poetry
    D. deal with superstition
    E. are more decisive than art

42. According to Shelley, poetry, sculpture, music, and painting have what characteristic in common?
    A. They are dependent on one another.
    B. They rely on grammatical forms.
    C. They are at odds with one another.
    D. They are eternal.
    E. They can only relate to a specific time and place.

43. In lines 19–20, the phrase "that imperial faculty, whose throne . . ." refers to
    A. legislators
    B. language
    C. synonyms
    D. nature
    E. poetry

44. According to Shelley, which of the following is not part of the nature of language?
    A. It is imaginative.
    B. It is a reflection of passion.
    C. It causes civil habits of action.
    D. It deals with the eternal self.
    E. It is connected only to thought.

45. In line 27, if the word "former" refers to language, then "latter" refers to
    A. art
    B. motion
    C. limits
    D. imagination
    E. metrics

46. Lines 27–28, beginning with, "The former . . ." contain *ALL* of the following literary devices *EXCEPT*
    A. parallel structure
    B. simile
    C. imagery
    D. personification
    E. metaphor

47. According to the final paragraph, the greatest attribute of the poet is his
    A. sensitivity to light and dark
    B. depiction of fantasy and reality
    C. perception of others
    D. ability to reflect the future
    E. creation of art

END OF SECTION I

The second part of the test is the 2-hour essay-writing section. You take this part of the exam after the break following your completion of the multiple-choice section. You will be required to write three different essays. In all likelihood, one of the questions will be based on a prose passage, one on a poem or two, and one will be what is called the free-response essay.

Do not write any essays at this time. Just take a careful look at each of the questions to get an idea of the types of writing assignments you are expected to be able to handle. Essay questions are called "prompts" by the AP.

Section II

Total time—2 hours

Question 1

(Suggested time 40 minutes. This question counts as one-third of the total score for Section II.)

In the following passage from the short story "The Dead," James Joyce presents an insight into the character of Gabriel. Write a well-organized essay in which you discuss various aspects of Gabriel's complex character that Joyce reveals to the reader and to Gabriel himself. Refer to such techniques and devices as imagery, point of view, motif, diction, and syntax.

The Dead

She was fast asleep.

Gabriel, leaning on his elbow, looked for a few moments
unresentfully on her tangled hair and half-open mouth, listening to her
deep-drawn breath. So she had had that romance in her life: a man had
died for her sake. It hardly pained him now to think how poor a part   5
he, her husband, had played in her life. He watched her while she slept
as though he and she had never lived together as man and wife. His
curious eyes rested long upon her face and on her hair and, as he thought
of what she must have been then, in that time of her first girlish beauty,
a strange friendly pity for her entered his soul. He did not like to say   10
even to himself that her face was no longer beautiful but he knew that it
was no longer the face for which Michael Furey had braved death.

Perhaps she had not told him all the story. His eyes moved to the
chair over which she had thrown some of her clothes. A petticoat string
dangled to the floor. One boot stood upright, its limp upper fallen down: 15
the fellow of it lay upon its side. He wondered at his riot of emotions of
an hour before. From what had it proceeded? From his aunt's supper,
from his own foolish speech, from the wine and dancing, the merry-making
when saying good-night in the hall, the pleasure of the walk along the river
in the snow. Poor Aunt Julia! She, too, would soon be a shade with the   20
shade of Patrick Morkan and his horse. He had caught that haggard look
upon her face for a moment when she was singing *Arrayed for the Bridal*.
Soon, perhaps, he would be sitting in the same drawing-room dressed in

black, his silk hat on his knees. The blinds would be drawn down and
Aunt Kate would be sitting beside him, crying and blowing her nose and   25
telling him how Julia had died. He would cast about in his mind for some
words that might console her, and would find only lame and useless ones.
Yes, yes: that would happen very soon.

Question 2

(Suggested time 40 minutes. This question counts as one-third of the total score for Section II.)

In "On the Subway," Sharon Olds brings two worlds into close proximity. Identify the complex contrasts that
develop both portraits in the poem and discuss the insights the narrator comes to as a result of the experience.
Refer to such literary techniques as tone, poetic devices, imagery, and organization.

On the Subway
by Sharon Olds

The boy and I face each other
His feet are huge, in black sneakers
laced with white in a complex pattern like a
set of intentional scars. We are stuck on
opposite sides of the car, a couple of   5
molecules stuck in a rod of light
rapidly moving through darkness.
He has the casual cold look of a mugger,
alert under hooded lids. He is wearing
red, like the inside of the body   10
exposed. I am wearing dark fur, the
whole skin of an animal taken and
used. I look at his raw face,
he looks at my fur coat, and I don't
know if I am in his power—   15
he could take my coat so easily, my
briefcase, my life—
or if he is in my power, the way I am
living off his life, eating the steak
he does not eat, as if I am taking   20
the food from his mouth. And he is black
and I am white, and without meaning or
trying to I must profit from his darkness,
the way he absorbs the murderous beams of the
nation's heart, as black cotton   25
absorbs the heat of the sun and holds it. There is
no way to know how easy this
white skin makes my life, this
life he could take so easily and
break across his knee like a stick the way his   30

own back is being broken, the
rod of his soul that at birth was dark and
fluid and rich as the heart of a seedling
ready to thrust up into any available light

Question 3

(Suggested time 40 minutes. This question counts as one-third of the total score for Section II.)

Often in literature, a literal or figurative journey is a significant factor in the development of a character or the meaning of the work as a whole. Choose a full-length work and write a well-organized essay in which you discuss the literal and/or figurative nature of the journey and how it affects characterization and theme. You may choose a work from the list below or another play or novel of literary merit.

As I Lay Dying	*Tom Jones*
Jane Eyre	*Heart of Darkness*
The Odyssey	*Moby Dick*
Don Quixote	*The Sun Also Rises*
Candide	*The Grapes of Wrath*
A Streetcar Named Desire	*The Stranger*
A Passage to India	*Ulysses*
Gulliver's Travels	*Their Eyes Were Watching God*
No Exit	*Obasan*
The Kite Runner	*Twelfth Night*

END OF SECTION II

Afterword

So that's what the Advanced Placement Literature and Composition exam looks like. If you're being honest with yourself, you're probably feeling a bit overwhelmed at this point. Good! This is primarily why we are going to deconstruct this entire Diagnostic/Master exam for you and with you throughout this book. By the time you reach Practice Exams 1 and 2, you should be feeling much more confident and comfortable about doing well on the AP Literature exam.

As you progress through this book, you will:

- Take each section of the Diagnostic/Master exam.
- Read the explanations for the answers to the multiple-choice questions.
- Read sample student essays written in response to each of the three prompts.
- Read the rubrics and ratings of the student essays.
- Evaluate your own performance in light of this information.

STEP 3

Develop Strategies for Success

CHAPTER 4   Section I of the Exam: The Multiple-Choice Questions
CHAPTER 5   The Prose Passage Essay
CHAPTER 6   The Poetry Essay
CHAPTER 7   The Free-Response Essay

CHAPTER 4

Section I of the Exam: The Multiple-Choice Questions

IN THIS CHAPTER

Summary: Become comfortable with the multiple-choice section of the exam. If you know what to expect, you can prepare.

Key Ideas
- ✪ Review the types of multiple-choice questions asked on the exam
- ✪ Learn strategies for approaching the multiple-choice questions
- ✪ Prepare yourself for the multiple-choice section of the exam
- ✪ Take the multiple-choice section of the exam
- ✪ Score yourself by checking the answer key and explanations for the multiple-choice section of the Diagnostic/Master exam

Introduction to the Multiple-Choice Section of the Exam

Multiple choice? Multiple guess? Multiple anxiety? The day after the exam, students often bemoan the difficulties and uncertainties of Section I of the AP Literature exam.

"It's unfair."

"It's crazy."

"Was that in English?"

"Did you get four Ds in a row for the second poem?"

"I just closed my eyes and pointed."

Is it really possible to avoid these and other exam woes? We hope that by following along with us in this chapter, you will begin to feel a bit more familiar with the world of multiple-choice questions and, thus, become a little more comfortable with the multiple-choice section of the exam.

What Is It About the Multiple-Choice Questions That Causes Such Anxiety?

Basically, a multiple-choice literature question is a flawed method of gauging understanding because, by its very nature, it forces you to play a cat-and-mouse game with the test maker, who demands that you concentrate on items that are incorrect before you can choose what is correct. We know, however, that complex literature has a richness that allows for ambiguity. When you are taking the exam, you are expected to match someone else's take on a work with the answers you choose. This is what often causes the student to feel that the multiple-choice section is unfair. And maybe, to a degree, it is. However, the test is designed to allow you to shine, *not* to be humiliated. To that end, you will not find "cutesy" questions, and the test writers will not play games with you. What they will do is present several valid options as a response to a challenging and appropriate question. These questions are designed to separate the perceptive and thoughtful reader from the superficial and impulsive one.

This said, it's wise to develop a strategy for success. Practice is the key to this success. You've been confronted with all types of multiple-choice questions during your career as a student. The test-taking skills you have learned in your social studies, math, and science classes may also apply to the AP Literature exam.

What Should I Expect in Section I?

For this first section of the AP Literature exam, you are allotted 1 hour to answer approximately 55 objective questions on four or five prose and poetry selections. The prose passage will comprise works of fiction or drama. You can expect the poems to be complete and from different time periods and of different styles and forms. In other words, you will not find two Shakespearean sonnets on the same exam.

These are *not* easy readings. They are representative of the college-level work you have been doing throughout the year. You will be expected to

- Follow sophisticated syntax
- Respond to diction
- Be comfortable with upper-level vocabulary
- Be familiar with literary terminology
- Make inferences
- Be sensitive to irony and tone
- Recognize components of style

The good news is that the selection is self-contained. This means that if it is about the Irish Potato Famine, you will not be at a disadvantage if you know nothing about it prior to the exam. Frequently there will be biblical references in a selection. This is especially true of works from an earlier time period. You are expected to be aware of basic allusions to biblical and mythological works often found in literature, but the passage will never require you to have any specific religious background.

Do not let the subject matter of a passage throw you. Strong analytical skills will work on any passage.

How Should I Begin to Work with Section I?

Take no more than a minute and thumb through the exam, looking for the following:

- The length of the selections
- The time periods or writing styles, if you can recognize them
- The number of questions asked
- A quick idea of the type of questions

This brief skimming of the test will put your mind into gear because you will be aware of what is expected of you.

How Should I Proceed Through This Section of the Exam?

"Creating my own multiple-choice questions was a terrific help to me when it came to doing close readings and correctly answering multiple-choice questions on the exam."
—Bill N.
  AP student

Timing is important. Always maintain an awareness of the time. Wear a watch. (Some students like to put it directly in front of them on the desk.) Remember, this will not be your first encounter with the multiple-choice section of the test. You've probably been practicing timed exams in class; in addition, this book provides you with three timed experiences. We're sure you will notice improvements as you progress through the timed practice activities.

Depending on the given selections, you may take less or more time on a particular passage, but you must know when to move on. The test *does not* become more difficult as it progresses. So, you will want to give yourself adequate opportunity to answer each set of questions.

Work at a pace of about one question per minute. Every question is worth the same number of points, so don't get bogged down on those that involve multiple tasks. Don't panic if a question is beyond you. Remember, it will probably be beyond a great number of other students as well. There has to be a bar that determines the 5's and 4's for this exam. Just do your best.

Reading the text carefully is a must. Begin at the beginning and work your way through. Do not waste time reading questions before you read the selection.

Most people read just with their eyes. We want you to slow down and read with your senses of sight, sound, and touch.

- Underline, circle, bracket, or highlight the text.
- Read closely, paying attention to punctuation and rhythms of the lines or sentences.
- Read as if you were reading the passage aloud to an audience, emphasizing meaning and intent.
- As corny as it may seem, hear those words in your head.
- This technique may seem childish, but it works. Using your finger as a pointer, under-score the line as you are reading it aloud in your head. This forces you to slow down and to really notice the text. This will be helpful when you have to refer to the passage.
- Use all the information given to you about the passage, such as title, author, date of publication, and footnotes.
- Be aware of foreshadowing.
- Be aware of thematic lines and be sensitive to details that will obviously be material for multiple-choice questions.
- When reading poetry, pay particular attention to enjambment and end-stopped lines because they carry meaning.
- With poetry, it's often helpful to paraphrase a stanza, especially if the order of the lines has been inverted.

> You can practice these techniques any time. Take any work and read it aloud. Time yourself. A good rate is about 1½ minutes per page.

Types of Multiple-Choice Questions

Multiple-choice questions are not written randomly. There are certain formats you will encounter. The answers to the following questions should clarify some of the patterns.

Is the Structure the Same for All of the Multiple-Choice Questions?

No. Here are several basic patterns that the AP test makers often employ:

1. **The straightforward question,** such as:
   - The poem is an example of a
     C. lyric
   - The word "smooth" refers to
     B. his skin

2. **The question that refers you to specific lines and asks you to draw a conclusion or to interpret.**
   - Lines 52–57 serve to
     A. reinforce the author's thesis

3. **The "all . . . except" question** requires extra time because it demands that you consider every possibility.
   - The AP Literature exam is all of the following *except*:
     A. It is given in May of each year.
     B. It is open to high school seniors.
     C It is published in the *New York Times*.
     D. It is used as a qualifier for college credit.
     E. It is a 3-hour test.

   NOTE: There are fewer and fewer of this type of question on the exam.

4. **The question that asks you to make an inference or to abstract a concept that is not directly stated in the passage.**
   - In the poem "My Last Duchess," the reader can infer that the speaker is
     E. arrogant

The infamous Roman Numeral question has been eliminated from the exam.

What Kinds of Questions Should I Expect on the Exam?

The multiple-choice questions center around form and content. The test makers want to assess your understanding of the meaning of the selection as well as your ability to draw inferences and perceive implications based on it. They also want to know whether you understand *how* a writer develops his or her ideas.

The questions, therefore, will be factual, technical, analytical, and inferential. The two tables that follow illustrate the types of key words and phrases in these four categories that you can expect to find in questions for both the prose and the poetry selections.

Note: Do not memorize these tables. Also, do not panic if a word or phrase is unfamiliar to you. You may or may not encounter any or all of these words or phrases on any given exam. You can, however, count on meeting up with many of these in the practice exams in this book.

Prose: Key Words and Phrases Found in Multiple-Choice Questions

FACTUAL	TECHNICAL	ANALYTICAL	INFERENTIAL
words refer to	sentence structure	rhetorical strategy	effect of diction
allusions	style	shift in development	tone
antecedents	grammatical purpose	rhetorical stance	inferences
pronoun referents	dominant technique	style	effect of last paragraph
genre	imagery	metaphor	effect on reader
setting	point of view	contrast	narrator's attitude
	organization of passage	comparison	image suggests
	narrative progress of passage	cause/effect	effect of detail
	conflict	argument	author implies
	irony	description	author most concerned with
	function of	narration	symbol
		specific-general	
		how something is characterized	
		imagery	
		passage is primarily concerned with	
		function of	

Poetry: Key Words and Phrases Found in Multiple-Choice Questions

FACTUAL	TECHNICAL	ANALYTICAL	INFERENTIAL
all except	imagery	character portrayal	mood
definition	literary devices	imagery	attitude of
thesis	paradox	literary devices	poet's attitude
sequence of events	organizational pattern	paradox	purpose of
the object of ___ is ___	syntax	purpose of	tone of the poem
allusion	metrics	rhetorical shifts	theme of the poem
the subject of dramatic situation	parallel structure	ironies presented	reader may infer
	rhetorical shifts	least important	best interpreted as
paraphrasing	ironies presented	most important	effect of diction
subject	function of diction		speaker implies
references	dramatic moment		___ is associated with ___
	meaning conveyed by		context
			symbol

A word about jargon. Jargon refers to words that are unique to a specific subject. A common language is important for communication, and there must be agreement on the basic meanings of terms. Even though it is important to know the universal language of a subject, it is also important that you *not* limit the scope of your thinking to a brief definition. All the terms used in the tables are interwoven in literature. They are categorized only for easy reference. They also work in many other contexts. *In other words, think beyond the box.*

Scoring the Multiple-Choice Section

How Does the Scoring of the Multiple-Choice Section Work?

The College Board has implemented a new scoring process for the multiple-choice section of the AP English Literature and Composition exam. No longer are points deducted for incorrect responses, so there is no longer a penalty for guessing incorrectly. Therefore, it is to your advantage to answer ALL of the multiple-choice questions. Your chances of guessing the correct answer improve if you skillfully apply the process of elimination to narrow the choices.

Multiple-choice scores are based solely on the number of questions answered correctly. If you answered 36 questions correctly, then your raw score is 36. This raw score, which is 45 percent of the total, is combined with that of the essay section to make up a composite score. This is then manipulated to form a scale on which the final AP grade is based.

Areas of Multiple-Choice Questions

Short Fiction: 42–49 percent of the questions
Poetry: 36–45 percent of the questions
Longer Works: 15–18 percent of the questions

Strategies for Answering the Multiple-Choice Questions

You've been answering multiple-choice questions most of your academic life, and you've probably figured out ways to deal with them. However, there may be some points you have not considered that will be helpful for this particular exam.

General Guidelines

- Work in order. This is a good approach for several reasons:
  - It's clear.
  - You will not lose your place on the scan sheet.
  - There may be a logic to working sequentially that will help you answer previous questions. But, this is your call. If you are more comfortable moving around the exam, do so.
- Write on the exam booklet. Mark it up. Make it yours. Interact with the test.
- Do not spend too much time on any one question.
- Focus on your strengths. If you are more comfortable working with poetry, answer the poetry questions first.
- Don't be misled by the length or appearance of a selection. There is no correlation between length or appearance and the difficulty of the questions.
- Don't fight the question or the passage. You may know other information about the subject of the text or a question. It's irrelevant. Work within the given context.
- Consider all the choices in a given question. This will keep you from jumping to a false conclusion. It helps you to slow down and to really look at each possibility. You may find that your first choice is not the best or most appropriate one.
- Maintain an open mind as you answer subsequent questions in a series. Sometimes the answer to a later question will contradict your answer to a previous one. Reconsider both answers. Also, the phrasing of a question may point to an answer in a previous question.
- Remember that all parts of an answer must be correct.
- When in doubt, go to the text.

Specific Techniques

- **Process of elimination:** This is your primary tool, except for direct knowledge of the answer.
  1. Read the five choices.
  2. If no choice immediately strikes you as correct, you can
     - Eliminate those choices that are obviously wrong
     - Eliminate those choices that are too narrow or too broad
     - Eliminate illogical choices
     - Eliminate answers that are synonymous
     - Eliminate answers that cancel each other out

3. If two answers are close, do one *or* the other of the following:
   • Find the one that is general enough to cover all aspects of the question
   • Find the one that is limited enough to be the detail the question is looking for

• **Substitution/fill in the blank**
   1. Rephrase the question, leaving a blank where the answer should go.

   2. Use each of the choices to fill in the blank until you find the one that is the best fit.

• **Using context**
   1. Consider the context when the question directs you to specific lines, words, or phrases.

   2. Locate the given word, phrase, sentence, or poetic line and read the sentence or line before and after the section of the text to which the question refers. Often this provides the information or clues you need to make your choice.

• **Anticipation:** As you read the passage for the first time, mark any details and ideas that you would ask a question about. You may be able to anticipate the test makers this way.

• **Intuition or the educated guess:** You have a wealth of skills and knowledge in your literary subconscious. A question or a choice may trigger a "remembrance of things past." This can be the basis for your educated guess. Have the confidence to use the educated guess as a valid technique. Trust your own resources.

> ## Survival Plan
>
> If time is running out and you haven't finished the fourth selection:
>
> 1. Scan the remaining questions and look for:
>   • The shortest questions
>   • The questions that direct you to a specific line
>
> 2. Look for specific detail/definition questions.
>
> 3. Look for self-contained questions. For example: "The sea slid silently from the shore" is an example of C. alliteration. You do not have to go to the passage to answer this question.

If I Don't Know an Answer, Should I Guess?

You can't be seriously hurt by making *educated guesses* based on a careful reading of the selection. Be smart. Understand that you need to come to this exam well prepared. You must have a foundation of knowledge and skills. You cannot guess through the entire exam and expect to do well.

This is not Lotto. This book is **not** about how to "beat the exam." We want to maximize the skills you already have. There is an inherent integrity in this exam and your participation in it. With this in mind, when there is no other direction open to you, it is perfectly fine to make an educated guess.

Is There Anything Special I Should Know About Preparing for the Prose Multiple-Choice Questions?

After you have finished with the Diagnostic/Master exam, you will be familiar with the format and types of questions asked on the AP Lit exam. However, just practicing answering multiple-choice questions on specific works will not give you a complete understanding of this questioning process. We suggest the following to help you hone your multiple-choice answering skills with prose multiple-choice questions:

- Choose a challenging passage from a full-length prose work.
- Read the selection a couple of times and create several multiple-choice questions about specific sections of the selection.
- Make certain the section is self-contained and complex.
- Choose a dialogue, monologue, introductory setting, set description, stage directions, philosophical passage, significant event, or moment of conflict.
- Create a variety of question types based on the previous chart.
- Refer to the prose table given earlier in this chapter for suggested language and type.
- Administer your mini-quiz to a classmate, study group, or class.
- Evaluate your results.
- Repeat this process through several different full-length works during your preparation for the exam. The works can certainly come from those you are studying in class.

Here's what should happen as a result of your using this process:

- Your expectation level for the selections in the actual test will be more realistic.
- You will become familiar with the language of multiple-choice questions.
- Your understanding of the process of choosing answers will be heightened.
- Questions you write that you find less than satisfactory will trigger your analytical skills as you attempt to figure out "what went wrong."
- Terminology will become more accurate.
- *Bonus:* If you continue to do this work throughout your preparation for the AP exam, you will have created a mental storehouse of literary information. So when you are presented with a prose or free-response essay in Section II, you will have an extra resource at your disposal.

"One of my biggest challenges in preparing for the exam was to learn not to jump to conclusions when I was doing the multiple-choice questions."
—Samantha S.
AP student

Your Turn

To Do:

1. Circle/highlight/underline the words and/or phrases that appear to be important for the meaning of the excerpt.

2. Carefully consider each of the given sample questions.

3. Construct your own question that is an example of the specific type.

from Mark Twain's *Huckleberry Finn*

Sometimes we'd have the whole river all to ourselves for the longest time. Yonder was the banks and the islands, across the water; and maybe a spark—which was a candle in a cabin window—and sometimes on the water you could see a spark or two—on a raft or a scow, you know; and maybe you could hear a fiddle or a song coming over from one of them crafts. It's lovely to live on a raft. We had the sky, up there, all speckled with stars, and we used to lay on our backs and look up at

5

*them, and discuss about whether they was made, or only just happened—Jim he
allowed they was made, but I allowed they happened; I judged it would have took
too long to make so many. Jim said the moon could a laid them; well, that looked
kind of reasonable, so I didn't say nothing against it, because I've seen a frog lay* 10
*most as many, so of course it could be done. We used to watch the stars that fell,
too, and see them streak down. Jim allowed they'd got spoiled and was hove out
of the nest.*

Title: *Huckleberry Finn*
Author: Mark Twain
Type of passage: Narrative description

Sample <u>Factual</u> Question: In lines 10–11, "I've seen a frog lay most as many" refers to

<u>Answer:</u> stars

<u>Rationale:</u> The implied comparison has Huck inferring
that the number of stars in the sky is similar
to the number of eggs a frog lays.

Your <u>Factual</u> Question:

<u>Answer:</u>   <u>Rationale:</u>

Sample <u>Technical</u> Question: A primary function of the sentence "It's lovely to live on a raft" is

<u>Answer:</u> to contrast with the lyrical
description in the passage

<u>Rationale:</u> The straightforward break in the middle of
the passage emphasizes the key point of the
description.

Your <u>Technical</u> Question:

<u>Answer:</u>   <u>Rationale:</u>

Sample <u>Analytical</u> Question: The primary purpose of using dialect is most likely to

<u>Answer:</u> reinforce the innocence and natural state of Huck and Jim

<u>Rationale:</u> The regional dialect illustrates the lack of the stereotypical education and background of the period.

Your <u>Analytical</u> Question:

<u>Answer:</u>   <u>Rationale:</u>

Sample <u>Inferential</u> Question: The tone of the passage can best be described as

<u>Answer:</u> nostalgic and philosophical

<u>Rationale:</u> The diction supports their reverie and their curiosity about their place in the universe.

Your <u>Inferential</u> Question:

<u>Answer:</u>   <u>Rationale:</u>

Is There Anything Special I Should Do to Prepare for the Poetry Questions?

The points made about prose hold true for the poetry multiple-choice questions as well. But there are a few specific pointers that may prove helpful:

- Choose thoughtful and interesting poems of some length. (See our suggested reading list.)
- Read the poems several times. Practice reading the poems aloud.
- The greatest benefit will be that as you read any poem, you will automatically begin to respond to areas of the poem that would lend themselves to a multiple-choice question.

- Here is a list of representative poets you may want to read.

  - Shakespeare
  - John Donne
  - Philip Larkin
  - Emily Dickinson
  - Sylvia Plath
  - Dylan Thomas
  - May Swenson
  - Theodore Roethke
  - Sharon Olds
  - Billy Collins
  - Pablo Neruda

  - Richard Wilbur
  - Adrienne Rich
  - Edmund Spenser
  - W. H. Auden
  - W. B. Yeats
  - Gwendolyn Brooks
  - Elizabeth Bishop
  - Langston Hughes
  - Galway Kinnell
  - Marianne Moore
  - May Sarton

> You might want to utilize this process throughout the year with major works studied in and out of class and keep track of your progress. See the Bibliography of this book.

Your Turn

To Do:

4. Circle/highlight/underline the words and/or phrases that appear to be important for the meaning of the poem.

5. Carefully consider each of the given sample questions.

6. Construct your own question that is an example of the specific type.

It Sifts from Leaden Sieves
By Emily Dickinson

It sifts from leaden sieves,
It powders all the wood,
It fills with alabaster wool
The wrinkles of the road.

It makes an even face   5
Of mountain and of plain, –
Unbroken forehead from the east
Unto the east again.

It reaches to the fence,
It wraps it, rail by rail,   10
Till it is lost in fleeces,
It flings a crystal veil

On stump and stack and stem, –
The summer's empty room,
Acres of seams where harvests were,   15
Recordless, but for them.

It ruffles wrists of posts,
As ankles of a queen, –
Then stills its artisans like ghosts,
Denying they have been.   20

Title: "It Sifts from Leaden Sieves"
Poet: Emily Dickinson

Sample <u>Factual</u> Question: The subject of the poem's dramatic situation is
<u>Answer:</u> the falling snow   <u>Rationale:</u> The images all support the snow metaphor.

Your <u>Factual</u> Question:

<u>Answer:</u>   <u>Rationale:</u>

Sample <u>Technical</u> Question: The primary literary device used in the poem is
<u>Answer:</u> metaphor   <u>Rationale:</u> Metaphor is used in every stanza.

Your <u>Technical</u> Question:

<u>Answer:</u>   <u>Rationale:</u>

Sample Analytical Question: Paradox is most readily seen in

Answer: the softness imagery vs. the   Rationale: There is a shift from description
last two lines of the poem   to the effect of the cold in
                                                                  the last two lines.

```
┌─────────────────────────────────────────────────────────────┐
│                                                               │
│   Your Analytical Question:                                   │
│                                                               │
│                                                               │
│                                                               │
│   Answer:                            Rationale:               │
│                                                               │
│                                                               │
│                                                               │
│                                                               │
│                                                               │
└─────────────────────────────────────────────────────────────┘
```

Sample Inferential Question: Based on the poem, the reader could infer that

Answer: the power of nature is   Rationale: Nothing in the poem is excluded
all-encompassing   from the power of the snow.

```
┌─────────────────────────────────────────────────────────────┐
│                                                               │
│   Your Inferential Question:                                  │
│                                                               │
│                                                               │
│                                                               │
│   Answer:                            Rationale:               │
│                                                               │
│                                                               │
│                                                               │
│                                                               │
│                                                               │
└─────────────────────────────────────────────────────────────┘
```

The Time Is at Hand

It is now time to try the Diagnostic/Master exam, Section I. Do this section in *one* sitting. Time yourself! Be honest with yourself when you score your answers.

Note: If the 1 hour passes before you finish all the questions, stop where you are and score what you have done up to this point. Afterwards, answer the remaining questions, but do not count the answers as part of your score.

When you have completed all the multiple-choice questions in this Diagnostic/Master exam, carefully read the explanations of the answers. Spend time here and assess which types of questions give you trouble. Use this book to learn from your mistakes.

ANSWER SHEET FOR DIAGNOSTIC
MULTIPLE-CHOICE QUESTIONS

1. _____   13. _____   25. _____   37. _____

2. _____   14. _____   26. _____   38. _____

3. _____   15. _____   27. _____   39. _____

4. _____   16. _____   28. _____   40. _____

5. _____   17. _____   29. _____   41. _____

6. _____   18. _____   30. _____   42. _____

7. _____   19. _____   31. _____   43. _____

8. _____   20. _____   32. _____   44. _____

9. _____   21. _____   33. _____   45. _____

10. _____   22. _____   34. _____   46. _____

11. _____   23. _____   35. _____   47. _____

12. _____   24. _____   36. _____

I _____ did _____ did not finish all the questions in the allotted 1 hour.

I had _____ correct answers. I had _____ incorrect answers. I left _____ questions blank.

I have carefully reviewed the explanations of the answers, and I think I need to work on the following types of questions:

THE MULTIPLE-CHOICE SECTION OF THE DIAGNOSTIC/MASTER EXAM

The multiple-choice section of the Diagnostic/Master exam follows. You have seen the questions in the "walk through" in Chapter 3.

Advanced Placement Literature and Composition

Section 1

Total time—1 hour

Carefully read the following passages and answer the accompanying questions. Questions 1–10 are based on the following poem.

Now Goes Under . . .
by Edna St. Vincent Millay

Now goes under, and I watch it go under, the sun
    That will not rise again.
Today has seen the setting, in your eyes cold
    and senseless as the sea,
Of friendship better than bread, and of bright charity   5
That lifts a man a little above the beasts that run.

That this could be!
That I should live to see
Most vulgar Pride, that stale obstreperous clown,
So fitted out with purple robe and crown   10
To stand among his betters! Face to face
With outraged me in this once holy place,
Where Wisdom was a favoured guest and hunted
Truth was harboured out of danger,
He bulks enthroned, a lewd, and insupportable stranger!   15

I would have sworn, indeed I swore it:
The hills may shift, the waters may decline,
Winter may twist the stem from the twig that bore it,
But never your love from me, your hand from mine.

Now goes under the sun, and I watch it go under.   20
Farewell, sweet light, great wonder!
You, too, farewell—but fare not well enough to dream
You have done wisely to invite the night before the darkness came.

1. The poem is an example of a(n)
   A. sonnet
   B. lyric
   C. ode
   D. ballad
   E. dramatic monologue

2. The setting of the sun is a symbol for
   A. the beginning of winter
   B. encountering danger
   C. the end of a relationship
   D. facing death
   E. the onset of night

3. The second stanza is developed primarily by
   A. metaphor
   B. simile
   C. personification
   D. hyperbole
   E. allusion

4. "He" in line 15 refers to
   A. Wisdom
   B. Truth
   C. I
   D. Pride
   E. charity

5. According to the speaker, what separates man from beast?
   A. love
   B. friendship
   C. charity
   D. truth
   E. wisdom

6. For the speaker, the relationship has been all of the following *except*
   A. honest
   B. dangerous
   C. spiritual
   D. ephemeral
   E. nourishing

7. The reader can infer from the play on words in the last stanza that the speaker is
   A. dying
   B. frantic
   C. wistful
   D. bitter
   E. capricious

8. "This once holy place" (line 12) refers to
   A. the sunset
   B. the relationship
   C. the sea
   D. the circus
   E. the Church

9. The cause of the relationship's situation is
   A. a stranger coming between them
   B. the lover not taking the relationship seriously
   C. the lover feeling intellectually superior
   D. the lover's pride coming between them
   E. the lover being insensitive

10. The speaker acknowledges the finality of the relationship in line(s)
   A. 1–2
   B. 7
   C. 8
   D. 16
   E. 18–19

Questions 11–23 are based on the following passage.

The sea-reach of the Thames stretched before us like the beginning of an
interminable waterway. The air was dark above Gravesend, and farther back still
seemed condensed into a mournful gloom, brooding motionless over the biggest and
the greatest town on earth.
   "I was thinking of very old times, when the Romans first came here, nineteen
hundred years ago—the other day . . . Light came out of this river since—you say knights?
Yes; but it is like a running blaze on a plain, like a flash of lightning in the clouds. We live
in the flicker—may it last as long as the old earth keeps rolling! But darkness was here
yesterday. Imagine the feelings of a commander of a fine—what d'ye call 'em?—trireme
in the Mediterranean, ordered suddenly to the north; run overland across the Gauls in a

5

10

hurry; put in charge of one of these craft the legionnaires—a wonderful lot of handy men they must have been, too—used to build, apparently by the hundred, in a month or two, if we may believe what we read. Imagine him here—the very end of the world, a sea the color of lead, a sky the color of smoke, a kind of ship about as rigid as a concertina—and going up this river with stores, or orders, or what you like. Sandbanks, marshes, forests, savages— 15 precious little to eat for a civilized man, nothing but Thames water to drink. No Falernian wine here, no going ashore. Here and there a military camp lost in a wilderness, like a needle in a bundle of hay—cold, fog, tempests, disease, exile, and death—death skulking in the air, in the water, in the bush. They must have been dying like flies here. Oh yes—he did it. Did it very well, too, no doubt, and without thinking much about it either, except 20 afterwards to brag of what he had gone through in his time, perhaps. They were men enough to face darkness. And perhaps he was cheered by keeping his eye on a chance of promotion to the fleet at Ravenna by and by, if he had good friends in Rome and survived the awful climate. Or think of a decent young citizen in a toga—perhaps too much dice, you know— coming out here in the train of some prefect, or tax-gatherer, or trader even, to mend his 25 fortunes. Land in a swamp, march through the woods, and in some inland post feel the savagery, the utter savagery, had closed round him—all that mysterious life of the wilderness that stirs in the forest, in the jungles, in the hearts of wild men. There's no initiation either into such mysteries. He has to live in the midst of the incomprehensible, which is also detestable. And it has a fascination, too, that goes to work upon him. The fascination of the 30 abomination—you know, imagine the growing regrets, the longing to escape, the powerless disgust, the surrender, the hate."

He paused.

"Mind," he began again, lifting one arm from the elbow, the palm of the hand outwards, so that, with his legs folded before him, he had the pose of a Buddha preaching in 35 European clothes and without a lotus flower—"Mind, none of us would feel exactly like this. What saves us is efficiency—the devotion to efficiency. But these chaps were not much account, really. They were no colonists; their administration was merely a squeeze, and nothing more, I suspect. They were conquerors, and for that you want only brute force— nothing to boast of, when you have it, since your strength is just an accident arising from the 40 weakness of others. They grabbed what they could get for the sake of what was to be got. It was just robbery with violence, aggravated murder on a great scale, and men going at it blind— as is very proper for those who tackle a darkness. The conquest of the earth, which mostly means taking it away from those who have a different complexion or slightly flatter noses than ourselves, is not a pretty thing when you look at it too much. What redeems it is the idea 45 only. An idea at the back of it; not a sentimental pretense but an idea; and an unselfish belief in the idea—something you can set up, and bow down before, and offer a sacrifice to . . . "

11. In the passage, *darkness* implies all of the following *except*
A. the unknown
B. savagery
C. ignorance
D. death
E. exploration

12. The setting of the passage is
A. Africa
B. Ancient Rome
C. the Thames River
D. the Mediterranean
E. Italy

13. The tone of the passage is
  A. condescending
  B. indignant
  C. scornful
  D. pensive
  E. laudatory

14. Later events may be foreshadowed by all of the following phrases *except*
  A. "Imagine the feelings of a commander . . . "
  B. " . . . live in the midst of the incomprehensible . . . "
  C. " . . . in some inland post feel the savagery . . . "
  D. "They must have been dying like flies here."
  E. " . . . the very end of the world . . . "

15. The narrator draws a parallel between
  A. light and dark
  B. past and present
  C. life and death
  D. fascination and abomination
  E. decency and savagery

16. In this passage, "We live in the flicker..." (lines 7–8) may be interpreted to mean *ALL* of the following *EXCEPT*
  A. In the history of the world, humanity's span on earth is brief.
  B. Future civilizations will learn from only a portion of the past.
  C. Periods of enlightenment and vision appear only briefly.
  D. The river has been the source of life throughout the ages.
  E. A moment of present-day insight about conquest.

17. One may conclude from the passage that the speaker
  A. admires adventurers
  B. longs to be a crusader
  C. is a former military officer
  D. recognizes and accepts the presence of evil in human experience
  E. is prejudiced

18. In the context of the passage, which of the following phrases presents a paradox?
  A. "The fascination of the abomination . . . "
  B. " . . . in the hearts of wild men"
  C. "There's no initiation . . . into such mysteries"
  D. " . . . a flash of lightning in the clouds"
  E. " . . . death skulking in the air . . . "

19. The lines "Imagine him here . . . concertina . . . " (lines 13–14) contain examples of
  A. hyperbole and personification
  B. irony and metaphor
  C. alliteration and personification
  D. parallel structure and simile
  E. allusion and simile

20. According to the speaker, the one trait which saves Europeans from savagery is
  A. sentiment
  B. a sense of mystery
  C. brute force
  D. religious zeal
  E. efficiency

21. According to the speaker, the only justification for conquest is
  A. the "weakness of others"
  B. it's being "proper for those who tackle a darkness . . . "
  C. their grabbing "what they could get for the sake of what was to be got"
  D. " . . . an unselfish belief in the idea . . . "
  E. "The fascination of the abomination . . . "

22. In the statement by the speaker, "Mind, none of us would feel exactly like this" (line 36), "this" refers to
  A. " . . . a Buddha preaching in European clothes . . . " (lines 35–36)
  B. " . . . imagine the growing regrets . . . the hate." (lines 31–32)
  C. "What redeems it is the idea only." (lines 45–46)
  D. " . . . think of a decent young citizen in a toga . . . " (line 24)
  E. "I was thinking of very old times . . . " (line 5)

23. The speaker presents all of the following
reasons for exploration and conquest *except*
  A. military expeditions
  B. " . . . a chance of promotion"
  C. " . . . to mend his fortunes"
  D. religious commitment
  E. punishment for a crime

Questions 24–35 are based on the following poem.

> That time of year thou mayst in me behold
> When yellow leaves, or none, or few, do hang
> Upon those boughs which shake against the cold,
> Bare ruin'd choirs, where late the sweet birds sang.
> In me thou see'st the twilight of such day   5
> As after sunset fadeth in the west;
> Which by and by black night doth take away,
> Death's second self, that seals up all in rest.
> In me thou see'st the glowing of such fire,
> That on the ashes of his youth doth lie,   10
> As the deathbed whereon it must expire,
> Consum'd with that which it was nourish'd by.
> This thou perceiv'st, which makes thy love more strong,
> To love that well which thou must leave ere long.

24. "That time of year" (line 1) refers to
  A. youth
  B. old age
  C. childhood
  D. senility
  E. maturity

25. "Death's second self" (line 8) refers to
  A. "That time of year"
  B. "sunset fadeth"
  C. "the west"
  D. "ruin'd choirs"
  E. "black night"

26. Line 12 is an example of
  A. paradox
  B. caesura
  C. parable
  D. hyperbole
  E. metonymy

27. "Twilight of such day" (line 5) is supported by
all of the following images *except*
  A. "sunset fadeth"
  B. "the glowing of such fire"
  C. "west"
  D. "Death's second self"
  E. "ashes of his youth"

28. "This thou perceiv'st" (line 13) refers to
  A. the beloved's deathbed
  B. the sorrow of unrequited love
  C. the passion of youth expiring
  D. the beloved's acknowledgment of the
     speaker's mortality
  E. the speaker sending the lover away

29. The poem is an example of a(n)
  A. elegy
  B. Spenserian sonnet
  C. Petrarchan sonnet
  D. Shakespearean sonnet
  E. sestina

30. The poem is primarily developed by
   A. metaphor
   B. argument
   C. synecdoche
   D. alternative choices
   E. contradiction

31. The irony of the poem is best expressed in line
   A. 5
   B. 7
   C. 10
   D. 11
   E. 14

32. "It" in line 12 can best be interpreted to mean
   A. a funeral pyre
   B. spent youth
   C. the intensity of the speaker's love
   D. the impending departure of his beloved
   E. the immortality of the relationship

33. An apt title for the poem could be
   A. Love Me or Leave Me
   B. Death Be Not Proud
   C. The End Justifies the Means
   D. Love's Fall
   E. Grow Old Along with Me

34. The tone of the poem can best be described as
   A. contemplative
   B. defiant
   C. submissive
   D. arbitrary
   E. complaining

35. The speaker most likely is
   A. jealous of the beloved's youth
   B. pleased that the lover will leave
   C. unable to keep up with the young lover
   D. unwilling to face his own mortality
   E. responsive to the beloved's constancy

Questions 36–47 are based on the following passage.

Poets and Language
by Percy Bysshe Shelley

Poets, according to the circumstances of the age and nation in which they appeared, were called, in the earlier epochs of the world, legislators, or prophets: a poet essentially comprises and unites both these characters. For he not only beholds intensely the present as it is, and discovers those laws according to which present things ought to be ordered, but he beholds the future in the present, and his thoughts are the germs of the flower and the   5
fruit of latest time. Not that I assert poets to be prophets in the gross sense of the word, or that they can foretell the form as surely as they foreknow the spirit of events; such is the pretense of superstition, which would make poetry an attribute of prophecy, rather than prophecy an attribute of poetry. A poet participates in the eternal, the infinite, and the one; as far as relates to his conceptions, time and place and number are not. The grammatical   10
forms which express the moods of time, and the difference of persons, and the distinction of place, are convertible with respect to the highest poetry without injuring it as poetry; and the choruses of Aeschylus, and the book of Job, and Dante's Paradise, would afford, more than any other writings, examples of this fact, if the limits of this essay did not forbid citation. The creations of sculpture, painting, and music, are illustrations still more decisive.   15
Language, colour, form, and religious and civil habits of action, are all the instruments and materials of poetry; they may be called poetry by that figure of speech which considers the effect as a synonym for a cause. But poetry in a more restricted sense expresses those arrangements of language, and especially metrical language, which are created by that imperial faculty, whose throne is curtained within the invisible nature of man. And this   20

springs from the nature itself of language, which is a more direct representation of the actions and passions of our internal being, and is susceptible of more various and delicate combinations, than colour, form, or motion, and is more plastic and obedient to the control of that faculty of which it is the creation. For Language is arbitrarily produced by the imagination, and has relation to thoughts alone; but all other materials, instruments, and conditions of art, have relations among each other, which limit and interpose between conception and expression. The former is a mirror which reflects the latter as a cloud which enfeebles, the light of which both are mediums of communication . . .

25

Poets are the hierophants* of an unapprehended inspiration; the mirrors of the gigantic shadows which futurity casts upon the present, the words which express what they understand not; the trumpets which sing to battle, and feel not what they inspire; the influence which is moved not, but moves. Poets are the unacknowledged legislators of the world.

30

---

*Hierophants: chief priests, advocates

36. The passage is an example of
  A. the opening of a novel
  B. the opening of an autobiography
  C. an essay
  D. an ode
  E. a dramatic monologue

37. According to Shelley, a poet is a combination of
  A. historical figure and patriot
  B. artist and priest
  C. grammarian and poet
  D. sculptor and musician
  E. lawmaker and seer

38. In lines 5 and 6, "the germs of the flower and the fruit of latest time" can best be interpreted to mean
  A. the guardian of the future
  B. that the poet's thoughts destroy conventional thinking
  C. that the poet is clairvoyant
  D. that the poet is the gardener of thought
  E. that the current thoughts of the poet presage the future

39. According to Shelley, "the pretense of superstition" (lines 7–8) is
  A. the ability to "foreknow" events
  B. the ability to control the future
  C. to grant immortality to the poet
  D. to be a legislator
  E. the ability to change the future

40. Shelley asserts that grammatical forms (lines 10–15) serve all the following purposes *except*
  A. to indicate verb tense
  B. to clarify pronoun agreement
  C. to solidify relative pronouns
  D. to forbid citation
  E. to enhance poetry

41. The reader may infer that the book of Job and the works of Aeschylus and Dante
  A. are too far in the past to be of value today
  B. are examples of Shelley's theories
  C. have injured poetry
  D. deal with superstition
  E. are more decisive than art

42. According to Shelley, poetry, sculpture, music, and painting have what characteristic in common?
  A. They are dependent on one another.
  B. They rely on grammatical forms.
  C. They are at odds with one another.
  D. They are eternal.
  E. They can only relate to a specific time and place.

43. In lines 19–20, the phrase "that imperial faculty, whose throne . . . " refers to
  A. legislators
  B. language
  C. synonyms
  D. nature
  E. poetry

44. According to Shelley, which of the following is not part of the nature of language?
A. It is imaginative.
B. It is a reflection of passion.
C. It causes civil habits of action.
D. It deals with the eternal self.
E. It is connected only to thought.

45. In line 27, if the word "former" refers to language, then "latter" refers to
A. art
B. motion
C. limits
D. imagination
E. metrics

46. Lines 27–28, beginning with, "The former . . ." contain *ALL* of the following literary devices *EXCEPT*
A. parallel structure
B. simile
C. imagery
D. personification
E. metaphor

47. According to the final paragraph, the greatest attribute of the poet is his
A. sensitivity to light and dark
B. depiction of fantasy and reality
C. perception of others
D. ability to reflect the future
E. creation of art

STOP.

THIS IS THE END OF THE MULTIPLE-CHOICE SECTION OF THE DIAGNOSTIC/MASTER EXAM

Answers and Explanations

Now Goes Under . . .
by Edna St. Vincent Millay

1. **B.** This question requires the student to know the characteristics of various poetic forms. (See Chapter 9.) Using the process of elimination, the correct answer B is readily confirmed. Lyric poetry is emotional and personal.

2. **C.** Although the setting sun is often associated with winter, death, and darkness, these answers are not symbolic of the literal topic of the poem—the end of the love relationship.

3. **C.** The poet uses personification in lines 9–15: "vulgar Pride," "Where Wisdom was a favoured guest," "hunted Truth" as characters to develop the conflicts apparent in the poem. [TIP: Capitalization of nouns often indicates personification.]

4. **D.** This is an antecedent question. The student must retrace the reference "He" back to its origins to locate the correct answer. Try asking "who is enthroned, lewd and unsupportable?" Since truth, charity, and wisdom are described positively, only *vulgar* pride qualifies as the answer.

5. **C.** This question requires you to find the antecedent. Ask yourself, "Who or what lifts man?" The answer, *charity*, should be obvious.

6. **B.** Sometimes you can find information from a previous question. In question 2, "danger" was eliminated as a choice; therefore, it probably wouldn't be suitable for this question either. Try finding proof of the others. Truth = honest; holy = spiritual; bread = nourishment. Therefore, *dangerous* has to be the answer.

7. **D.** This is a tone question based on a repetitive contradictory phrase. She does *not* wish him well; therefore, she is bitter and resigned. There is nothing playful, wistful, or frantic in the conclusion.

8. **B.** This is a relationship question. You should realize this by the intensity of the opposing lewd force, pride, which destroyed the sanctity of the love. (If you see this, you could validate your answer to question 9.)

9. **D.** The cause is developed in the longest stanza, lines 7–15. Find the proof for your answer in lines 7–12.

10. **A.** Interestingly enough, the speaker reveals the conclusion in the first two lines of the poem. "The sun that will not rise again" establishes the totality of the circumstances.

Heart of Darkness
by Joseph Conrad

11. **E.** Here's an easy question to start you off. For years you heard your English teachers and your classmates discussing all the elements that could be associated with *darkness*. All the choices given in this question would qualify except for *exploration*.

12. **C.** Line 1 gives you the answer. The Thames is the river that runs through the heart of London.

13. **D.** A careful reading of the passage will introduce you to a speaker who is *thinking* about the past, *thinking* about exploration and conquest, and *thinking* about the conqueror and the conquered.

14. **A.** Here, the speaker is asking his listeners to picture the past. Therefore, it is *not* pointing to the future. The feelings of a commander have nothing to do with a future event; whereas each of the other choices hints at a future concept.

15. **B.** The second paragraph is about ancient Rome and its conquests. The third paragraph has the speaker considering "us" and what saves "us." This is past and present.

16. **B.** The first ten lines support inclusion of A. Choice B is NOT part of the speaker's conversation. Choice C is supported in the second paragraph. Choice D may be found in lines 5–8. Lines 36–47 support Choice E.

17. **D.** Lines 26–30 and 39–45 indicate the speaker's attitude toward the human condition. There is no evidence in the passage to support any of the other choices.

18. **A.** The question assumes you know the definition of *paradox*. Therefore, you should

be able to see that to be fascinated by that which is repulsive, awful, and horrible is a paradox.

19. D. "A sea," "a sky," "a kind," "or orders," "or what" are examples of parallel structure. The simile is "ship about as rigid as a concertina."

20. E. This is a straightforward, factual question. The answer is found in line 37.

21. D. In lines 45–47 the speaker is philosophizing about what it is that "redeems" the "conquest of the earth." It is the *idea*.

22. B. This question asks you to locate the antecedent of "this." You could use the substitution method here. Just replace "this" with the word or phrase. Or, you could look carefully at the text itself. The omniscient narrator is describing the speaker as a Buddha. Lines 45–46 come after "this." D and E are not real possibilities. Also, they are too far away from the pronoun.

23. E. A careful reading of the passage allows you to find references to A and D and to locate the quoted phrases in B and C. What you will *not* find are any references to "punishment for a crime."

Sonnet 73
by William Shakespeare

24. B. The difficulty with this question lies in the similarity between B and E. However, it should be apparent from the numerous references to death and the contrast to youth that the poet is speaking of a literal time period in life and not of a state of emotional development.

25. E. Use the process of substitution and work backward in the poem to find the antecedent. Recognize the appositive phrase, which is set off by commas, to spot the previous image— "black night." Another trick is to recast the line into a directly stated sentence instead of the poetic inversion. Asking "who or what is Death's second self" will help you locate the subject of the line.

26. A. Once again you are being tested on terminology and your ability to recognize an example. Deconstruct the line and find its

essence; here it is obvious that "consumed" and "nourished" are contradictory.

27. B. Even without returning to the poem, you should notice that A, C, D, and E suggest death or diminishment. The only image of intensity and life appears in choice B.

28. D. The keys to this question can be found in lines 10–12 and line 14, which restate the irony of the beloved's devotion and the speaker's mortality. A good technique is to always check the previous and subsequent lines in order to clarify your answer. Also, careful reading would eliminate A and B. Passion is not mentioned in the poem.

29. D. For the prepared student, this question is a giveaway. Definitions of these terms in Chapter 9 clarify the differences among the types of sonnets. The rhyme scheme should lead you to choose D.

30. A. The sonnet depends on several extended comparisons with nature—the seasons, day and night, and fire. Although there may be a contradiction in the final three lines, the primary means of development is metaphor. (See Chapter 8 for examples of synecdoche.)

31. E. Since contradiction and paradox are techniques that create irony, you should be able to see that choice E restates the essential opposing forces in the sonnet.

32. C. You must reread and interpret the entire third quatrain to clearly figure out this question. You need to decode the metaphor and realize that fires must be fed and that they expire when they exhaust the source of fuel.

33. D. Even though E is a lovely thought, the speaker never expresses the desire to have the beloved age along with him. This answer depends on the pun in the title of choice D— fall. Here it may refer to the season of age as well as to the decline of the speaker and the relationship. No other choice is supported in the sonnet.

34. A. At first glance, one might think the speaker is submissive to the greater force of death; however, at no time does he acquiesce to the demands of mortality. The speaker thinks about and reflects on his circumstances.

35. E. You should notice that three of the five choices are negative. If you have read carefully, you will be aware that the poem is laudatory and positive with regard to the depth of the beloved's love. And, at no time is the speaker looking forward to his lover's departure.

Poets and Language
by Percy Bysshe Shelley

36. C. This question is an example of how important the knowledge of definitions of literary terms is if you hope to do well on the AP Lit exam. Using your knowledge and experience, you would obviously choose C after reading just a few of the opening lines.

37. E. Lines 2–3 give you the answer to this factual question. You simply have to know a couple of synonyms for "legislators" and "prophets."

38. E. Here, you are being asked to make some serious associations with germination and flowering of buds and plants that lead to the future production of fruit. Also, the word "latest" should lead you to choose E.

39. A. This question centers around a literary definition and requires you to look at the words preceding and following the given phrase. "Foreknow the spirit of events" and "attribute of prophecy" point only to A.

40. D. A careful reading of lines 10–15 will lead you to conclude that all choices *except* "forbid citation" can be seen as a function of

grammatical forms. Citation is associated with the limits of the essay.

41. B. In line 14, "examples of this fact" refers to Aeschylus, the book of Job, and Dante. The word "examples" must lead you to choose B.

42. D. This is a rather difficult question. In lines 9–10, the reader is told that the poet participates in the eternal. Lines 11–12 state that grammatical forms will not injure poetry, and the reader is given examples of this. At the end of the paragraph, Shelley states that sculpture, etc. is even "more decisive," meaning indicative of the eternal.

43. E. Simply, the antecedent of "that" is "poetry." If in doubt, use substitution.

44. C. Lines 21–24 indicate all the characteristics given except for C.

45. A. This question demands nothing more than knowing the meanings of two words and locating an antecedent. To find the answer, you must go to the preceding sentence. In line 26, you will see the *last* item is "art."

46. D. Comparing language to a mirror and all other materials to a cloud are examples of metaphor and simile being used to construct imagery. Comparing an inanimate object to a living being is not a part of this image.

47. D. Carefully read the words in lines 29–30, beginning with "the mirrors" and ending with "upon the present." Here, Shelley compares poets to mirrors of the future. Mirrors reflect.

CHAPTER 5

The Prose Passage Essay

IN THIS CHAPTER

Summary: Complete explanation of the prose passage essay and its purpose as it is presented on the AP English Literature exam

Key Ideas

✪ Learn the types of prose passage prompts you might encounter on the AP English Literature exam
✪ Learn about the rubrics and rating of the AP English Literature prose passage essay
✪ Learn the basics of reading and notating a given passage
✪ Learn the basics of constructing your response to the prompt
✪ Examine the student models that respond to the diagnostic exam's prose passage essay prompt
✪ Learn how the rubrics were used to rate the student sample essays

Introduction to the Prose Passage Essay

This section of the exam gives you an opportunity to read and analyze a prose piece of literature. This is your chance to become personally involved in the text and to demonstrate your literary skills.

What Is an AP Literature Prose Passage?

Generally, it is a one-page excerpt from a work of fiction. More often than not, the selection will be from a novel or short story. Be aware that the exam may also present an excerpt from a drama.

What Is the Purpose in Writing an Essay About a Prose Piece?

First, the people at the College Board want to determine your facility in reading and interpreting a sustained piece of literature. It requires you to understand the text and to analyze those techniques and devices the author uses to achieve his or her purpose.

Second, the AP exam is designed to allow you to demonstrate your ease and fluency with terminology, interpretation, and criticism. Also, the level of your writing should be a direct reflection of your critical thinking.

Third, the AP exam determines your ability to make connections between analysis and interpretation. For example, when you find a metaphor, you should identify and connect it to the author's intended purpose or meaning. You should not just list items as you locate them. You must connect them to your interpretation.

> Before beginning to work with an actual prose passage, read the review of processes and terms in the Comprehensive Review section of this book. You should also have completed some of the activities in that section.

Types of Prose Passage Essay Questions

Let's look at a few prose passage questions that have been asked on the AP Literature exam in the past:

- Analyze narrative and literary techniques and other resources of language used for characterization.
- How does a narrator reveal character? (i.e., tone, diction, syntax, point of view)
- How does the author reveal a character's predicament? (i.e., diction, imagery, point of view)
- Explain the effect of the passage on the reader.
- Compare/contrast two passages concerning diction and details for the effect on the reader.
- How does the passage provide characterization and evaluation of one character over another? (i.e., diction, syntax, imagery, tone)
- What is the attitude of the speaker toward a particular subject?
- Analyze the effect of revision when given both the original and the revised version of a text.
- Analyze style and tone and how they are used to explore the author's attitudes toward his or her subject.
- How is the reader prepared for the conclusion of the piece?

You should be prepared to write an essay based on any of these prompts. Practice. Practice. Practice anticipating questions. Keep a running list of the kinds of questions your teacher asks.

> Don't be thrown by the complexity of a passage. Remember, *you* choose the references you wish to incorporate into your essay. So, even if you haven't understood everything, you are still able to write an intelligent essay—*as long as you address the prompt* and refer to the parts of the passage you do understand.
>
> Watch out for overconfidence when you see what you believe to be an easy question with an easy passage. You are going to have to work extra hard to find the nuances in the text that will allow you to write a mature essay.

Rating the Prose Passage Essay

You will be relieved to know that the rating of your essay is *not* based on whether or not the reader likes you or agrees with your point of view.

How Do the Test Readers Evaluate My Essay?

It's important to understand just what it is that goes into rating your essay. This is called a *rubric*, but don't let that word frighten you. A rubric is a word that simply refers to the <u>rating standards that are set and used by the people who read the essays</u>. These standards are fairly consistent, no matter what the prompt might be. The primary change is in the citing of the specifics in a particular prompt.

Let us assure you that, as experienced readers of the AP English exams, we know that the readers are trained to reward those things you do well in addressing the question. They are *not* looking to punish you. They are aware of the time constraints, and they read your essay just as your own instructor would read the first draft of an essay you wrote on a 40-minute exam. <u>These readers look forward to an interesting, insightful, and well-constructed essay</u>.

So, let's take a look at the following rubrics:

Prose Passage Essay Rubric

- 1 point for thesis/claim/introduction that is appropriate to the prompt
- 4 points for evidence/support of the thesis/claim
  - Clear and appropriate references to the text
  - Clear presentation of how the references relate to the thesis
- 1 point for complexity of the commentary and syntax

Remember, the essay is really a first draft. The test readers know this and approach each essay with this in mind.

Timing the Essay

Timing is crucial. With that in mind, here's a workable strategy:

- 1–3 minutes reading and "working the prompt."
- 5 minutes reading and making marginal notes about the passage. Try to isolate 2 quotations that strike you. This may give you your opening and closing.
- 5–10 minutes preparing to write. (Choose one or two of the following methods that you feel comfortable with.)
  - Underlining, bracketing, circling
  - Marginal notations
  - Charts or key word/one word/line number outlining
- 20–25 minutes to write your essay, based on your preparation.
- 3 minutes for proofreading.

Using a highlighter is not allowed during the exam. However, it is a strong tool for practice in critical reading.

Note: Throughout this book, the term **highlight** will also refer to underlining, circling, or bracketing.

In the margin, note what time you should be finished with each essay. For example, the test starts at 1 P.M. You write 1:40 in the margin. Time to move on.

Working the Prompt

You can't write clearly unless you know *Why* you are writing and *What's Expected* of you. When you "Work the Prompt," you are maximizing both of these areas.

How Should I Go About Reading the Prose Prompt?

To bring the answer home to you, we will deconstruct a prompt for you now. (This is the same question that is in the Diagnostic/Master exam.) Plan to spend 1–3 minutes carefully reading the question. This will give you time to really digest what the question is asking you to do.

Here's the prompt:

In the following passage from the short story "The Dead," James Joyce presents an insight into the character of Gabriel. Write a well-organized essay in which you discuss various aspects of Gabriel's character that Joyce reveals to the reader and to Gabriel himself. Refer to such techniques and devices as imagery, point of view, motif, diction, and syntax.

Here are three reasons why you should do a 1–3-minute careful analysis of the prompt.

1. Once you know what is expected, you will read in a more directed manner.

2. Once you internalize the question, you will be sensitive to those details that will apply.

3. Once you know all the facets that need to be addressed, you will be able to write a complete essay demonstrating adherence to the topic.

Topic adherence, which means sticking to the question, is key to achieving a high score.

Do this now. Underline, circle, or bracket the essential terms and elements in the prompt. Time yourself. How long did it take you? _____ Don't worry if it took you longer than 1–3 minutes in this first attempt. You will be practicing this technique throughout this review, and it will become almost second nature to you.

Compare our working of the prompt with yours.

In the following passage from the <u>short story</u> "<u>The Dead</u>," <u>James Joyce</u> presents an <u>insight</u> into the <u>character</u> of Gabriel. Write a well-organized essay in which you <u>discuss</u> various <u>aspects of Gabriel's complex character</u> that Joyce <u>reveals to the reader and to Gabriel himself</u>. Refer to such <u>techniques</u> and devices as <u>imagery</u>, <u>point of view</u>, <u>motif</u>, <u>diction</u>, and <u>syntax</u>.

In this prompt, anything else you may have highlighted is extraneous.

When the question uses the expression "such as," you are *not* required to use only those ideas presented; you are free to use your own selection of techniques and devices. Notice that the prompt requires more than one technique. One will not be enough. You *must* use more than one. If you fail to use more than one technique, no matter how well you present your answer, your essay will be incomplete.

Reading and Notating the Prose Passage

Depending on your style and comfort level, choose one of these approaches to your reading:

1. A. Read quickly to get the gist of the passage.
   B. Reread, using the visual and marginal notes approach.
2. A. Read slowly, using highlighting and making marginal notes.
   B. Reread to confirm that you understand the full impact of the passage.

Note: In both approaches, you *must* highlight and make marginal notes. There is no way to avoid this. Ignore what you don't immediately understand. It may become clear to you after you finish reading the passage. Practice. Practice. Concentrate on those parts of the passage that apply to what you highlighted in the prompt.

There are many ways to read and interpret any given passage. You have to choose which one to use and which specifics to include for support. Don't be rattled if there is leftover material.

We've reproduced the passage for you below so that you can practice both the reading and the process of deconstructing the text. Use highlighting, arrows, circles, underlining, notes, numbers, and whatever you need to make the connections clear to you.

Do this now. Spend 8–10 minutes working the material. *Do not skip this step*. It is time well spent and is a key to the high-score essay.

The Dead

She was fast asleep.

Gabriel, leaning on his elbow, looked for a few moments
unresentfully on her tangled hair and half-open mouth, listening to her
deep-drawn breath. So she had had that romance in her life: a man had
died for her sake. It hardly pained him now to think how poor a part   5
he, her husband, had played in her life. He watched her while she slept
as though he and she had never lived together as man and wife. His
curious eyes rested long upon her face and on her hair and, as he thought
of what she must have been then, in that time of her first girlish beauty,
a strange friendly pity for her entered his soul. He did not like to say   10
even to himself that her face was no longer beautiful but he knew that it
was no longer the face for which Michael Furey had braved death.

Perhaps she had not told him all the story. His eyes moved to the
chair over which she had thrown some of her clothes. A petticoat string
dangled to the floor. One boot stood upright, its limp upper fallen down: 15
the fellow of it lay upon its side. He wondered at his riot of emotions of
an hour before. From what had it proceeded? From his aunt's supper,
from his own foolish speech, from the wine and dancing, the merry-making
when saying good-night in the hall, the pleasure of the walk along the river
in the snow. Poor Aunt Julia! She, too, would soon be a shade with the   20
shade of Patrick Morkan and his horse. He had caught that haggard look
upon her face for a moment when she was singing *Arrayed for the Bridal.*
Soon, perhaps, he would be sitting in the same drawing-room dressed in
black, his silk hat on his knees. The blinds would be drawn down and
Aunt Kate would be sitting beside him, crying and blowing her nose and   25
telling him how Julia had died. He would cast about in his mind for some
words that might console her, and would find only lame and useless ones.
Yes, yes: that would happen very soon.

KEY IDEA ▶ Now, compare your reading notes with what we've done below. Yours may vary from
ours, but the results of your note-taking should be similar in scope.

The Dead

who? — *alike?*

Bible?
angel? — Gabriel, leaning on his elbow, <u>looked</u> for a few <u>moments</u> — *time* / *he hears*
death?
time — <u>unresentfully</u> on her <u>tangled</u> hair and <u>half-open mouth</u>, <u>listening</u> to her — *not him*
last? — deep-drawn breath. So she <u>had had</u> that <u>romance in her life: a man had</u>
<u>died for her sake</u>. It <u>hardly pained him now to think</u> how <u>poor a part</u> — *he thinks*
detached? — he, her husband, had played in her life. <u>He watched her</u> while <u>she slept</u> — *he sees*
death — as though he and she <u>had never lived together as man and wife</u>. His — *death-like?*
time — <u>curious</u> eyes <u>rested</u> long upon her face and on her hair and, as <u>he thought</u>
<u>of what she must have been</u> <u>then</u>, in that <u>time</u> of her <u>first girlish</u> beauty, — *time—again*

She was fast <u>asleep</u>. ◀——— *short sentence*

he's kind? — a <u>strange friendly pity</u> for her entered his <u>soul</u>. <u>He did not like to say</u> — back to death

weak — <u>even to himself</u> that <u>her face was no longer beautiful</u> but he knew that it — time

coward? — was <u>no longer</u> the face for which Michael <u>Furey</u> had <u>braved death</u>. — fury?

self-image   time — Perhaps she had not told him all the story. His eyes moved to the — not a coward

chair over which she had thrown some of her clothes. A petticoat string — weak?

dangled to the floor. One boot stood upright, its <u>limp</u> upper <u>fallen down</u>: — lack of control?

the fellow of it lay upon its side. He wondered at his <u>riot</u> of emotions of — afraid to let go?

time — an <u>hour before</u>. From what had it proceeded? From his aunt's supper,

self-image — from his own <u>foolish speech</u>, from the wine and dancing, the merry-making

death? — when saying <u>good-night</u> in the hall, the pleasure of the walk along the river

cold death? — in the <u>snow</u>. Poor Aunt Julia! She, too, would <u>soon</u> be a <u>shade</u> with the — time

ghost? — <u>shade</u> of Patrick Morkan and his horse. He had caught that haggard look — cold

cold   time — upon her face for a <u>moment</u> when she was singing *Arrayed for the Bridal*.

time — <u>Soon</u>, perhaps, he would be sitting in the same drawing-room <u>dressed in</u> — mourning

death — <u>black, his silk hat on his knees</u>. The <u>blinds would be drawn down</u> and — closed off   mourning

Aunt Kate would be sitting beside him, <u>crying and blowing</u> her nose and — self-image

death — telling him how <u>Julia had died</u>. <u>He would cast about in his mind for some</u> — detached

weak? — <u>words that might console her</u>, and would find only <u>lame and useless</u> ones.

uncertain? — Yes, yes: that would happen very <u>soon</u>. — time — weakness

After you have marked the passage, review the prompt. You are asked to look for ways Joyce reveals Gabriel's character. When you consult your notes, certain categories will begin to pop out at you. These can be the basis for the development of the body of your essay. For example, we saw details and images that support the concepts of:

- Death
- Time
- Insecurity
- Passivity
- Detachment

In addition, stylistically, we noticed the use of short sentences.

Here's how one category developed using the notations made on the passage. Notice that we have ignored notes that did not apply to the prompt.

Concept: Time

Words/Phrases from the Text:

"a few moments"
"had had that romance"
"he thought of what she must
  have been then"
"girlish beauty"
"no longer beautiful"

"no longer the face"
"an hour before"
"soon be a shade"
"for a moment"
"soon"
"that would happen very soon"

Conclusion: Gabriel moves from the distant past to the near future. He becomes aware of the change in the marital relationship with his wife and with his own passage.

Your Turn

Now you choose a concept you are able to explore and defend that reveals Gabriel's character.

Concept:

Words/Phrases from the Text:

Conclusion:

In response to the prompt, we have decided that the techniques/devices we will analyze are:

• Imagery	• Style
• Diction	• Motif

Here's one technique/device and how it is developed in the passage. Again, notice that we use our margin notes to trace this development.

Technique/Device: Imagery

Words/Phrases from the Text:

the title "The Dead"	Gabriel's very name
"entered his soul"	"braved death"
"fallen down"	"good-night"
"in the snow"	"would soon be a shade"
"dressed in black"	"the blinds would be drawn"
"crying and blowing her nose"	

Conclusion: These images foreshadow and emphasize that there is a coldness and a loss in relationships and self-image.

Your Turn

Now you choose the technique/device you are able to explore and defend that reveals Gabriel's character.

Technique/Device:

Words/Phrases from the Text:

Conclusion:

If you expand the above techniques/devices and categories into interpretive statements and support those statements with appropriate details that you've already isolated, you will be writing a detailed essay.

Writing the Opening Paragraph

Your opening statement is the one that sets the tone of your essay and possibly raises the expectations of the reader. Spend time on your first paragraph to maximize your score.

Make certain that your topic is very clear. This reinforces the idea that you fully understand what is expected of you and what you will communicate to the reader. Generally, identify both the text and its author in this first paragraph.

A suggested approach is to relate a direct quotation from the passage to the topic.

Consider the "philosophy of firsts." It is a crucial strategy to spend focused time on the first part of the question and on the first paragraph of the essay because:

1. It establishes the direction and tone of your essay.

2. It gives you the guidelines for what to develop in your essay.

3. It connects you to the reader.

Remember our philosophy: **In the Beginning:** if you focus on the beginning, the rest will fall into place. A wonderful thing happens after much practice, highlighting, and note-taking. Your mind starts to focus automatically. Trust us on this. It is the winning edge that can take an average essay and raise it to a higher level.

Do this now. Take 5 minutes to write your opening paragraph for "The Dead" prompt. Write quickly, referring to your notes.

Let's check what you've written:

Highlight these points to see if you've done them. You may be surprised at what is actually there.

• Have you included author and title? _____ Yes _____ No

• Have you addressed the character of Gabriel? _____ Yes _____ No

• Have you specifically mentioned the techniques you will refer to in your essay?

_____ Yes _____ No

Here are four sample opening paragraphs that address all of the criteria:

A

In "The Dead" by James Joyce, the character Gabriel is revealed through diction, point of view, and imagery as he watches his wife sleep.

B

Poor Gabriel! Who would have thought he knew so little about himself and his life. And yet, in "The Dead," James Joyce, through diction, point of view, and imagery, makes it clear to the reader and to Gabriel that there is much to reveal about his character.

C

"Yes, yes: that would happen very soon." And, yes, very soon the reader of the excerpt from Joyce's "The Dead" gets to know the character of Gabriel. Through diction, point of view, and imagery, we are introduced to Gabriel and what he thinks of himself.

D

"The Dead." How apt a title. James Joyce turns his reader into a fly on the wall as Gabriel is about to realize the many losses in his life. Death pervades the passage, from his sleeping wife to his dying aunt.

Each of these opening paragraphs is an acceptable beginning to an AP Literature exam essay. Note what each of these paragraphs accomplishes:

• Each has identified the title and author.
• Each has stated which techniques/devices will be used.
• Each has stated the purpose of analyzing these techniques/devices.

Now, note what is different about each opening paragraph:

• Sample **A** restates the question without anything extra. It is to the point, so much so that it does nothing more than repeat the question. It's correct, but it does not really pique the reader's interest. (Use this type of opening if you feel unsure of or uncomfortable with the prompt.)
• Sample **B** reveals the writer's attitude toward the subject. The writer has already determined that Gabriel is flawed and indicates an understanding of how Gabriel's character is revealed in the passage.
• Sample **C**, with its direct quotation, places the reader immediately into the passage. The reader quickly begins to hear the writer's voice through his or her choice of words (diction).
• Sample **D**, at first glance, reveals a mature, confident writer who is not afraid to *imply* the prompt's criteria.

Note: There are many other types of opening paragraphs that could do the job as well. The paragraphs above are just a few samples.

Into which of the above samples would you classify your opening paragraph?

Writing the Body

When you write the body of your essay, take only 20–25 minutes. Time yourself and try your best to finish within that time frame.

Since this is practice, don't panic if you can't complete the essay within the allotted time. You will become more and more comfortable with the tasks presented to you as you gain experience with this type of question.

What Should I Include in the Body of the Prose Passage Essay?

1. Obviously, this is where you present your interpretation and the points you wish to make that are related to the prompt.

2. Use specific references and details from the passage.
   • Don't always paraphrase the original; refer directly to it.
   • Place quotation marks around those words and phrases that you extract from the passage.

3. Use "connective tissue" in your essay to establish adherence to the question.
   • Use the repetition of key ideas from your opening paragraph.
   • Try using "echo words" (i.e., synonyms, such as death/loss/passing or character/persona/personality).
   • Create transitions from one paragraph to the next.

To understand the process, carefully read the following sample paragraphs. Each develops one of the categories and techniques/devices asked for in the prompt. Notice the specific references and the "connective tissue." Also, notice that details that do not apply to the prompt have been ignored.

A
This paragraph develops **imagery**.

Joyce creates imagery to lead his reader to sense the cloud of death that pervades Gabriel's world. From its very title "The Dead," the reader is prepared for loss. Just what has Gabriel lost: his wife, his confidence, his job, a friend, a relative, what? As his "wife slept," Gabriel sees her "half-open mouth" and "listens" to her "deep-drawn breath." The reader almost senses this to be a death watch. The images about the room reinforce this sense of doom. One boot is "limp" and the other is "upon its side." Picturing the future, Gabriel sees a "drawing-room dressed in black" with blinds "drawn down" and his Aunt Kate "crying" and "telling him how Julia had died." And to underscore his own feelings of internal lifelessness, he can only find "lame and useless" words of comfort.

B
This paragraph develops the **motif of time**.

Time is a constant from the beginning to the end of the passage. In the first paragraph, Gabriel is in the present while thinking of the past. He is an observer, watching his wife as he, himself, is observed by the narrator, and as we, as readers, observe the entire scene. Time moves the reader and Gabriel through the experience. Immediately, we spend a "few moments" with Gabriel as he goes back and forth in time assessing his relationship with his wife. He recognizes she "had had romance in her life." But, "it hardly pains him now." He thinks of what she had been "then" in her "girlish" beauty, which may indicate his own aging. His "strange friendly pity," because she is "no longer beautiful," may be self-pity, as well. In the next paragraph, we are with Gabriel as he reflects on his emotional "riot" only an hour before. However, he jumps to the future because he can't sustain self-examination. He chooses to allow himself to jump to this future and a new subject—Aunt Julia's death. In this future, he continues to see only his inability and incompetence. For Gabriel, all this will happen "very soon."

C
This passage develops **diction**.

Gabriel appears to be a man who is on the outside of his life. Joyce's diction reveals his passive nature. Gabriel "looked on" and "watched" his wife sleeping. He spent time "listening to her breath" and was "hardly pained by his role in her life." His eyes "rest" on her, and he "thinks of the past." All of Gabriel's actions are as weak as a "limp" and "fallen down" boot, "inert in the face of life." He is in direct contrast to Michael Furey, who has "braved death." And he knows this about himself. The narrator's diction reveals that Gabriel "did not like to say even to himself," implying that he is too weak to face the truth.

Later in the text, Gabriel's word choice further indicates his insecurity. He is troubled by his "riot of emotions," his "foolish speech." It is obvious that Gabriel will not take such risks again.

D
This passage develops **style**.

Joyce's very straightforward writing style supports the conclusions he wishes the reader to draw about the character of Gabriel. Most sentences are in the subject/verb, simple sentence form, reflecting the plain, uncomplicated character of Gabriel.

Joyce employs a third person narrator to further reinforce Gabriel's detachment from his own circumstances. We watch him observing his own life with little or no connection on his part. He wonders at his "riot of emotions." All this is presented without Joyce using obvious poetic devices. This punctuates the lack of "romance" in Gabriel's life when compared with that of Michael Furey.

> Start a study group. Approach an essay as a team. After you've deconstructed the prompt, have each person write a paragraph on a separate area of the question. Then come together and discuss what was written. You'll be amazed at how much fun this is because the work will carry you away. This is a chance to explore exciting ideas.
>
> Again, sharing your writing with members of your class or study group will allow you to gain experience and find a comfort zone with requirements and possibilities.

We urge you to spend more time developing the body paragraphs than worrying about a concluding paragraph, especially one that begins with "In conclusion," or "In summary." In such a brief essay, the reader will have no problem remembering what you have already stated. It is not necessary to repeat yourself in a summary-type final paragraph.

If you want to make a final statement, try to link your ideas to a particularly effective line or image from the passage.

Note: Look at the last line of Sample **B** on motif. For Gabriel, all this will happen "very soon." This final sentence would be fine as the conclusion to the essay. A conclusion does not have to be a paragraph. It can be the writer's final remark or observation presented in a sentence or two.

Do this now. Write the body of your essay. Time yourself. Allow 15–20 minutes to complete this task.

Sample Student Essays

Following are two actual student essays followed by a rubric and comments on each. Read both of the samples in sequence to clarify the differences between "high" and "mid-range" essays.

Student Essay A

A picture is worth a thousand words, but James Joyce manages to paint a pretty vivid one in only two short paragraphs. Joyce offers tremendous insight into the character of Gabriel in the short story "The Dead." He captures the essence of a scene laden with death and laced with tones of despair and hopelessness. By employing third person narration alternating with a stream of consciousness, Joyce demonstrates his abilities to delve deep into Gabriel's mind, illustrating this somewhat detached disposition and low self-image.

The passage takes us through Gabriel's reflections upon past, present, and future events while his inner character unfolds. Joyce's careful use of diction suggests that Gabriel has emotionally closed himself off to the world as he tries to cope with some aforementioned incident. He was "hardly pained" to think about a situation which caused a "riot of emotions" just a little earlier on that evening. Here, Joyce is emphasizing Gabriel's way of coping with an unfavorable event by blocking it out. He continues to "unresentfully" reflect upon what had occurred, closing himself off from any pain he obviously experienced a short while ago.

With the powerful omniscience of a third-person narrator, Joyce is able to describe the workings of Gabriel's inner consciousness without writing from the first-person point of view. Gabriel further detaches himself as he thinks about his wife. He watches her from the point of view of an outsider, as if they were never married. The mere fact that Gabriel is able to do this suggests that he and his wife do not have a truly loving relationship. This assertion is underscored by the "friendly" pity Gabriel feels for his wife, emphasizing the lack of true love in their relationship. Gabriel later questions his wife's honesty, further emphasizing a troubled relationship. The reader may be inclined to infer that Gabriel is completely devoid of compassion; however, this idea is refuted. Gabriel proceeds to express an element of sorrow when he thinks back to his wife's youth and beauty.

The evening's events had evidently triggered some type of emotional outburst which Gabriel cannot stop thinking about. His mental state is paralleled by the chaotic state of disorder in the room he is in. With a masterful control of language and syntax, Joyce describes in short, choppy sentences the array of clothing strewn around the room. This is followed by one of the longest sentences in the passage. Joyce reveals this series of events all at once, paralleling Gabriel's release of a multitude of emotions at once.

Joyce weaves a motif of darkness and death into the story. His aunt's "haggard" appearance ironically catches Gabriel's attention during the recitation of Arrayed for the Bridal, a seemingly happy song. This image of happiness and marriage is further contrasted with images of the woman's funeral and a detailed description of how Gabriel will mourn for her. Joyce also takes time to underscore Gabriel's low self-esteem, in that he will only think of "lame and useless" words at a time when comforting tones are necessary. He is essentially describing himself, since it has been established that he failed as a husband and that he is emotionally distraught even though he blocks out the pain he feels. "The blinds would be drawn down," Gabriel says, as he describes both the room at his aunt's funeral and his mental state of affairs.

The true originator of "stream-of-consciousness" techniques, Joyce delves deep into Gabriel's mind, describing his wide range of emotions and state of mind. His powerful diction reveals a great deal about Gabriel's character while his implied insights penetrate into the reader's mind, reinforcing the abstract meanings behind the actions and events that transpire throughout the course of his story.

Student Essay B

In the excerpt from the short story "The Dead" from Dubliners by James Joyce, the author describes some personality traits of the character Gabriel as he sits watching a sleeping woman. The point of view from which this excerpt is expressed helps the reader to get to know Gabriel because the narrator is omniscient and knows how Gabriel perceives things and what he is thinking. With the use of many literary devices such as imagery, diction, and syntax, the reader is able to see that Gabriel is an observant and a reflective person, but he is also detached.

Gabriel comes across as observant, because throughout the entire passage he is observing a woman, his wife, sleeping. He scans the room looking over everything and taking note of everything. An example of this is looking at "her tangled hair and half-open mouth, listening to her deep-drawn breath." The author uses the technique of syntax ("deep-drawn breath" and "half-open mouth") in the above quotation to show us exactly what Gabriel is seeing. Gabriel notices many details, and they are described so that the reader can clearly formulate a picture of what he is gazing at. This imagery can be seen in lines such as the one where the woman's boots are being described. "One boot stood upright, its limp upper fallen down: the fellow of it lay upon the side." The diction used such as "limp" and "upright," are concrete words that create clear pictures. Another reason that Gabriel comes across as observant is because he catches and notices little things. For example, he "caught" the "haggard look" on his Aunt Julia's face.

Resulting from the fact that Gabriel is observant, he is also reflective. He thinks over past events that had happened and wonders what caused them and why he did what he did. In the first paragraph he reflects on his wife's "fading beauty," what she used to look like, and the story of the death of Michael Furey. He realizes that it is a possibility that she had not told him the entire story concerning the boy's death. He further reflects when he is thinking about his emotional outburst. He asks himself many questions including "From what had it proceeded?"

A feeling of detachment is also present. The way he looks at his wife "as though he and she had never lived together as man and wife" shows that he is viewing his own life from an objective standpoint. He is able to look at his own life as though it wasn't his. The sentence that reads "it hardly pained him now to think how poor a part he, her husband, had played in her life," further exemplifies this feeling of detachment. Feelings that he used to feel no longer even touched him. He was able to recognize them, yet remain separate. In the second paragraph Gabriel continues

to come across as remote. He is able to picture and describe in great detail the
death and funeral of his Aunt Julia. He narrates the future drastic event in a
matter-of-fact way. Gabriel goes so far as to describe what he will be thinking at
the time of his Aunt Julia's death which is "he would cast about in his mind for some
words that might console her (his Aunt Kate), and would find only lame and useless
ones." This statement finalizes the idea that Gabriel is a person who is, at least to
some degree, detached from his own life.

    Even though the passage is fairly short, the author is able to impart a fair
amount of information concerning the character Gabriel. It becomes apparent that
he possesses the qualities of observance, reflection, and detachment. These
qualities are all interconnected because of the fact that he is observant leading to
his ability to reflect on his actions and actions of others. This in turn leads to his
detachment, because when he reflects on his life he does it from the standpoint of a
third-person narrator. The author's use of literary techniques helps to convey these
personality traits of Gabriel to a reader.

35

40

45

    Let's take a look at a set of rubrics for this prose passage essay. (If you want to see
actual AP rubrics as used in a recent AP Lit. exam, log on to the College Board website:
<www.collegeboard.org/ap>). As you probably know, essays are rated on a 6–1 scale, with
6 the highest and 1 the lowest. Since we are not there with you to personally rate your
essay and to respond to your style and approach, we are going to list the criteria for high-,
middle-, and low-range papers. These criteria are based on our experience with rubrics and
reading AP Literature essays.

    A HIGH-range essay can be a 6 or a 5. MIDDLE refers to essays in the 4–3 range. And
the LOW-scoring essays are rated 2–1.

    After reading the following rubrics, evaluate the two essays that you have just read.

Rating the Student Essays

High-Range Essay (5, 6)

- Indicates complete understanding of the prompt.
- The thesis clearly presents a possible interpretation and indicates how the support will
  be developed.
- Distinguishes between what Gabriel acknowledges about himself and what the reader
  comes to know about him.
- Explores the complexity of Gabriel's character.
- Identifies and analyzes Joyce's literary techniques, such as imagery, diction, point of view,
  motif, and style.
- Cites specific references to the passage.
- Illustrates and supports the points being made.
- Is clear, well-organized, and coherent.
- Reflects the ability to manipulate language at an advanced level.
- Contains only minor errors or flaws, if any.

Middle-Range Essay (3, 4)

- Refers accurately to the prompt.
- Refers accurately to the literary devices used by Joyce.
- Provides a less thorough analysis of Gabriel's character than the higher-rated paper.
- Is less adept at linking techniques to the purpose of the passage.
- Demonstrates writing that is adequate to convey the writer's intent.
- May not be sensitive to the implications about Gabriel's character.

Low-Range Essay (1, 2)

- Does not respond adequately to the prompt.
- Demonstrates insufficient and/or inaccurate understanding of the passage.
- Does not link literary devices to Gabriel's character.
- Underdevelops and/or inaccurately analyzes literary techniques.
- Fails to demonstrate an understanding of Gabriel's character.
- Demonstrates weak control of the elements of diction, syntax, and organization.
  How would you rate these essays?
  Now, compare your evaluation of the two student essays with ours.

Student Essay A

This is a high-range paper for the following reasons:

- Is on task.
- Shows complete understanding of the prompt and the passage.
- Indicates perceptive, subtle analysis (line 8).
- Maintains excellent topic adherence (lines 9, 17, 28, 39).
- Uses good "connective tissue" (repetition of key words).
- Chooses good specific references (lines 11, 12, 21, 35).
- Knows how to distinguish between the author and the narrator.
- Understands point of view well.
- Makes suggestions and inferences (lines 7, 20).
- Demonstrates good critical thinking.
- Is perceptive about syntax and the style of the author (lines 27–33).
- Links techniques with character (line 34).
- Demonstrates mature language manipulation (line 34).
- Understands function of diction and motif (lines 40–44).

> **TIP** It's best to omit extraneous judgmental words from your essay (line 45).

This is obviously a mature, critical reader and writer. Using subtle inferences and implications, the writer demonstrates an understanding of the character of Gabriel both as Joyce presents him and as Gabriel views himself. There is nothing extraneous or repetitious in this essay. Each point leads directly and compellingly to the next aspect of Gabriel's character.

This is definitely a strong, high-range essay.

Student Essay B

This is a middle-range essay for the following reasons:

- Sets up an introduction which indicates the techniques that will be developed, but neglects to clearly set up the required discussion of how Gabriel views himself.
- Immediately establishes that the essay will address Gabriel's character as drawn by the narrator and seen by the reader.
- Addresses three aspects of Gabriel's character without fully developing the analysis of literary techniques.
- Adheres to the essay's topic.
- Uses "connective tissue" (lines 21, 28).
- Uses "echo words" (lines 8, 9, 10).
- Uses citations from the passages.
- Isolates some details to illustrate Gabriel's character (lines 31–32, 39).
- Confuses syntax with diction (lines 12–13).
- Lacks development of literary technique in paragraph 4.
- Displays faulty diction and syntax.
- Does not develop an important part of the prompt—how Gabriel views himself.
- Incorporates faulty logic at times (lines 44–49).

This essay is a solid, middle-range paper. The writer has a facility with literary analysis. Even though there are flashes of real insight, they are not sustained throughout the essay. There is a strong opening paragraph which makes it clear to the reader what the topic of the paper is. The writer obviously grasps Gabriel's character and the needed details to support the character analysis. But the weakness in this paper is the writer's incomplete development of the relationship of literary techniques to character analysis.

Note: Both essays have concluding paragraphs that are repetitive and largely unnecessary. It is best to avoid this type of ending.

Your Turn

How about sharing these samples with members of your class or study group and discussing possible responses?

Try a little reverse psychology. Now that you are thoroughly familiar with this passage, construct two or three alternative prompts. (Walk a little in the examiner's shoes.) This will help you gain insight into the process of test-making. Create two questions of your own. (See the Types of Prose Passage Essay Questions section of this chapter for ideas.)

1ˢᵗ alternative prompt for "The Dead"

_____

_____

_____

_____

_____

2ⁿᵈ alternative prompt for "The Dead"

_____

_____

_____

_____

_____

Rapid Review

After you've absorbed the ideas in this chapter, the following points will provide you with a quick refresher when needed:

- Familiarize yourself with the types of prose questions (prompts).
- Highlight the prompt and understand all the required tasks.
- Time your essay carefully.
- Spend sufficient time "working the passage" before you begin writing.
- Mark up the passage.
- Create a strong opening paragraph.
- Refer often to the passage.
- Use concrete details and quotes to support your ideas.
- Always stay on topic.
- Avoid plot summary.
- Include transitions and echo words.
- Check the models and rubrics for guidance for self-evaluation.
- Practice—vary the question and your approach.
- Share ideas with others.

The Poetry Essay

IN THIS CHAPTER

Summary: Examination of the poetry essay and its purpose as it is presented in the AP English Literature exam

Key Ideas
- ✪ Learn the types of poetry prompts you might encounter in the AP English Literature exam
- ✪ Learn the basics of reading and notating a given poem
- ✪ Learn the basics of constructing your response to the poetry prompt
- ✪ Learn about the rubrics and rating of the AP poetry essays
- ✪ Examine model student essays
- ✪ Learn how rubrics were used to rate student essays

Introduction to the Poetry Essay

It's obvious to any reader that poetry is different from prose. And, writing about each is different also. This chapter will guide you through the expectations and processes associated with the AP Poetry section.

What Is the Purpose of the Poetry Essay?

The College Board wants to determine your facility in reading and interpreting a sustained piece of literature. You are required to understand the text and to analyze those techniques and devices the poet uses to achieve his or her purpose.

The AP Lit exam is designed to allow you to demonstrate your ease and fluency with terminology, interpretation, and analysis. The level of your writing should be a direct reflection of your critical thinking.

The AP Lit exam is looking for connections between analysis and interpretation. For example, when you find a metaphor, you should identify it and connect it to the poet's intended purpose or meaning. You shouldn't just list items as you locate them. You must connect them to your interpretation.

Before beginning to work with an actual poem, read the review of processes and terms in the Comprehensive Review section of this book. Make certain to complete some of the activities in that section.

Types of Prompts Used for the Poetry Essay

Not every poetry essay prompt is the same. Familiarizing yourself with the various types is critical. This familiarity will both increase your confidence and provide you with a format for poetry analysis.

What Kinds of Questions Are Asked for the Poetry Essay?

Let's look at several typical questions that have been used as prompts for the poetry essay on the AP Literature exam in the past:

- How does the language of the poem reflect the speaker's perceptions, and how does that language determine the reader's perception?
- How does the poet reveal character? (i.e., diction, sound devices, imagery, allusion)
- Discuss how poetic elements, such as language, structure, imagery, and point of view, convey meaning in a poem.
- Relate the imagery, form, or theme of a particular section of a poem to another part of that same poem. Discuss changing attitude or perception of speaker or reader.
- Analyze a poem's extended metaphor and how it reveals the poet's or speaker's attitude.
- Discuss the way of life revealed in a poem. Refer to such poetic elements as tone, imagery, symbol, and verse form.
- Discuss the poet's changing reaction to the subject developed in the poem.
- Discuss how the form of the poem affects its meaning.
- NOTE: There will be NO "paired poem prompts" on the exam.

You should be prepared to write an essay based on any of these prompts. Apply these questions to poems you read throughout the year. Practice anticipating questions. Keep a running list of the kinds of questions your teacher asks. Practice. Practice.

Timing and Planning the Poetry Essay

Successful writing is directly related to both thought and structure, and you will need to consider the following concepts related to pre-writing.

How Should I Plan to Spend My Time Writing the Poetry Essay?

Remember, timing is crucial. With this in mind, here's a workable strategy:

- 1–3 minutes reading and "working the prompt."
- 5 minutes reading and making marginal notes about the poem. Try to isolate two references that strike you. This may give you your opening and closing.
- 5–10 minutes preparing to write. (Choose one or two of the following methods that you feel comfortable with.)
  - Highlighting, underlining, circling, bracketing
  - Marginal mapping (see Chapter 5 for samples)
  - Key word/one word/line number outlining
  - Numerical clustering
- 20–25 minutes to write your essay, based on your preparation.
- 3 minutes for proofreading.

Working the Prompt

It is important to understand that the quality of your essay greatly depends upon your correctly addressing the prompt.

How Should I Go About Reading the Poetry Prompt?

As we did in the prose section, we will deconstruct a poetry essay prompt for you now. (This is the same question that is in the Diagnostic/Master exam earlier in this book.)

You should plan to spend 1–3 minutes carefully reading the question. This will give you time to really digest what the question is asking you to do.

Here's the prompt:

In "On the Subway," Sharon Olds brings two worlds into close proximity. Identify the contrasts that develop both portraits in the poem and discuss the insights the narrator comes to as a result of the experience. Refer to such literary techniques as tone, poetic devices, imagery, and organization.

In the margin, note what time you should be finished with this essay. For example, the test starts at 1 P.M. You write 1:40 in the margin. Time to move on.

Here are three reasons why you should do a 1–3-minute careful analysis of the prompt:

1. Once you know what is expected, you will read in a more directed manner.

2. Once you internalize the question, you will be sensitive to the details that will apply as you read the poem.

3. Once you know all the facets that need to be addressed, you will be able to write a complete essay that demonstrates adherence to the topic.

Do this now. Highlight, circle, or underline the essential terms and elements in the prompt. Time yourself. How long did it take you?

Compare our highlighting of the prompt with yours.

In "On the Subway," Sharon Olds brings two worlds into close proximity. Identify the contrasts that develop both portraits in the poem and discuss the insights the narrator comes to as a result of the experience. Refer to such literary techniques as tone, poetic devices, imagery, and organization.

In this prompt, anything else you may have highlighted is extraneous.

When the question uses the expression "such as," you are not required to use only those ideas presented; you are free to use your own selection of techniques and devices. Notice that the prompt requires more than one technique. One will not be enough. You must use more than one. If you fail to use more than one technique, no matter how well you present your answer, your essay will be incomplete.

Reading and Notating the Poetry Selection

Finally, read the poem. Depending on your style and comfort level, choose one of these approaches to your reading:

1. A. Read quickly to get the gist of the poem.
   B. Reread, using the highlighting and marginal notes approach.

2. A. Read slowly, as if speaking aloud. Let the structure of the poem help you with meaning. (See the terms *enjambment* and *caesura* in the Glossary at the back of this book.)
   B. Reread to confirm that you understand the full impact of the poem. Do your highlighting and make marginal notes.

Note: In both approaches, you *must* highlight and make marginal notes. There is no way to avoid this. Ignore what you don't immediately understand. It may become clear to you after reading the poem. Practice. Practice. Concentrate on those parts of the poem that apply to what you highlighted in the prompt.

There are many ways to read and interpret any poetry. You have to choose your own approach and which specifics to include for support. *Don't be rattled if there is leftover material.*

We've reproduced the poem for you below so that you can practice both the reading and the process of deconstructing the text. Use highlighting, arrows, circles, underlining, notes, numbers, and whatever you need to make the connections clear to you.

Do this now. Spend 8–10 minutes working the material. *Do not skip this step.* It is time well spent and is a key to the high-score essay.

On the Subway
by Sharon Olds

The boy and I face each other
His feet are huge, in black sneakers
laced with white in a complex pattern like a
set of intentional scars. We are stuck on

"When I read poetry out loud, it's easier for me to understand it."
—Jennifer L.
   AP student

opposite sides of the car, a couple of 5
molecules stuck in a rod of light
rapidly moving through darkness.
He has the casual cold look of a mugger,
alert under hooded lids. He is wearing
red, like the inside of the body 10
exposed. I am wearing dark fur, the
whole skin of an animal taken and
used. I look at his raw face,
he looks at my fur coat, and I don't
know if I am in his power— 15
he could take my coat so easily, my
briefcase, my life—
or if he is in my power, the way I am
living off his life, eating the steak
he does not eat, as if I am taking 20
the food from his mouth. And he is black
and I am white, and without meaning or
trying to I must profit from his darkness,
the way he absorbs the murderous beams of the
nation's heart, as black cotton 25
absorbs the heat of the sun and holds it. There is
no way to know how easy this
white skin makes my life, this
life he could take so easily and
break across his knee like a stick the way his 30
own back is being broken, the
rod of his soul that at birth was dark and
fluid and rich as the heart of a seedling
ready to thrust up into any available light

Now compare your reading notes with what we've done below. Yours may vary from ours, but the results of your note-taking should be similar in scope.

On the Subway
by Sharon Olds

first part = narrator as observer

first person   *oppositions*

The boy and I face each other

His feet are huge, in black sneakers

laced with white in a complex pattern like a — *dark*

light —— set of intentional scars. We are stuck on

violence? —— opposite sides of the car, a couple of   5

opposite sides of molecules stuck in a rod of light
the "tracks"

rapidly moving through darkness.   *light and dark metaphor*

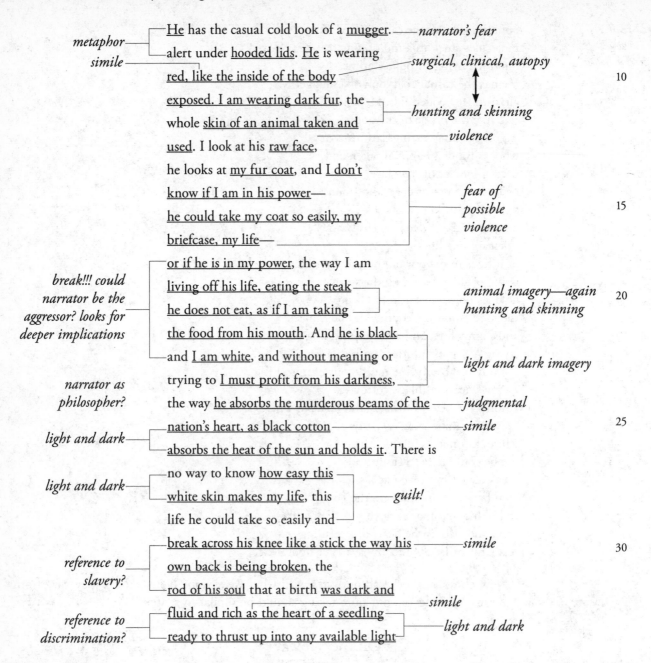

metaphor — He has the casual cold look of a mugger. — narrator's fear
simile — alert under hooded lids. He is wearing
red, like the inside of the body — surgical, clinical, autopsy ↕
exposed. I am wearing dark fur, the — hunting and skinning
whole skin of an animal taken and
used. I look at his raw face, — violence
he looks at my fur coat, and I don't
know if I am in his power— — fear of possible violence
he could take my coat so easily, my
briefcase, my life—

break!!! could narrator be the aggressor? looks for deeper implications — or if he is in my power, the way I am
living off his life, eating the steak — animal imagery—again hunting and skinning
he does not eat, as if I am taking
the food from his mouth. And he is black
and I am white, and without meaning or — light and dark imagery
narrator as philosopher? — trying to I must profit from his darkness,
the way he absorbs the murderous beams of the — judgmental
light and dark — nation's heart, as black cotton — simile
absorbs the heat of the sun and holds it. There is
light and dark — no way to know how easy this
white skin makes my life, this — guilt!
life he could take so easily and
reference to slavery? — break across his knee like a stick the way his — simile
own back is being broken, the
rod of his soul that at birth was dark and — simile
reference to discrimination? — fluid and rich as the heart of a seedling
ready to thrust up into any available light — light and dark

10

15

20

25

30

After you have marked the poem, review the prompt. When you look at your notes, certain categories will begin to pop out at you. These can be the basis for the development of the body of your essay. For example:

- Light and dark imagery
- Speaker's insights
- Contrast in status
- Metaphors

- Animal imagery
- Implied violence
- Shift in middle of poem
- Similes

Here's how we saw one category develop in the poem. Notice that we have ignored notes that did not apply to the prompt.

Category: Light and dark imagery

<u>Examples:</u>

"black sneakers"   "laced with white"   "rod of light"
"moving through darkness"   "profit from his darkness"   "he is black"
"and I am white"   "heat of the sun"   "murderous beams"
"black cotton"   "thrust up into any   "dark and fluid"
"how easy this white skin   available light"
   makes my life"

Comment: The use of black and white imagery emphasizes the opposite ends of the spectrum represented by the speaker and the boy.

Your Turn

Now you choose a category that seems to pop out at you and trace its use through the poem.

Category:

Examples:

Comment:

We chose to examine poetic devices used in "On the Subway."

Category: Poetic devices

Examples:

Simile	lines 3–4	"complex … scars"
Metaphor	lines 4–6	"We are … molecules"
Simile	lines 9–11	"He is wearing … exposed"
Simile	lines 24–26	"he absorbs … holds it"
Simile	lines 29–30	"he could … stick"
Simile	line 32	"rod of his soul"
Simile	lines 32–34	"rod of his soul … light"

Comment: By definition, similes and metaphors are comparisons. The poet uses these comparisons to develop and flesh out the juxtaposition of the life and situation of the speaker and the boy.

Your Turn

Refer to this chapter's earlier section about the types of poetry prompts to expect on the exam. Construct two alternative prompts for Sharon Olds's "On the Subway."

1st Alternative prompt:

2nd Alternative prompt:

Notice that we have ignored notes that did not apply to the prompt.

Now choose the techniques that develop the contrasting portraits and reveal the narrator's perceptions.

In response to the prompt, we have decided that the techniques/devices we will analyze are:

- Imagery
- Poetic devices
- Organization

If you expand the above techniques/devices and the above categories into interpretive statements and support those statements with appropriate details that you've already isolated, you will be writing a defended essay.

Writing the Opening Paragraph

Your opening statement is the one that sets the tone of your essay and possibly raises the expectations of the reader. Spend time on your first paragraph to maximize your score.

Make certain that your topic is very clear. This reinforces the idea that you fully understand what is expected of you and what you will communicate to the reader. Generally, identify both the text and the poet in this first paragraph.

Do this now. Take 5 minutes to write your opening paragraph for the prompt. Write quickly, referring to your notes.

Let's check what you've written.

Highlight these points to see if you've done them. You may be surprised at what is actually there.

- Have you included the poet and the title?
- Have you addressed the portraits, contrasts, and insights?
- Have you specifically mentioned the techniques you will refer to in your essay?

Here are three sample opening paragraphs that address each of the above criteria.

A

Sharon Olds in the poem, "On the Subway," presents a brief encounter between two people of different races which leads to several insights of one participant. This is accomplished through Olds's use of poetic devices, imagery, and imagination.

B

The observer and the observed. One has control over the other. In her poem, "On the Subway," Sharon Olds asks her readers to enter the mind of a white woman who observes a young, black man as they travel together, neither knowing the other. Using poetic devices, imagery, and organization, Olds takes the reader on a ride through the contrasts and images that spark the imagination of the white onlooker.

C

"And he is black and I am white" establishes the basic contrast and conflict in Sharon Olds's poem, "On the Subway." Through imagery, organization, and poetic devices, Olds creates two contrasting portraits. The narrator's confrontation becomes the reader's also as she reveals her troubling fears and insights through her images and comments concerning her encounter with the black youth.

These three introductory paragraphs identify the poet and the title and clearly indicate an understanding of the prompt. Now, let's note what is different about each.

Sample **A** is a straightforward, unadorned restatement of the prompt. It is correct, yet lacks a writer's voice. (If you are unsure of how to proceed, this is the type of opening you may want to consider.) This type of opening paragraph will at least allow you to get into the essay with as little complexity as possible.

Sample **B** immediately reveals the writer's confidence and mature writing style. The prompt is addressed in a provocative and interesting manner, letting the reader know the tone of the essay.

Sample **C** incorporates a direct quotation from the poem which indicates the writer is comfortable with citation. The writer also links the reader with the poem and feels confident that his or her judgments about the encounter are supportable.

Note: There are many other types of opening paragraphs that could do the job as well. The paragraphs above are just a few samples.

Does your opening paragraph resemble any of these samples?

_____Yes_____No

Writing the Body of the Poetry Essay

When you write the body of your essay, take only 15–20 minutes. Time yourself and try your best to finish within that time frame.

Since this is practice, don't panic if you can't complete the essay within the allotted time. You will become more and more comfortable with the tasks presented to you as you gain experience with this type of question.

What Should I Include in the Body of the Poetry Essay?

1. Obviously, this is where you present your interpretation and the points you wish to make that are related to the prompt.

2. Use specific references and details from the poem.
   - Refer directly to the original. Don't always paraphrase.
   - Place quotation marks around those words and phrases that you extract from the poem.

3. Use "connective tissue" in your essay to establish adherence to the question.
   - Use the repetition of key ideas from your opening paragraph.
   - Try using "echo words" (i.e., synonyms such as *insight* can be inference/observation/ perception; *fear* can be apprehension/insecurity).
   - Create transitions from one paragraph to the next.

To understand the process, carefully read the following sample paragraphs. Each develops one of the categories and techniques/devices asked for in the prompt. Notice the specific references and the "connective tissue." Also, notice that details that do not apply to the prompt have been ignored.

A

This paragraph develops **poetic devices**.

"Black sneakers laced with white in a complex pattern like a set of intentional scars" is the jarring simile Olds uses to establish the relationship between the woman and the "boy" on the subway. Immediately, the poetic device implies the bondage and pain of the oppressed minority and the deliberate complexity of race relations. This idea of inter-woven lives is further developed by the metaphor that links both as "molecules stuck in a rod of light." The youth, however, is compared to a reptile with "hooded lids," and all the fear and repulsion associated with this creature is transferred to the boy who is hiding his true intentions with such a look. The woman follows her fearful insights with still another extreme simile—worrying about "this life he could take so easily and break across his knee like a stick." Still, she proves the complexity of her thoughts by creating a sym-pathetic metaphor to ponder "the rod of his soul—the heart of a seedling" yearning to grow into the light.

B

This paragraph develops **imagery**.

The images in the poem are predominantly drawn from the contrast between light and dark. "Black sneakers," "white laces," "rod of light rapidly moving through darkness" are all images that immediately establish the contrast that is at the heart of the meaning of the poem. This juxtaposition becomes reality in lines 21–22 when we learn that "he is black and I am white." The problem is how the "white" profits from his "darkness." [line 23] What should be light, "the beams of the nation's heart," is murderous, and he "as black cotton," absorbs this heat. This angry contrast leads the speaker to her insight about her life in lines 26–28. Empathizing with the black youth, the narrator moves beyond her prejudices and finds promise in the last three lines which see the dark being born into the light.

C

This paragraph develops **organization**.

The organization of "On the Subway" is rather linear. Olds's narrator proceeds from a frightened observer to a philosophical questioner to finally a mature, sympathetic fore-caster of the promise of the young, black man. The first thirteen lines provide the interior monologue of a woman who sits across from a young, black male and looks him over from head to toe. In line 10 she begins to move deeply into the hidden person across from her, with this "introspection" ending in lines 14–16 with her questioning who actu-ally has power over whom. Line 18 presents a true shift from personal observation to an almost societal conscience which is sympathetic to the plight of all blacks in America as seen in lines 21–26. Bringing the reader back to the opening section of the poem, the speaker intimates at the promise of the young man with "the rod of his soul . . . rich as the heart of a seedling/ready to thrust up into any available light." [lines 32–34]

Refer to our list of recommended poets at the back of this book. Look for poems similar in length and complexity to those we've provided and apply a variety of prompts. You can try these alone, with a study group, or with your class.

Note: Look at the last sentence of Sample B on imagery: "Empathizing with the black youth, the narrator moves beyond her prejudices and finds promise in the last three lines which see the dark being born into the light."

This final sentence would be fine as the conclusion to the essay. A conclusion does not have to be a paragraph. It can be the writer's final remark, observation, or reference and may be only a sentence or two.

Do this now. Write the body of your essay. Time yourself. Allow 15–20 minutes to complete this task.

Sample Student Essays

Following are two actual student essays followed by a rubric and comments on each.

Student Essay A

The three sections of "On the Subway" by Sharon Olds express the complicated relationship between Caucasians and African-Americans. In the first section the author presents an exposition that contrasts a white person with a black (lines 1–13). In the second, the speaker begins to develop the apparent disparities so that inter-relationships emerge (lines 13–20). In the third, the narrator gains insight   5
into how this scene is representative of American culture at large (lines 20–34).

The imagery Olds uses in the first section emphasizes the difference between the white woman who is the narrator and the observer and the black boy, who is the observed, as they ride the subway. The shoes he is wearing are black "laced with white" (line 3). The speaker describes the white zigzags as "intentional scars"   10
(line 4). The scars allude to the discrimination against the black man by white society. The adjective "intentional" denotes that whites purposely harm blacks. The image contrasts whites with blacks: whites are powerful; blacks are subservient. Similarly, the two characters are described as being "stuck on opposite sides" of the subway car; they are separated permanently from each other (lines 4–5). The description of the   15
clothing is a third contrasting element. Here, the black man is "exposed," while the speaker is covered in fur (line 11). This image reinforces the opposition between the white woman and the black boy.

The second section sees a shift in tone. Where the first section is composed of finite physical descriptions, the second is more philosophical and indicates the   20
speaker's apprehension. She is uncertain and writes that "I don't/know if I am in his power . . . or if he is in my power" (lines 14–15, 18). Such a statement is important because it illustrates that the boundaries between whites and blacks are not as clearcut as they may seem. Perhaps the speaker begins to realize that the image of the subservient black and the powerful white presented in the first section of the poem   25
is incorrect. The repetition of the word "Life" is another way the interconnection between the two characters is developed. The narrator cannot decide whether her wealth usurps the power of the black man or whether his potential aggression usurps her power (lines 17, 19).

The tone, again, shifts in the third segment. Here, it is clear that the speaker is trying to gain an understanding of the relationship between the white world and that of the black boy. At first, she realizes that they are different because "he is black and I am white" (lines 21–22). The image of the "black cotton" alludes to slavery, once again referring to the scars, or distinctions, imposed by the white society. Yet, at the end of this section, the differences between the two people are strangely reconciled. This is accomplished using the technique of repetition. Instead of repeating a word as in the second section, an image is repeated. Lines 29–31 state that the black man could hurt the white woman; he could "break [her] across his knee . . . the way his own back is being broken." In other words, both whites and blacks can hurt; both races can be injured by either repression or aggression, and so they are connected through their pain and unrealized dreams.

Student Essay B

In the poem "On the Subway" by Sharon Olds, she contrasts the worlds of an affluent white person and a poor black person. The two people have many opposing characteristics, and the author uses literary techniques such as tone, poetic devices, and imagery to portray these differences. The narrator is the white woman, and she realizes how people get "stuck" in places of society based on their skin color. The word "stuck" is repeated twice to stress this idea.

The major difference between the two people is obviously their skin color. This one difference causes many aspects of each person's life to be unlike the other's. The white woman is above the black man in the eyes of much of society. The narrator states that "without meaning or trying to I must profit from his darkness." This is basically saying that the black man is living in a white man's world, where his skin color alone has given him a predisposition in the eyes of many. This idea is further supported when the speaker thinks "There is no way to know how easy this white skin makes my life." Olds uses the following simile to show the black man's situation: ". . . he absorbs the murderous beams of the nation's heart, as black cotton absorbs the heat of the sun and holds it."

Another contrast that is in the poem is the rawness of the black man versus the sheltered and refined look of the white woman. Olds uses a simile to describe the red that the black youth is wearing: "Like the inside of the body exposed." The white woman is the outside of the animal wearing a fur coat. The black man is the inside of the body, the true animal, while the white woman is not; she is simply wearing the outer covering of an animal.

As a result of this experience, the narrator realizes that there is a balance of power and control between her and the young man. She realizes that at times, and in certain situations, she rules, while in others the black man does. Her life, her "easier" life, can be taken away by the black youth. Who has the power on the train? The big, strong, raw black man or the weaker, but richer, white woman? Society has given the white woman a false sense of superiority and security. She is protected by wealth, her job, and her possessions, but when alone on the subway with this black man, she feels fear. She is confronted by her own vulnerability. The black youth who is being broken by society can break the white woman who is society.

Overall, this poem effectively contrasts the two people and exposes a fallacy of society. The black man must live in eternal darkness because he is never allowed to "thrust up into any available light."

Rating the Student Essays

Let's take a look at a set of rubrics for the poetry essay.

- 1 point for thesis/claim/introduction that is appropriate to the prompt
  - The thesis clearly presents a possible interpretation and indicates how the support will be developed.
- 4 points for evidence/support of the thesis/claim
  - Clear and appropriate references to the text
  - Clear presentation of how the references relate to the thesis
- 1 point for complexity of the commentary and syntax

> *Note:* The essay is really a first draft. The readers know this and approach each essay with this in mind.

Student Essay A

This is a high-range essay (5, 6) for the following reasons:

- A sophisticated, indirect indication of the task of the prompt and organization.
- Tightly constructed and thorough discussion of the contrasts and opposition in the poem.
- Effective analysis of imagery (lines 1–13, 15–17).
- Effective and coherent discussion of tone.
- Understanding of the subtleties of tone (lines 19–21).
- Strong support for assertions and interpretations (lines 22–29).
- Effective analysis of literary techniques (lines 11, 33–34, 36–38).

"Even though I hate doing it, my writing really improves when I spend the time revising what I've written."
—Mike T.
   AP student

This high-ranking essay is subtle, concise, and on target. There is nothing that takes away from the writer's focus. Each paragraph grows out of the previous one, and the reader always knows where the author is taking him or her. The syntax, diction, and organization are mature and confident.

Student Essay B

This is a middle-range essay (3, 4) for the following reasons:

- Clearly identifies the task, the poem, and the poet.
- States the techniques that will be discussed in the essay.
- Lacks a transition to the body of the essay (lines 6–7).
- Provides an adequate discussion of the insights of the speaker (lines 23–25).
- Cites appropriate specifics to support the thesis of the essay (lines 14–16).
- Uses standard style, diction, and structure, but does not reflect a sophisticated or mature writer.
- Attempts a universal statement within a rather repetitive and summary-like conclusion (lines 32–34).

How about sharing these samples with members of your class or study group and discussing possible responses?

While adhering to the prompt, this midrange essay is an adequate first draft. It shows promise but comes dangerously close to paraphrasing lines. The analysis is basic and obvious, depending on only one device, that of simile. The writer hints at the subtleties but misses the opportunity to respond to further complexities inherent in the poem.

Note: Both essays have concluding paragraphs which are repetitive and mostly unnecessary. It is best to avoid this type of ending.

Rapid Review

Need a Quick Review? Spend a minute or two reading through…that'll do.

- Review terms and techniques.
- Become familiar with types of poetry questions (prompts).
- Highlight the prompt to make certain you are aware of required tasks.
- Time your essay carefully.
- Read the poem a couple of times.
- Spend sufficient time "working the poem" before writing.
- Mark up the poem.
- Create a strong opening paragraph, including prompt information.
- Refer often to the poem for concrete details and quotes to support your ideas.
- Always stay on topic.
- Avoid simply paraphrasing.
- Include transitions and echo words.
- Practice—vary the prompt and your response.
- Consult the models and rubrics for self-evaluation.
- Share ideas with others.

CHAPTER 7

The Free-Response Essay

IN THIS CHAPTER

Summary: Examination of the free-response essay and its purpose as it is presented in the AP English Literature exam

Key Ideas
- ✪ Learn the types of free-response prompts you might encounter in the AP English Literature exam
- ✪ Practice various ways of organizing the information based on your chosen literary work
- ✪ Learn the basics of constructing your response to the free-response prompt
- ✪ Learn about the rubrics and rating of the AP free-response essays
- ✪ Examine model student essays
- ✪ Learn how rubrics were used to rate student essays
- ✪ Learn how the synthesis essay differs from the argumentative and analysis essays
- ✪ Learn the process of dealing with many texts

Introduction to the Free-Response Essay

Nothing in life is free, but this essay does indicate that the end is near. So, hang in there. However, a cliché-clogged essay is *not* the indicator of the high-range essay. This chapter will provide the information and the practice you need to "knock their socks off."

What Is a Free-Response Essay?

The free-response essay is based on a provocative question that highlights specific insights applicable to a broad range of literary texts. The question provides for varied personal interpretations and multiple approaches. It allows students to truly create the specific substance of their own essay.

What Is the Purpose of the Free-Response Essay?

The College Board wants to assess your ability to discuss a work of literature in a particular context. The illustrations you include in your essay will demonstrate your insights and critical thinking as well as your writing ability.

What Makes This Essay "Free"?

Although the question is the same for all students, you have total freedom to choose the piece of literature to which you will refer. Once chosen, you have total freedom to select the specifics that will support your thesis. Unlike the other two essays, which have rubrics based on certain concrete interpretations and directions of the text, your free-response essay will be uniquely your own.

If This Is Total Freedom of Expression, How Can I Ever Get Less Than a 6?

The test reader is expecting an essay that demonstrates a mature understanding and defense of the prompt. Your paper must be specific and well organized. It must also adhere to the topic. You will lose major credit for providing only plot summary. Your illustrations should be cogent and insightful rather than obvious or superficial. For a high score, you must bring something specific and relevant to the page.

What Are the Pitfalls of the Free-Response Essay?

It is our experience that the free-response question is a double-edged sword. Students can suffer from overconfidence because of the open nature of this essay. They depend on memory rather than on preparation and often go for the most obvious illustrations. They tend to ramble on in vague and unsupported generalities, and they frequently provide incorrect information. *The failure to plan and limit can undermine this essay.*

Students often have trouble choosing the appropriate work and lose valuable time pondering a variety of choices. It is important to be decisive and confident in your presentation.

What Kinds of Works May I Refer to in This Essay?

Generally, you are asked to choose a full-length work, almost always a novel or play. However, if the prompt says "choose a work," you may use a poem, short story, novella, or work of nonfiction. *Note*: You may *never* use a film.

NOTE: The list of suggested texts for FRQ3 will have 36–42 works on it, NONE of which will be works in translation or ancient texts (e.g., *The Odyssey*, *The Iliad*). Students will be allowed to write about works in translation (e.g., *Crime and Punishment*, *Madame Bovary*), but translated works will not be listed in the prompt.

- What constitutes "literary merit" will no longer be an issue. Works of literature characterized by "complexity" will be acceptable choices.
- Literary nonfiction (e.g., *The Bell Jar*, *In Cold Blood*, *Night*) will be acceptable choices.

Must I Use the List of Works Provided at the Bottom of the Prompt?

Absolutely not! Since this is a free-response essay, the choice of a literary work is up to you. You should choose a work that is appropriate to the prompt, one that is appropriate to AP students, and one that is comfortable for you.

Must I Use Works Read This Year?

No, but why would you choose any work that could be a faded memory or unsuitable for AP-level analysis? We always recommend using works that you studied in class and have read and discussed throughout the year. One exception occurs when you have written a lengthy literary research paper or a sustained critical analysis. In this situation, you may have real in-depth familiarity with a work that you could adapt to a free-response question. By all means, go for it!

How Do I Prepare for the Free-Response Essay?

You need to tell yourself in September or October that you will be taking the exam next May. This will emphasize the point that throughout the year you will have to keep some type of record of the works you have read and some specific points you want to make about each of them. (In Chapter 8, we introduce several techniques and processes that will enable you to keep these records.)

By the time of the exam in May, you need to be thoroughly conversant with at least three to five full-length works from different genres, eras, and literary movements.

You also need to practice. Practice writing questions, practice choosing appropriate works, and practice writing responses to questions. Practice!

What Criteria Do the AP Readers Use to Rate a Free-Response Essay?

The readers are looking for literary insights and awareness of character, comprehension of theme, and the ability to transfer specific ideas and details to a universal concept. In addition, the readers are hoping to see a writer who reveals and understands the relationships among form, content, style, and structure and their effects on the meaning of the work. The essay should indicate the writer's ability to choose appropriate illustrations from a full-length work and to connect them in a thoughtful way. The sophisticated writer will refer to plot but will not summarize. As always, the reader is looking for a well-organized essay written in a mature voice.

What Happens If I Use a Work That the Reader Doesn't Know?

This should not be a major concern to you. Throughout the year, your AP instructor has provided you with appropriate literary experiences suitable for addressing this prompt. In addition, be assured that any work we mention in this book will be appropriate. Be sure to consult our suggested reading list to increase your range of choices. Any other works by the same author would probably be on an appropriate AP level. For the most part, the AP prefers works from the literary canon because they exhibit breadth and complexity for literary scholarship. Don't fight these requirements. You do yourself a disservice when you insist on trying to outwit or beat the system.

Having said all this, if by chance you do choose an obscure work and present it well, the reader will respond accordingly.

Types of Free-Response Prompts

Here are some topics that could be the basis for a free-response prompt. We also include some suggested works for these.

- The journey as a major force in a work. (*Gulliver's Travels, As I Lay Dying, The Stranger, The Kite Runner,* etc.)
- What happens to a dream deferred? (*Hedda Gabler, Desire Under the Elms, Their Eyes Were Watching God,* etc.)
- Transformation (literal and/or figurative). (*Dr. Jekyll and Mr. Hyde, Black Like Me, Metamorphosis,* etc.)
- Descent into madness/hell. (*Medea, Heart of Darkness, Secret Sharer,* etc.)
- An ironic reversal in a character's beliefs or actions. (*Heart of Darkness, The Stranger, Oedipus,* etc.)
- Perception and reality—"What is, is not." (*Twelfth Night, Hamlet, Who's Afraid of Virginia Woolf?,* etc.)
- A child becomes a force to reveal _____ . (*Jane Eyre, Huckleberry Finn, Lord of the Flies,* etc.)
- Ceremony or ritual plays an important role. (*The Stranger, Lord of the Flies, The Sun Also Rises, Suddenly Last Summer,* etc.)
- The role of the fool, comic character, or wise servant who reveals _____ . (*King Lear, The Importance of Being Earnest, Tartuffe,* etc.)

   Note: Fill in works you would use to respond to the above prompts.

_____

_____

_____

_____

_____

"I really like hearing and reading how the other students do the same questions. It helps me evaluate my own ideas and essays."
—Adam S.
   AP student

Here's another set of possible free-response prompts for development:

- How an opening scene or chapter establishes the character, conflict, or theme of a major literary work.
- How a minor character is used to develop a major character.
- How violence relates to character or theme.
- How time is a major factor.
- The ways in which an author changes the reader's attitude(s) toward a subject.
- The use of contrasting settings.
- Parent/child or sibling relationships and their significance.
- The analysis of a villain with regard to the meaning of the work.
- The use of an unrealistic character or element and its effect on the work.
- The relevance of a nonmodern work to the present day.
- The conflict between passion and responsibility.
- The conflict between character and society.

Note: To our knowledge, a free-response question has never been repeated. Therefore, we suggest:

1. Use the prompts cited earlier when you discuss works you read or when you write about those works throughout the year.

2. Generate a list of topics that would also be suitable for free-response prompts. Discuss, outline, or prepare sample essays utilizing these questions.

Anticipating prompts and responses is a productive way to prepare for this exam.

General Rubrics for the Free-Response Essay

Let's take a look at a set of rubrics for the free-response essay.

- 1 point for thesis/claim/introduction that is appropriate to the prompt
  - The thesis clearly cites a major work related to the prompt and indicates how the support will be developed.
- 4 points for evidence/support of the thesis/claim
  - Clear and appropriate references to the text
  - Clear presentation of how the references relate to the thesis
- 1 point for complexity of the commentary and syntax

Timing and Planning the Free-Response Essay

This essay is the real challenge of the exam. Keep in mind that with the other two essay questions, half the job was done for you; the material was limited and provided for you. But now you are faced with the blank page that you must fill. Therefore, you must plan this essay carefully and completely. With this in mind, here's a workable strategy:

- 1–3 minutes working the prompt. (At this point, you might even chart the prompt.)
- 3–5 minutes choosing your work. (You should mentally run through two or three works that might be appropriate.) This is a crucial step for laying the foundation for your essay.
- 5–10 minutes for brainstorming, charting, mapping, outlining, and so on the specifics you plan to use in your essay. (Remember, a vague, general, unsupported essay will cost you points.)
- 20–25 minutes to write your essay based on your preparation.
- 3 minutes for proofreading.

Working the Prompt from the Diagnostic/Master Exam

Before you read the prompt, immediately cover the list of suggested works. There are several good reasons for this:

- It requires time to read the list.
- Chances are you will have read very few works on the list. If you are like many students, this could make you feel insecure and rattle your confidence.
- If you are familiar with a work or two, you may be predisposed to use the work to answer the question even if it is not necessarily your best choice. You may find yourself considering a work that you would not have considered if it were not listed, and you may find yourself taking precious time to fit that choice unsuccessfully to the prompt.

Here is the PROMPT:

Often in literature, a literal or figurative journey is a significant factor in the development of a character or the meaning of the work. Choose a full-length work and write a well-organized essay in which you discuss the literal and/or figurative nature of the journey and how it affects characterization and theme. You may choose from the list below or another full-length work of literary merit.

As I Lay Dying	*Tom Jones*
Jane Eyre	*Heart of Darkness*
The Odyssey	*Moby Dick*
Don Quixote	*The Sun Also Rises*
Candide	*The Grapes of Wrath*
A Streetcar Named Desire	*The Stranger*
A Passage to India	*Ulysses*
Gulliver's Travels	*Their Eyes Were Watching God*
No Exit	*Obasan*
The Kite Runner	*Twelfth Night*

Notating the Prompt

We recommend that you chart or map the prompt. This is a simple visualization of your task. Before you look at our samples, you might want to try charting or mapping the prompt on your own.

Following is a sample chart:

Jane Eyre

	JOURNEY	EFFECT ON CHARACTER	EFFECT ON THEME
LITERAL			
FIGURATIVE			

Here is a sample map:

Following is a sample topic outline:

Journey

- Literal effect
  - character
  - theme
- Figurative effect
  - character
  - theme

Your Turn

Carefully read and highlight the following prompt.

Frequently, the tension in a literary work is created by the conflict between a character and society. Choose a full-length literary work and discuss the nature of the conflict, its effect on the character, on society, and on the resulting thematic implications.

A. **Construct a chart** that addresses the requirements of the prompt.

Title of literary work:

	NATURE OF CONFLICT	EFFECT OF CONFLICT
ON CHARACTER		
ON SOCIETY		
ON THEMATIC IMPLICATIONS		

B. Using the same literary work you chose for the chart, **create a map**.

(character) _____   (society) _____   (thematic) _____

_____   _____   _____

_____   _____   _____

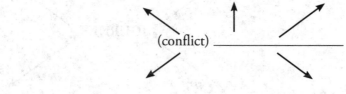

(conflict) _____

(effect on character) _____   (effect on society) _____

_____   _____

_____   _____

C. With the same literary work and prompt in mind, **construct an outline**.

Conflict

Nature of conflict
– On character:
– On society:

Effect of conflict
– On character:
– On society:

Thematic implications
– On character:
– On society:

When you provide the specifics, either mentally or by writing them down, you will ensure that you have addressed all parts of the prompt. This also will provide the basic structure of your essay.

Note: Although it may feel awkward and contrived at first, if you actually practice this technique, it will become automatic and help you to immediately get into the writing of your essay.

KEY IDEA

Now that you are familiar with the prompt, take a few moments to think about works that might be appropriate for this question. One or two will immediately pop into your mind. Mentally examine them for scenes or details that you might be able to use. *If you can't think of specifics, abandon this choice.*

If you wish, now take a look at the list of suggested works, because:

- You may find your choice there, and you will feel very validated.
- You may see a different work by the same author, which may also boost your confidence.
- You might see another work or author you recognize you had not considered that could possibly spark a better response to the prompt.

This process should only take a minute or so.

Do this now. Spend 8–10 minutes working your choice to fit the requirements of the prompt. For example, prior to the exam, you will have prepared a cross section of works from various genres, time periods, and literary movements. Since these are works with depth, you will be able to take your basic scene or references and modify them to suit the task of the given prompt.

Using *Hamlet* as an example, let's assume you reviewed the graveyard scene prior to the exam. This scene would be appropriate to illustrate your thoughts on such varied prompts as:

- The use of humor—the gravedigger.
- The role of a minor character—Horatio.
- The concept of death as the great leveler—motif.
- Use of ritual—funeral.
- The impact of a character *not* seen in the work—Yorick.
- The use of coincidence or irony in the work—Ophelia's grave.
- The use of setting to develop theme or character—"To be or not to be."

You get the point. Obviously, you could not answer a question about the effectiveness of a work's conclusion by using this scene, which is exactly why you prepare *several* different literary examples.

We know that Shakespeare is so universal that any work could be used to answer almost any free-response question. Therefore, we urge you to prepare at least one Shakespearean play as a "safe" work.

There is another reason to spend several minutes planning your essay. Frequently, your first responses and examples are the obvious and common ones. This is not to say that you could not write an adequate essay using these. But, if they came to you this quickly, they probably also came to many thousands of other students taking the exam. It is usually more challenging and rewarding to find a unique focus for your essay. For example: choosing the gravedigger's scene in *Hamlet* rather than the "To be or not to be" scene may reveal a more creative thinker.

Sometimes, as you are planning, you realize that your work will answer only part of the prompt and that it would be better to switch to another work. If you have prepared well prior to the test, you will be able to do this without taking up much time. Sometimes it's better to abandon your initial choice in favor of the second and more productive one. This is why you have not yet begun to write.

Developing the Opening Paragraph

STRATEGY

Now you are ready to write. Remember, your opening paragraph is the one that raises the expectations of the reader and sets the tone of your essay. Spend time on your first paragraph to maximize your score.

Make certain that your topic is very clear to the reader. This reinforces the idea that you fully understand what is expected of you and what you will communicate to the reader. Generally, identify both the text and the author in this first paragraph.

Do this now. Take 5 minutes and write your opening paragraph for this prompt. Write quickly, referring to your notes.

Let's check what you've written:

Actually highlight these to see if you've done it. You may be surprised at what is actually there.

• Have you included the author and title?
• Have you addressed the literal and figurative journeys?
• Have you addressed characterization and theme?

Here are three sample opening paragraphs that address each of the above criteria.

A

"There was no possibility of taking a walk that day" says young Jane in Chapter One of Charlotte Bronte's novel, *Jane Eyre*. Little did she know that her very existence would evolve from her personal odyssey as she journeyed from Gateshead to Lowood to Thornfield and beyond; from child to adolescent to woman. This literal and figurative journey enables Bronte to develop both the character and the theme of her work.

B

Up the hill, down the street, across the road from cafe to cafe, the characters in Ernest Hemingway's novel, *The Sun Also Rises*, wander interminably. Hemingway employs this aimless journey to reveal the lost nature of his characters and his theme of the search for meaning and direction in their post–World War I existence.

C

In *Heart of Darkness* by Joseph Conrad, a literal journey from England to Africa becomes a nightmare of realization and epiphany for the main character, Marlowe. Conrad develops his themes through Marlowe's observations and experiences on his figurative journey from innocence to corruption, idealism to cynicism, and optimism to despair.

Note: These three introductory paragraphs identify the author and the title and clearly indicate an understanding of the prompt. Let's note what is different about each.

Sample **A** begins with an appropriate, direct quotation. It clearly delineates the two types of journeys and their relationship to the character. The writer indicates an understanding of the difference between literal and figurative interpretation.

Sample **B** has a clear writer's voice. The writer is not afraid to be judgmental. The tone of the essay is apparent and sustained.

Sample **C** alludes to the content of the body of the essay and touches on vague generalities. However, the maturity of the vocabulary and thought indicate the writer's understanding of Conrad's complex themes and their relationship to the prompt.

Note: There are many other types of opening paragraphs that could also do the job. The paragraphs above are just a few samples. Does your opening paragraph resemble any of these samples? When you write the body of your essay, take only 15–20 minutes. Time yourself and try your best to finish within that time frame.

Developing the Body of the Essay

Time to pump some mental iron and to firm up and tone those flabby ideas and turn them into examples of intellectual fitness.

What Should I Include in the Body of the Free-Response Essay?

1. Obviously, this is where you present your interpretation and the points you wish to make that are related to the prompt.

2. Use specific references and details from the chosen work.
   • Incorporate direct quotations when possible.
   • Place quotation marks around those words or phrases taken directly from the work.

3. Use connective tissue in your essay to establish adherence to the question.
   • Use the repetition of key ideas in the prompt and in your opening paragraph.
   • Try using "echo words" (i.e., synonyms such as journey/wanderings/travels or figurative/symbolic/metaphoric).
   • Use transitions from one paragraph to the next.

To understand the process, carefully read the following sample paragraphs. Each illustrates an aspect of the prompt. Notice the specific references and the connective tissue.

A

At Gateshead, despite its material comforts, Jane was an orphaned outcast who felt "like a discord." She was, like Cinderella, abused by her cousins and aunt and nurtured only by Bessie, a servant. Jane's immaturity and rebellious nature cause her to be jealous and vengeful which culminates in a violent confrontation with her repulsive cousin, John. Her subsequent eviction from Gateshead forces her to embark on a journey that will affect her forever. The stark privations of Lowood humble Jane and open her to the true riches of friendship with Helen Burns. It is here she learns the academic, religious, and social skills that will enable her to move on to her destiny at Thornfield.

B

Throughout the novel Jake escorts the reader on the journeys that become the only purpose the group exhibits. The trip to San Fermin for the fiesta is also a journey to hell, away from civilization and morality. The fiesta "explodes" and for seven days any behavior is acceptable, for there is no accountability during this time. No one "pays the bill," yet. Brett is worshiped as a pagan idol; garlic is strung around her neck, and men drink to her powers. She is compared to Circe, and, indeed, she turns her companions into swine as they fight over her. This trip to the fiesta reinforces the lack of spirituality and direction that is a theme of the novel.

C

Referring to the map of the Congo, Marlowe states that "the snake had charmed me." This primal description prepares us for the inevitable journey up the river that will change the very core of his character. The snake implies temptation, and Marlowe is seduced by the mysteries of Africa and his desire to meet Kurtz in the interior. He is too naive and pure to anticipate the abominations that await him at the inner station. Like a descent into hell, the journey progresses. The encounters with Fresleven, the workers without rivets, the pilgrims shooting into the jungle, all foreshadow Marlowe's changing understanding of the absurdity of life and the flawed nature of man. Only when he is totally aware of "the horror, the horror" can he journey back to "another dark place of the universe," London, to see the Intended and to corrupt his own values for her sake.

Let's examine these three body paragraphs.

Sample **A** is about *Jane Eyre*. It addresses one aspect of the prompt—Jane's character at the beginning of the journey—and continues with the first major change in her life. The writer demonstrates familiarity with the novel through concrete details and quotations. Theme is implied and leads the reader to anticipate further development in the rest of the body of the essay.

Sample **B** refers to *The Sun Also Rises*. This paragraph uses a single incident to develop the discussion of the journey as it affects character and theme. The writer includes very specific details of the San Fermin fiesta to support comments about Brett and Jake. The integration of these details is presented in a cohesive, mature style.

Sample **C** delves into *Heart of Darkness*. This paragraph is a philosophical approach, which assumes the reader is familiar with the novel. It focuses on theme and how the development of the character is used to illustrate that theme. The ending of the paragraph presents an insight that invites the reader to "stay tuned."

Do this now. Write the body of your essay. Time yourself. Allow 15–20 minutes to complete this task.

Sample Student Essays

Here are two actual student essays that are followed by a rubric and comments on each essay.

Student Essay A

The journey taken by Edna in Kate Chopin's <u>The Awakening</u> exemplifies the journey that is a very common feature in many works of literature. This journey is not a commonplace journey; it is one that brings about development and change in the story's main character. In <u>The Awakening</u>, the spiritual journey that Edna takes changes the way she thinks, acts, and lives. The ramifications of her journey change her life.   5

The story takes place in New Orleans around the turn of the century. The women of society were treated as possessions, either of their fathers or their husbands, or even of their religion. The story's protagonist, Edna, is introduced as the respectable wife. She is a good mother and is faithful to her husband. The   10 family vacations for the summer in Grand Isle. While there, Edna befriends Robert who every summer devotes himself to being an attendant to one of the married women, Edna being his current choice. While there, she undergoes a series of "awakenings" which begin her journey. One such push was Edna's learning to swim. Although she was previously afraid of the water and of swimming, one day   15 she tried, and is successful. Her newfound ability signifies the steps she is taking towards no longer being a possession. It is one of the first signs that Edna is ready to break free and to be her own person. The water gives her a sense of freedom, and she relishes this sensation.

Edna's growing love for Robert alerts her of the journey upon which she has unknowingly embarked. After Robert leaves, giving very short notice, she misses him tremendously. She realizes that she is in love with him but has no such love for her husband, Leonce. While Robert gives into her every whim, Leonce only cares about Edna as if she were his possession. He does not consider her feelings and emotions, only his own. He leaves the family often to go into the city for work, sending candy and chocolates to Edna and her children in order to compensate for his absence. He constantly neglects Edna's emotional needs, and as a result, intensifies the strength of her journey. However, Leonce is not the only person who sees Edna merely as a possession. Even Robert, who is in love with her, feels that Edna belongs to Leonce. Because he knows that she cannot be his, Robert refuses to let their relationship progress any further than it has, and the only way for him to achieve this is to go away and cut off contact with Edna.

When the family returns to their home in New Orleans, Edna is not content with her life and begins to neglect performing some of her expected activities and duties, such as entertaining the wives of her husband's clients. Edna's refusal to accompany her husband on a business trip is the pinnacle of her journey. Leonce is shocked and appalled by her noncompliance, but he feels that she is going through a phase and will soon come to her senses.

While her husband is gone, Edna's children are sent to live with their grandmother. During this time, Edna is free and independent. She meets a variety of new people who she begins to spend time with. One of these people is Alcee Arobin, who becomes her lover. This relationship is important in Edna's journey because it represents a further rift from her previous life as a possession. More and more, Edna becomes her own person. Moreover, although he tries to make her his own possession as well, Edna refuses to let Alcee have the upper hand in their relationship. She refuses to let anyone control her life ever again. She even goes so far as to close up her house and rent a much smaller place to dwell in. Edna's actions come as a shock to many people, especially her husband, but she is really just trying to assert her individuality. However, no one understands what she is going through. In fact, many people, including her husband, blame her behavior on mental illness. Edna realizes that she cannot continue to live in this manner.

At the novel's conclusion, Edna decides to commit suicide. She swims into the ocean and drowns herself. It is fitting that she chooses the ocean, the place where she feels she has the most freedom, to end the journey. Edna decides that she would rather not live at all than to live a life where she cannot be her own person.

Student Essay B

It is easy to interpret the novel, <u>Things Fall Apart</u>, as a denouncement of white colonization, or simply as a detailed portrayal of African culture. But that would be all too banal; it has already been said and done by many authors. What makes this novel distinctive is the development and depiction of Okonkwo's journey through life and how his journey effects the novel's themes.

Given Okonkwo's rugged personality, he encounters many conflicts on his journey to self-awareness. Okonkwo clashes with his father, his wives, his children,

his village, and perhaps every other character, but his greatest struggle is with himself. It seems as if Okonkwo's enemy is his father's flaws, but in reality, Okonkwo's hidden enemy is his fear of his father's reflection upon himself. Okonkwo spends his 10
whole life on a journey away from the values of his father, so much up to the point where he ruins his life as well as the lives of those around him. His tragic flaw is his obsessive aversion to his father's laid back character. Okonkwo is so engulfed by his life's mission to become a rejection of his father's character, that he fails to see Unoka's positive traits such as tenderness, wisdom, and a passion for life, which 15
Okonkwo lacks.

Even though Okonkwo is the protagonist in this book, he is also the antagonist; clearly, he is on a trip to disaster. He has not journeyed inside himself to understand what makes him act the way he does. He is extremely rash and explosive and does not think twice about throwing a fatal punch. He foolishly thinks that his aggressiveness 20
is the only way for a man to act; it is this misconception that ultimately ruins him. Unfortunately for Okonkwo, he never realizes his flaw, and in the end, it is as if he cannot flee his father's reflection, for just like his father, he dies with shame and disgrace.

He had the ambition; he had the intelligence; he had the passion; but he had 25
all of these for the wrong reasons. Perhaps <u>Things Fall Apart</u> portrays Okonkwo's lack of development rather than his development through time. From his early youth he forms this strong aversion to weakness and ineptitude, and this controls all his actions throughout his life. In actuality, the fact that he is totally ruled by this fear of ineptitude underscores how internally weak Okonkwo is. In the end, when he 30
realizes that there is no possible way to triumph, that he cannot control people with his violent actions, and that he cannot control his fate, what does he do? He gives up and commits the most cowardly act of suicide.

Rating the Student Essays

Let's take a look at ranking comments about each of these essays. Student Essay A is a borderline high-range essay for several reasons:

- It addresses all aspects of the prompt.
- It is highly detailed (lines 13–14, 25–26, 34–35).
- It demonstrates strong topic adherence (lines 5–6, 14–15, 20, 36–37, 50–51).
- There is strong integration of specifics to support the thesis (lines 16–17, 29–32, 42–43).
- There is perceptive character analysis (lines 33–36, 49–51).
- There is clear linear development of the essay (lines 9, 13–14, 33, 39, 48).
- The essay is frequently repetitive and needs echo words.
- There are some syntax and diction errors.

This is an example of a strong midrange essay which could make the jump into the high-range area because of its organization, its use of detail, and its insights. It's obvious that the writer thoroughly understands the work and presents various specifics to support the thesis. The diction and syntax are, at times, not as mature as would be found on more sophisticated essays.

Student Essay B is a basic midrange essay for the following reasons:

"Peer review groups unite the class as they begin to form a writing community that is open to ideas, criticism, and revision."
—Sandi F.
    AP teacher

- It does begin to address the basic tasks of the prompt.
- It identifies character and theme.
- It refers to the character's journeys but does not really develop any of them (paragraphs 2–3).
- There are many generalizations which need more specific support (lines 10–16, 25–27).
- The essay loses its clear connection to the prompt at times (paragraph 4).
- The diction and syntax, although adequate, lack a maturity seen in higher-level papers.

This lower, midrange essay demonstrates that the writer understands the prompt. It does contain several perceptive insights which are unevenly developed. This is obviously a first draft in need of further revision. The essay would have benefited from more thorough preparation of the work prior to the exam. As it stands, it relies too heavily on generalizations.

Final Comments

Warning! Although the free-response essay may appear to be the easiest and most accessible on the exam, it is fraught with danger. The worst danger is relying on vague references and general statements that are not supported by specific details or lines. In addition, you have to develop the organizational pattern of the essay and control its progression. All too often the essays read like capsule summaries of the plots.

Your lifesaver in this essay situation is preparation. We say this again because it bears repeating:

- Review full-length works you've read during the year.
- Choose a minimum of five works you've connected with.
- Classify the five works to ensure a broad spectrum of types, literary movements, and themes.
- Isolate several *pivotal* scenes, moments, or episodes from each of the five works and examine the suitability of those scenes for a variety of questions.
- Select quotations and details from these pivotal scenes.
- If necessary, reread only the pivotal scenes before you take the exam.

Rapid Review

- Remember the pitfalls of the free-response essay: vagueness and plot summary.
- Choose AP-level full-length novels or plays that you thoroughly recall and understand.
- Generally, use this year's material.
- Familiarize yourself with sample free-response prompts.
- Anticipate free-response prompts.
- Develop specific review materials for several full-length works.
- Practice applying your knowledge to a variety of prompts.
- Highlight the prompt to make certain you are addressing the requirements of the question.

- Do not waste time looking at the suggested works. Choose from your own memory bank.
- Plan the essay thoroughly before you begin writing.
- Briefly chart your response. Fill in with concrete details and quotes, if possible.
- Write an engaging opening paragraph that reflects the question's requirements.
- Stay on topic.
- *Avoid plot summary.*
- Include transitions and echo words.
- Review our models and rubrics for self-evaluation.
- Share your ideas with others.

STEP **4**

Review the Knowledge You Need to Score High

CHAPTER **8**   Comprehensive Review—Prose
CHAPTER **9**   Comprehensive Review—Poetry

Introduction to Review Section

Why a Review Section? Why Not Just Provide a Series of Practice Exams?

Since the AP Lit exam is the culminating, evaluative tool for your high school English career, it would be wonderful if it could be truly representative of all that you have learned. But, it is only a 3-hour test. Therefore, it must of necessity be general, and it must be wide ranging enough to provide equity and opportunity for every student who takes the exam. What the test makers assume about the students who take the AP Lit exam is a common background of terminology and skills.

The following two chapters are not a replacement for your serious in-class study and practice. Instead, they provide a resource for terminology and skills when you need clarification or explanation. We want the information to enhance your analytical skills and to present you with direction you might not have considered.

CHAPTER 8

Comprehensive Review—Prose

IN THIS CHAPTER

Summary: A brief review of terms and processes associated with prose analysis

Key Ideas
- ✪ Understand the components of a narrative
- ✪ Explore various types of novels
- ✪ Learn literary terminology related to analysis
- ✪ Understand various levels of interpretation

Introduction to Prose

Our desire to know ourselves and others, to explore the unknown mysteries of existence, to make sense out of chaos, and to connect with our own kind are all primary reasons for engaging in the process of literary analysis.

The benefits to self and society that result from this interaction include a sense of wonder at the glory of humanity's imagination, a sense of excitement at the prospect of intellectual challenge, and a sense of connection with the universe.

You have already engaged in these lofty experiences. This section will provide a brief review of terms and processes associated with the study of literature. Included are some suggested activities for you to try which will help you prepare for the exam.

What Is Prose?

As you know, prose is the written equivalent of the spoken language. It is written in words, phrases, sentences, paragraphs, and chapters. It utilizes punctuation, grammar, and vocabulary to develop its message. Prose is made up of fiction and nonfiction. For the AP Lit exam, you are required to be well read in the areas of:

- Fiction, which includes:
  - Novels
  - Short stories
- Nonfiction, which includes:
  - Essays
  - Autobiographies and biographies
  - Speeches
  - Journals
  - Articles

Note: A brief word about drama. Since this section is a review of prose designed to prepare you for the AP Lit exam, it is not feasible to address every literary distinction and definition. Therefore, we wish to stress the following:

- Specific terminology can be found in the Glossary at the back of this book.
- All the techniques examined for prose can be used to analyze drama as well.
- The overlapping nature of the analytical skills makes them suitable for prose, poetry, and drama.

Five Aspects of Every Narrative

There is a certain degree of universality regarding definitions of terms when analyzing literature. For clarity and understanding, you should be aware of the following terms.

Plot

The plot is a series of episodes in a *narrative* carried out by the *characters*. Here are the primary terms related to plot. You should be familiar with all of them. Obviously each work manipulates these concepts in its own unique way.

- *Initial incident:* the event that puts the story in gear.
- *Rising action:* the series of complications in the narrative.
- *The climax:* the highest point of interest, action, or tension. More subtly, it is a turning point in the protagonist's behavior or thoughts.
- *Falling action:* the series of events occurring after the climax.
- *Denouement:* the resolution that ties up the loose ends of the plot.

These form the skeleton of a discussion about plot. But there are also other elements that add to your comprehension.

- *Foreshadowing:* hints at future events.
- *Flashbacks:* cut or piece a prior scene into the present situation.
- *In medias res:* literally, to be in the middle. This is a device that places the reader immediately into the action.

- *Subplot:* secondary plot that explores ideas that are different from the main story line.
- *Parallel plot:* a secondary story line that mimics the main plot.

Setting

Traditionally, setting is the time and place of a work, but it is also so much more. Setting is not accidental. It is a vital part of the narrative, and it can serve many functions. You should consider setting in light of the following:

- *General:* to underscore the universality of the work ("The Open Boat")
- *Specific:* to create a definitive ambiance that impacts on the work's possibilities (*Gone with the Wind*)
- *Character or foil:* in relation to the protagonist (*The Perfect Storm*)
- *Limiting factor:* to allow the plot, character, and theme to develop (*Lord of the Flies*)
- To *reveal style* (*The Secret Sharer*)
- To *reveal character* (*Hedda Gabler*)
- To *reveal theme* (*Heart of Darkness*)

Your Turn

Choose a literary text you've read during the past two years and examine a particularly effective setting.

1. Jot down the major specifics of the setting.

2. Identify the function(s) of that setting.

Title: _____

Setting: _____

_____

Details/Specifics   **Function(s)**

Character

Character development can be both simple and complex. The author has a variety of methods from which to choose. Here's a mnemonic device that may help you analyze character: Use the word **STAR**.

- **S**—what the character *says*;
- **T**—what the character *thinks*;
- **A**—how the character *acts* and interacts; and
- **R**—how the character *reacts*.

Traditionally, characters carry out the plot, and it is around the characters that the plot revolves and the theme is developed. There can be many types of characters in a given work:

- *Protagonist:* the main character who is the central focus of the story. For example, Hamlet is the eponymous protagonist.
- *Antagonist:* the opposing force. It does not always have to be a person. For example, the sea or the fish in *The Old Man and the Sea.*
- *Major:* the character or characters who play a significant role in the work.
- *Minor:* the characters who are utilized for a specific purpose, such as moving the plot along or contrasting with a major character.
- *Dynamic:* refers to characters who undergo major changes, such as Jane Eyre.
- *Static:* generally refers to characters who remain the same throughout the story. For instance, Brutus in *Julius Caesar* always considers himself to be an "honorable man."
- *Stereotype:* a character who is used to represent a class or a group.
- *Foil:* a character who provides the opportunity for comparison and contrast. For example, in Shakespeare's *Julius Caesar*, Brutus and Cassius are foils for each other.

Character as Hero

Once again, you may encounter many variations on the concept of hero:

"Be consistent and persistent in maintaining a literary journal. Students who do this have greater recall of information that they can incorporate into their literary essays."
—Charles V.
    AP teacher

- Aristotelian tragic hero:
  - Of noble birth; larger than life
  - Basically good
  - Exhibits a fatal flaw
  - Makes error in judgment
  - Possesses hubris (excessive arrogance or pride) which causes the error in judgment
  - Brings about his own downfall
  - Has a moment of realization, an epiphany
  - Lives and suffers
  - Examples: Creon in *Antigone*, Oedipus in *Oedipus*, Jason in *Medea*

- Classical hero: a variation on the tragic hero:
  - Examples: Macbeth in *Macbeth*, Lear in *King Lear*, Hamlet in *Hamlet*

- Romantic hero:
  - Larger than life
  - Charismatic
  - Possesses an air of mystery
  - "Saves the day" or the heroine

- Embodies freedom, adventure, and idealism
- Often outside the law
- Examples: Robin Hood, Ivanhoe, James Bond, Mr. Rochester in *Jane Eyre*

- Modern hero:
  - May be everyman
  - Has human weaknesses
  - Caught in the ironies of the human condition
  - Struggles for insight
  - Examples: Willy Loman in *Death of a Salesman*, Tom Joad in *Grapes of Wrath*

- Hemingway hero:
  - Brave
  - Endures
  - Maintains a sense of humor
  - Exhibits grace under pressure
  - Examples: Santiago in *The Old Man and the Sea*, Jake Barnes in *The Sun Also Rises*, Butch and Sundance in *Butch Cassidy and the Sundance Kid*

- Antihero: Protagonist is notably lacking in heroic qualities:
  - Examples: Meursault in *The Stranger*, Randall McMurphy in *One Flew Over the Cuckoo's Nest*, Homer Simpson of cartoon fame

Theme

Theme is the main idea, the moving force, what it's all about, the "why" behind the "what," the universal concept or comment, the big picture, the major insight, the *raison d'être*. But theme is much more than a simple checklist. And, we cringe each time we hear, "What is the theme?" Remember, the enlightened, complex mind questions, ponders, responds. A literary work evolves and can be validly interpreted in so many ways that it would be a disservice to limit it to any single, exclusive theme.

Keeping an open mind, understand that the following is an overview of ways of assessing themes. All elements of a literary work point toward the development of the theme. Therefore, you will apply all that you have been learning and practicing in your search for a discernible, supportable theme.

Motif   In its most general sense, motif is the repetition of an image. It may be closely connected to symbol, or it may be a thematic restatement.

The following is a preparation process for discovering and analyzing the function of motif. You can try this with any work.

- Isolate some general motifs you've noticed in a work.
- Provide specific examples to illustrate the motif.
- Draw inferences from your observations.

These rough inferences may lead you to a better understanding of character and theme. The following is a sample worksheet that uses the above process to analyze motif in Tennessee Williams's *A Streetcar Named Desire*.

Motif in *A Streetcar Named Desire*

MOTIF	EXAMPLE	THEMATIC IMPLICATIONS
Color	White woods (Blanche DuBois) Blue piano Red pajamas—Stanley Allan Grey	Red/white/blue = American theme Blue/gray—Civil War? Rape of Old South? Destruction of a way of life
Music	The blues "Only a Paper Moon" (if you believed in me) Captive maiden	Loss/sorrow, betrayal Lack of reality—insanity Control/slavery

Animals	Blanche:
	    fine feathered/wildcat
	    trapped bird/tiger
	    moth to light
	Stanley:
	    rooster/pig
	    ape
	    goat/Capricorn
		ego/id
		duality
		self-destruction
		
		survival of the fittest
		Darwinism/primitivism
		Dionysian—rape

Here's another way to work through an idea about theme. Sometimes it's easier to input a theme and then prove it with support from a work. If you can defend an idea with several specifics, you probably have identified a theme. Let's look at Shakespeare's *Hamlet*:

Hamlet

POSSIBLE THEME	EVIDENCE
What is, is not	1. Hamlet is not mad, only north-northwest. 2. Polonius is not Claudius in Gertrude's chamber. 3. Ophelia is not disinterested in Hamlet's overtures. 4. Rosencrantz and Guildenstern are not Hamlet's "friends."
Vengeance	1. Old Hamlet's charge to Hamlet to redress his murder. 2. Laertes's vow to avenge his father's death. 3. Fortinbras's victory to avenge his father.

Obviously, we have provided the organization in our samples, but these two techniques are solid, reliable processes. They will work on the exam, too, especially as you interrelate ideas for your essays or identify points that may be the topic of multiple-choice questions.

Keep a section in your notes where you enter important motifs, images, and so on and their implications from works you study. These concrete details will be invaluable when you write the free-response essay. Keep in mind that motif, imagery, symbol, and theme build on one another and are interrelated.

Point of View

Point of view is the method the author utilizes to tell the story. It is the vantage point from which the narrative is told. You've had practice with this in both reading and writing.

- *First person*: The narrator is the story's protagonist. (I went to the store.)
- *Third-person objective*: The narrator is an onlooker reporting the story. (She went to the store.)
- *Third-person omniscient*: The narrator reports the story and provides information unknown to the character(s). (She went to the store unaware that in three minutes she would meet her long-lost mother selling apples on the corner.)
- *Stream of consciousness*: This is a narrative technique that places the reader in the mind and thought processes of the narrator, no matter how random and spontaneous that may be (e.g., James Joyce's *Ulysses*).
- *Chorus*: Ancient Greek plays employed a chorus as a narrative device. The chorus, as needed, could be a character, an assembly, the playwright's voice, the audience, an omniscient forecaster. This function can be seen in modern works as well.
- *Stage manager*: This technique utilizes a character who comments omnisciently (e.g., *Our Town*, *The Glass Menagerie*).
- *Interior monologue*: This technique reflects the inner thoughts of the character.

Note: In modern literature, authors often use multiple forms of narration. For example, in *As I Lay Dying* by William Faulkner, every chapter has a different narrator.

Types of Novels

KEY IDEA

There are many types of novels you will encounter during your study of English literature. Some novels exhibit several qualities. A few of the most common genres are:

- *Epistolary*: These novels utilize the convention of letter writing and are among the earliest novel forms (e.g., *Pamela*, *Dracula*, *The Color Purple*).
- *Picaresque*: This early, episodic novel form concentrates on the misadventures of a young rogue (e.g., *Huckleberry Finn*, *Don Quixote*, *Tom Jones*, *Candide*).
- *Autobiographical*: This readily identifiable type is always told in the first person and allows the reader to directly interact with the protagonist (e.g., *David Copperfield*, *Catcher in the Rye*).
- *Gothic*: This type of novel is concerned with the macabre, supernatural, and exotic (e.g., *Frankenstein*, *Interview with a Vampire*, *Dr. Jekyll and Mr. Hyde*).
- *Historical*: This form is grounded in a real context and relies heavily on setting and factual detail (e.g., *A Tale of Two Cities*, *War and Peace*).
- *Romantic*: This novel form is idealistic, imaginative, and adventuresome. The romantic hero is the cornerstone of the novel, which often includes exotic locales (e.g., *Wuthering Heights*, *Madame Bovary*).
- *Allegorical*: This type of novel is representative and symbolic. It operates on at least two levels. Its specifics correspond to another concept (e.g., *Animal Farm*, *Lord of the Flies*).

Consider this. *Jane Eyre* has elements of all these types, as do many other novels. List and loosely categorize some of the major novels you've read.

_____

_____

_____

_____

_____

Literary Terminology

Literary analysis assumes the working knowledge of a common vocabulary.

The Kaleidoscope of Literary Meaning

Literary meaning is developed and revealed through various devices and techniques. What follows is a brief listing of those terms and devices most often used in prose, poetry, and drama.

- *Allusion*: An allusion is a reference to another work, concept, or situation which generally enhances the meaning of the work that is citing it. There are many types of allusions, and they may be implicit or explicit, highly limited or broadly developed. Often, modern readers may miss the context of a particular reference because they have a limited frame of reference. A few common categories of allusion follow:
  - *Mythological allusions*: These often cite specific characters. Common allusions might refer to the beauty of Aphrodite or the power of Zeus. "She followed like Niobe, all tears" (*Hamlet*). Sometimes the entire work may refer to a mythological event. The play *Desire Under the Elms* is a sustained allusion to the Phaedra legend, as well as the Oedipal myth.
  - *Biblical allusions*: These references may deal with circumstances as familiar as "the mark of Cain," "the fall from paradise," "the tribulations of Job," or "destruction by flood or fire." A character may have the "strength of Samson" or the "loyalty of Ruth."
  - *Historical allusions*: These kinds of allusions might refer to major historical events, such as Napoleon meeting his Waterloo or Nixon dealing with Watergate.
  - *Literary allusions*: Often works will refer to other well-known pieces. For example, *West Side Story* expects you to think of *Romeo and Juliet*. To describe a character as "quixotic" refers to Cervantes's great novel *Don Quixote*.
  - *Political allusions*: These references would be sustained in works like *Gulliver's Travels* or *Alice in Wonderland*. They might also be used briefly. If a character were called the next Julius Caesar, we might sense that he would be betrayed in some manner. *The Crucible* is a historical allusion to the Salem witch trials and is also a statement about McCarthyism in the 1950s.
  - *Contemporary allusions*: These are often lost when the current context is no longer in the public eye. For example, "valley girls" or "Beavis and Butthead" may not remain in vogue, and, therefore, references to them would lose their effectiveness.

- *Ambiguity*: This is the seemingly incongruous and contradictory interpretations of meaning in a work. James Joyce and William Faulkner utilize ambiguity often in their writing.

- *Allegory*: A work that operates on another level. The characters and events may be interpreted for both literal and symbolic meaning. For example, *Of Mice and Men* by Steinbeck is an indictment of the exploitation of the masses and a call to unionism as well as a story of doomed friendship. Other allegorical works include *The Old Man and the Sea* by Hemingway, *Animal Farm* by Orwell, *Candide* by Voltaire, and *Pilgrim's Progress* by John Bunyan.

- *Parable*: A parable is an allegorical story that is intended to teach. It generally provides a moral lesson or illustrates a guiding principle. "The Nun's Priest's Tale" in *The Canterbury Tales* by Chaucer is a parable about vanity and pride.

- *Symbol*: This is an image that also represents something else. Some symbols appear to be extremely specific. In Hawthorne's *The Scarlet Letter* the scarlet letter is a symbol of Hester's impropriety. It can also represent Hester's pride, talent, responsibility, and shame. The reader should always be open to the broadest interpretation of the concept of symbol, whether about character, setting, situation, detail, or whatever. Another example of symbol is the splitting of the chestnut tree in *Jane Eyre*. Here Bronte symbolizes the breach in the relationship between Jane and Rochester. The white hat in *The Secret Sharer* by Conrad is a symbol of man's compassion and pity for his own kind.

- *Connotation*: This is the implication that is suggested by a word or phrase rather than the word or phrase's actual, literal meaning. For example, the use of "antique land" instead of "ancient land" brings a richer connotation to Shelley's "Ozymandias." The reader must be especially open to the varied levels of meaning in poetry.

- *Denotation*: The literal meaning of a word or phrase. If a reader is attempting to present a valid interpretation of a literary work, he or she must pay attention to both the denotation and the connotation of the language.

- *Tone*: Tone is difficult to define but is relatively easy to assess. It is a subtle feeling that the author creates through diction. The following is a short list of words often used to describe tone. Notice that they are adjectives.

bitter	objective	idyllic
sardonic	naive	compassionate
sarcastic	joyous	reverent
ironic	spiritual	lugubrious
mocking	wistful	elegiac
scornful	nostalgic	gothic
satiric	humorous	macabre
vituperative	mock-serious	reflective
scathing	pedantic	maudlin
confidential	didactic	sentimental
factual	inspiring	patriotic
informal	remorseful	jingoistic
facetious	disdainful	detached
critical	laudatory	

- *Transition*: Do not be fooled into thinking that "transition" is an unimportant term. An author will give you a road map through his or her story's journey, and one of the best indicators of direction is the transition word or phrase. Transitions help to move the reader smoothly from one part of the text to another. Below is a list of the most effective commonly used transitions:

and	also	as a result	after
but	besides	for example	although
for	consequently	in addition	because
nor	furthermore	in the same way	once
or	however	on the contrary	since
so	likewise	on the other hand	unless
yet	moreover	otherwise	until
	nonetheless	unlike the former	while
	similarly		
	still		
	therefore		

Prose Analysis

A word about this section: There are many processes that will help you to understand prose, poetry, and drama.

These approaches may not all be suitable for every work, but they certainly are worth considering as methods for responding to subtleties that are in the work.

Name Analysis

KEY IDEA

Consider your name. Did your folks have a specific reason for choosing it? Does it have a family significance or a special cultural meaning? What would you choose for your name and why? Remember, names and identity are closely linked.

Authors often choose names that bring another dimension to a character or place. A good reader is sensitive to the implications of names. Here are a few interesting names and observations about each:

• Oedipus—swollen foot, seeker of truth
• Billy Budd—simple, melodic, young growth, ready to bloom
• Jane Eyre—Janus/beginning, air, err, heir, ere, eerie, ire
• Helen Burns—fever, fervor, mythological inspiration
• Mr. Mason—the Masons are a secret fraternity; he holds the secret
• Stella—star, light
• Kurtz—short, curt
• Willy Loman—low man

Your Turn

Create your own listing of literary names and their interpretations and implications. (This could also include place names, etc.)

Literary Work	Name	Interpretations

It's an Open-and-Closed Case

The first thing that catches your attention should be the title. By all means, consider it carefully. *David Copperfield* lets you know it will be a novel about character. *As I Lay Dying* involves plot and theme. *One Flew Over the Cuckoo's Nest* involves you immediately in symbol, character, and theme.

Authors place special emphasis on the first and last impressions they make on a reader. The opening and closing lines of chapters or scenes are, therefore, usually very significant and should be closely examined. (This is much like an establishing shot in a movie that sets up the audience for future developments.)

Here's the opening line from Chapter 1 of *Jane Eyre*:

> *There was no possibility of taking a walk that day.*

Here are some implications of this one line: no independence, locked in, no sense of curiosity, outside force preventing a journey, not ready to leave. Obviously, the character is not ready to experience the outside world or to embark on her journey.

Contrast that with the last line of Chapter 1:

> *Four hands were laid upon me and I was borne upstairs.*

This line introduces a spiritual level to the novel. It also implies that a new Jane will emerge, and indeed she does.

Take a look at one of the last lines of the novel:

> *We wended our way into the wood.*

This lovely, alliterative line completes the journey. Jane and Edward have come full circle as they stroll their way together.

In a Shakespearean play, often a couplet at the end of a scene or act will neatly summarize or foreshadow events. In *Julius Caesar*, for example:

> *And after this, let Caesar seat him sure*
> *For we will shake him, or worse days endure (Julius Caesar)*

Keep a written record of opening and closing lines of complete literary works, chapters, scenes, acts. Not only will this develop your interpretative skills, but it will also provide you with a list of quotations for later use in essays.

Levels of Interpretation

Complex works of literature afford many avenues of interpretation. After you read a work, consider the following areas of exploration. We use Ibsen's *Hedda Gabler* as a model.

- *Literal level*: A young woman is frustrated in her life and eventually commits suicide.
- *Social level*: Ibsen explores the role of women in society and presents the despair connected with a male-dominated existence.
- *Psychological level*: The play traces a descent into madness and the motivations for aberrant human behavior.
- *Religious level*: The loss of a soul to temptation, the encounter with the devil, and the inspiration of godliness are all in the play.
- *Sexual level*: Gender issues, the Electra complex, phallic symbols, abortion, and homosexuality are all developed and explored through numerous love triangles.
- *Political level*: The play could be read as a treatise on socialism. It denigrates capitalism and pays homage to the ideas of Marx's *Communist Manifesto*.

Obviously, you need to supply the evidence from the works to develop your interpretations in a concrete manner.

Note: A word about ***subtext***:

Subtext refers to the implied meaning of a work or section of a work. It involves reading between the lines to discover subtle attitudes, comments, and observations within the piece. The exploration of subtext utilizes all of the interpretative skills you've been developing in your AP course.

Practice looking beyond the literal presentation of the plays, novels, and short stories you read. The following are richly suitable for such study:

Desire Under the Elms	Eugene O'Neill
Heart of Darkness	Joseph Conrad
Dubliners	James Joyce
The Grapes of Wrath	John Steinbeck
Les Miserables	Victor Hugo
The Kite Runner	Khaled Hosseini
Beloved	Toni Morrison

Final Comments

One of the most rewarding forms of preparation you can do involves developing a sensitivity to the words of a piece of literature.

Get a journal or set aside a section of your notebook for recording lines you respond to for their beauty, appeal, meaning, or relevance. For each work you read:

- Enter the lines.
- Identify the speaker and situation.

- Interpret, connect, comment, or reflect on your choice.
- Free-associate as well as relate the quotation to the original text.
- Make connections to other works you read.
- Project and expand on the lines.

For each full-length work, record at least ten references. Write these quotations out and include the page numbers so you can easily find them if you need to. Try to take them from throughout the work. Here is what is going to happen. Soon, you will automatically identify and respond to significant lines and passages. It will become second nature for you to identify lines of import and meaning in a work as you read. You will also begin to remember lines from a work and to connect them to important details, episodes, and themes. You will be able to understand and analyze a character in light of his or her own language. In other words, you will be interpreting literature based on text.

Rapid Review

- Every narrative is composed of plot, setting, character, theme, and point of view.
- Motifs develop characters and themes.
- Themes require specific illustrations to support them.
- There are many types of characters and heroes.
- There are many forms of narration.
- Novels may exhibit many characteristics.
- Meaning may be revealed via multiple approaches.
- Parables and allegories operate on symbolic levels. Connotations of words reveal the subtext of a work.
- Tone is a description of the attitude found in a piece of literature.
- Transitions aid movement and unity in a written work.
- Titles and names are important areas for analysis.
- First and last lines often carry great meaning in a work and demand careful attention.
- Works may be interpreted literally, socially, psychologically, sexually, politically, and so on.
- Quotations from works are an accurate way of understanding meaning and characterization. They also provide support for your interpretations.

CHAPTER 9

Comprehensive Review—Poetry

IN THIS CHAPTER

Summary: Overview, including definitions, examples, and practice with poetic forms

Key Ideas
- ✪ Learn the differences between poetry and prose
- ✪ Understand the structure of poetry
- ✪ Explore various types of poetry
- ✪ Practice interpreting selected poems
- ✪ Compare and contrast given poems

Introduction to Poetry

Poetry—the very word inspires fear and trembling, and well it should because it deals with the intensity of human emotion and the experiences of life itself. But there is no reason to fear that which elevates, elucidates, edifies, and inspires. Poetry is a gift of language, like speech and song, and with familiarity comes pleasure and knowledge and comfort.

However, it may still be intimidating to read poetry. After all, we've been speaking and reading prose our entire lives. This review assumes that by the time you reach an AP-level literature course, you have some experience and facility with poetry. We provide you with definitions, examples, and practice with interpretation. Hopefully, you will provide the interest, diligence, and critical thinking necessary for a joyful and meaningful experience.

Remember our philosophy of firsts? First, we believe that you should read as much poetry as possible. Early in the year, pick up an anthology of poetry and read, read, read. Open to any page and read for pleasure and interest. Don't try to "study" the poems; just respond to them on an emotional level. Consider the following:

- Identify subjects that move you or engage you.
- Are there certain themes you respond to? Are there certain poets you like? List them and read more poetry by them.
- Are there certain types or styles of poems you enjoy? What do they seem to have in common?
- Are there images or lines you love? Keep a record of some of your favorites.

Make this a time to develop a personal taste for poetry. Use this random approach to experience a broad range of form and content. You should find that you are more comfortable with poetry simply because you have been discovering it at your own pace.

When you are comfortable and have honestly tried reading it for pleasure, it is time to approach it on a more analytical level.

The Structure of Poetry

What Makes Poetry Different from Prose?

How do you know when you're working with poetry and not prose? Simple. Just look at it. It's shorter; it's condensed; it's written in a different physical form. The following might help you to visualize the basic differences:

Prose	Poetry
Words	Syllables
Phrases	Feet
Sentences	Lines
Paragraphs	Stanzas
Chapters	Cantos

It should not be news to you when we say that poetry sounds different from prose. It is more musical, and it often relies on sound to convey meaning. In addition, it can employ meter, which provides rhythm. Did you know that poetry is from the ancient oral tradition of storytelling and song? Rhyme and meter made it easier for the bards to remember the story line. Try to imagine Homer in a dimly lit hall chanting the story of Odysseus.

As with prose, poetry also has its own jargon. Some of this lingo is specifically related to form and meter. The analysis of a poem's form and meter is termed **scansion**.

The Foot

The **foot** is the basic building block of poetry. It is composed of a pattern of syllables. These patterns create the meter of a poem. **Meter** is a pattern of beats or accents. We figure out this pattern by counting the stressed and unstressed syllables in a line. Unstressed syllables are indicated with a ˘, and stressed syllables are indicated with a ´.

There are five common patterns that are used repeatedly in English poetry. They are:

- The *iamb* ˘ ´ (tŏ dáy) (bĕ cáuse)
- The *trochee* ´ ˘ (háp pў) (líght lў)
- The *anapest* ˘ ˘ ´ (ŏb vĭ oús) (rĕ gŭ lár)
- The *dactyl* ´ ˘ ˘ (cĭg ă rĕtte) (ín tĕr rŭpt)
- The *spondee* ´ ´ (dówn tówn) (slíp shód)

The Line

Unlike the prose sentence, which is determined by subject, verb, and punctuation, the poetic line is measured by the number of feet it contains.

- 1 foot   monometer
- 2 feet   dimeter
- 3 feet   trimeter
- 4 feet   tetrameter
- 5 feet   pentameter
- 6 feet   hexameter
- 7 feet   heptameter
- 8 feet   octameter
- 9 feet   nonometer

Your Turn

Now answer the following. How many stressed syllables are in a line of:

Iambic pentameter   _____
Dactylic trimeter   _____
Anapestic dimeter   _____
Spondaic monometer   _____
Trochaic tetrameter   _____

Note: Answers can be found at the end of the definition of "meter" in the Glossary of terms.

The Stanza

You should now understand that syllables form feet, feet form lines, and lines form stanzas. Stanzas also have names:

- 1 line   a line
- 2 lines   couplet
- 3 lines   tercet
- 4 lines   quatrain
- 5 lines   cinquain
- 6 lines   sestet
- 7 lines   septet
- 8 lines   octave

Your Turn

What is the total number that results from adding up all of the metric references in the following, make-believe poem?

- The poem is composed of 3 quatrains, 2 couplets, and 1 sestet.
- Each quatrain is written in iambic tetrameter.
- The couplets are dactylic dimeter.
- The sestet is trochaic trimeter.

The total number is _____.

Note: You can find the answer at the end of the definition of "rhythm" in the Glossary of terms.

You will never have to be this technical on the AP exam. However, you will probably find a question on meter, and technical terms may be included in the answer choices to the multiple-choice questions. In addition, sometimes in the poetry essay you may find an opportunity to use your knowledge of scansion, or your analysis of the rhyme and meter of the poem, to develop your essay. This can be very effective if it is linked to interpretation.

Rhyme

One of the first processes you should become familiar with concerns the identification of a poem's rhyme scheme. This is easily accomplished by assigning consecutive letters of the alphabet to each new sound at the end of a line of poetry. Traditionally, rhyme scheme is indicated with italicized, lowercase letters placed to the right of each line of the poem.

- *a* for the first
- *b* for the second
- *c* for the third
- *d*, *e*, and so forth

Try this with the opening stanza from "Peace" by George Herbert.

> *Sweet Peace, where dost thou dwell? I humbly crave,*
> > *Let me once know.*
> *I sought thee in a secret cave,*
> > *And asked if Peace were there.*
> *A hollow wind did seem to answer, "No,*
> > *Go seek elsewhere."*

You may restart the scheme with each new stanza or continue throughout the poem. Remember, the purpose is to identify and establish a pattern and to consider if the pattern helps to develop sound and/or meaning. Here's what the rhyme scheme looks like for the above selection: *a b a c b c*.

When you analyze the pattern of the complete poem, you can conclude that there is a very regular structure to this poem which is consistent throughout. Perhaps the content will also reflect a regular development. Certainly the rhyme enhances the sound of the poem and helps it flow. From now on we will refer to rhyme scheme when we encounter a new poem.

The rhymes we have illustrated are called **end rhymes** and are the most common. **Masculine rhyme** is the most frequently used end rhyme. It occurs when the last stressed syllable of the rhyming words matches exactly. ("The play's the thing/Wherein I'll catch the conscience of the king.") However, there are **internal rhymes** as well. These rhymes occur within the line and add to the music of the poem. An example of this is *dreary*, in Poe's "The Raven" ("Once upon a midnight dreary, while I pondered, weak and weary"). **Feminine rhyme** involves two consecutive syllables of the rhyming words, with the first syllable stressed. ("The horses were prancing / as the clowns were dancing.")

Types of Poetry

Because of its personal nature, poetry has evolved into many different forms, each with its own unique purpose and components. What follows is an examination of the most often encountered forms.

Most poetry falls into one of two major categories. ***Narrative poetry*** tells a story. ***Lyric poetry*** presents a personal impression.

The Ballad

The ***ballad*** is one of the earliest poetic forms. It is a narrative that was originally spoken or sung and has often changed over time. It usually:

- Is simple.
- Employs dialogue, repetition, minor characterization.
- Is written in quatrains.
- Has a basic rhyme scheme, primarily *a b c b*.
- Has a refrain which adds to its songlike quality.
- Is composed of two lines of iambic tetrameter which alternate with two lines of iambic trimeter.

The subject matter of ballads varies considerably. Frequently, ballads deal with the events in the life of a folk hero, like Robin Hood. Sometimes they retell historical events. The supernatural, disasters, good and evil, love and loss are all topics found in traditional ballads.

The following is a typical folk ballad. Read this poem out loud. Listen to the music as you read. Get involved in the story. Imagine the scene. Try to capture the dialect or sound of the Scottish burr.

Bonny Barbara Allan
by Anonymous

It was in and about the Martinmas time,
When the green leaves were falling,
That Sir John Graeme, in the West Country,
Fell in love with Barbara Allan.

He sent his man down through the town,   5
To the place where she was dwelling:
"O haste and come to my master dear,
Gin ye be Barbara Allan."

O hooly, hooly rose she up,
To the place where he was lying,   10
And when she drew the curtain by:
"Young man I think you're dying."

"O it's I'm sick, and very, very sick,
And 'tis a' for Barbara Allan."
O the better for me ye's never be,   15
Though your heart's blood were a-spilling.

"O dinna ye mind, young man," said she,
"When ye was in the tavern a drinking,

That ye made the healths gae round and round,
And slighted Barbara Allan?"   20

He turned his face unto the wall,
And death was with him dealing:
"Adieu, adieu, my dear friends all,
And be kind to Barbara Allan."

And slowly, slowly raise she up,   25
And slowly, slowly left him,
And sighing said, she could not stay,
Since death of life had reft him.

She had not gane a mile or twa,
When she heard the dead-bell ringing,   30
And every jow that the dead bell geid,
It cried, "Woe to Barbara Allan."

"O mother, mother, make my bed!
O make it saft and narrow!
Since my love died for me to-day,   35
I'll die for him to-morrow."

After you've read the ballad, consider the following:

1. Check the rhyme scheme and stanza form. You should notice it is written in quatrains. The rhyme scheme is a little tricky here; it depends on pronunciation and is what is called a ***forced rhyme***. If you soften the "g" sound in the word "falling," it more closely rhymes with "Allan." Try this throughout the ballad, recognizing that the spoken word can be altered and stretched to fit the intention of rhyme. This falls under the category of "poetic license."

2. Follow the plot of the narrative. Poor Barbara Allan, poor Sir John. They are a classic example of thwarted young lovers, a literary pattern as old as Antigone and Haemon or Romeo and Juliet. Love, unrequited love, and dying for love are all universal themes in literature.

3. Observe the use of repetition and how it unifies the poem by sound and structure. "Barbara Allan/Hooly, hooly/Adieu, adieu/Slowly, slowly/Mother, mother."

4. Notice that dialogue is incorporated into the poem for characterization and plot development.

> Don't be too inflexible when checking rhyme or meter. Remember, never sacrifice meaning for form. You're smart; you can make intellectual leaps.

Here are some wonderfully wicked and enjoyable ballads to read:

"Sir Patrick Spens"—the tragic end of a loyal sailor
"The Twa Corbies"—the irony of life and nature
"Edward"—a wicked, wicked, bloody tale
"Robin Hood"—still a great, grand adventure

"Lord Randall"—sex, lies, and death in ancient England
"Get Up and Bar the Door"—a humorous battle of the sexes
"La Belle Dame Sans Merci"—John Keats's fabulous tale of a demon lover

Have you read ballads? Traditional or modern? List them here. Jot down a few details or lines to remind you of important points. If you're musical, try singing one out loud.

_____

_____

_____

_____

_____

The Lyric

Lyric poetry is highly personal and emotional. It can be as simple as a sensory impression or as elevated as an ode or elegy. Subjective and melodious, it is often reflective in tone.

The following is an example of a lyric:

A Red, Red Rose
by Robert Burns

O my luve's like a red, red rose,
That's newly sprung in June;
O my luve's like the melodie
That's sweetly played in tune.

As fair art thou, my bonnie lass,   5
So deep in luve am I;
And I will luve thee still, my dear,
Till a' the seas gang dry.

Till a' the seas gang dry, my dear,
And the rocks melt wi' the sun: 10
O I will luve thee still, my dear,
While the sands o' life shall run.

And fare the weel, my only luve,
And fare the weel awhile!
And I will come again, my luve,   15
Though it were ten thousand mile.

Now answer the following questions:

1. The stanza form is _____

2. The rhyme scheme is _____

3. The meter of line 6 is _____

4. The first stanza depends on similes. Underline them. _____

5. Cite assonance in stanza one. _____

6. Line 8 is an example of _____

7. Highlight alliteration in the poem. _____

8. Did you recognize iambic trimeter? How about hyperbole? _____

The following are wonderful lyric poems. Read a few.

> Edna St. Vincent Millay—"Childhood Is the Kingdom Where Nobody Dies"
> Emily Dickinson—"Wild Nights, Wild Nights"
> Dylan Thomas—"Fern Hill"
> Matthew Arnold—"Dover Beach"
> Andrew Marvell—"To His Coy Mistress"

The Ode

The **ode** is a formal lyric poem that addresses subjects of elevated stature. One of the most beautiful odes in English literature is by Percy Bysshe Shelley.

Ode to the West Wind

O wild West Wind, thou breath of Autumn's being,
Thou, from whose unseen presence the leaves dead
Are driven, like ghosts from an enchanter fleeing,

Yellow, and black, and pale, and hectic red,   5
Pestilence-stricken multitudes: O thou,
Who chariotest to their dark wintry bed

The wingéd seeds, where they lie cold and low,
Each like a corpse within the grave, until
Thine azure sister of the Spring shall blow

Her clarion* o'er the dreaming earth, and fill   10
(Driving sweet buds like flocks to feed in air)
With living hues and odors plain and hill:

Wild Spirit, which art moving everywhere;
Destroyer and preserver; hear, oh, hear!

2

Thou on whose stream, mid the steep sky's commotion,   15
Loose clouds like earth's decaying leaves are shed,
Shook from the tangled boughs of Heaven and Ocean,

Angels of rain and lightning: there are spread
On the blue surface of thine aery surge,
Like the bright hair uplifted from the head   20

_____
*Melodious trumpet call

Of some fierce Maenad,* even from the dim verge
Of the horizon to the zenith's height,
The locks of the approaching storm. Thou dirge

Of the dying year, to which this closing night
Will be the dome of a vast sepulcher,   25
Vaulted with all thy congregated might

Of vapors, from whose solid atmosphere
Black rain, and fire, and hail will burst: oh, hear!

                              3
Thou who didst waken from his summer dreams
The blue Mediterranean, where he lay,   30
Lulled by the coil of his crystalline streams

Beside a pumice isle in Baiae's† bay,
And saw in sleep old palaces and towers
Quivering within the wave's intenser day,

All overgrown with azure moss and flowers   35
So sweet, the sense faints picturing them! Thou
For whose path the Atlantic's level powers

Cleave themselves into chasms, while far below
The sea-blooms and the oozy woods which wear
The sapless foliage of the ocean, know   40

Thy voice, and suddenly grow gray with fear,
And tremble and despoil themselves: oh, hear!

                              4
If I were a dead leaf thou mightest bear;
If I were a swift cloud to fly with thee;
A wave to pant beneath thy power, and share   45

The impulse of thy strength, only less free
Than thou, O uncontrollable! If even
I were as in my boyhood, and could be

The comrade of thy wanderings over Heaven,
As then, when to outstrip thy skiey speed   50
Scarce seem a vision; I would ne'er have striven

As thus with thee in prayer in my sore need.
Oh, lift me as a wave, a leave, a cloud!
I fall upon the thorns of life! I bleed!

---

*Frenzied dancer
†A village near Naples, Italy

A heavy weight of hours has chained and bowed   55
One too like thee: tameless, and swift, and proud.

5

Make me thy lyre,* even as the forest is:
What if my leaves are falling like its own!
The tumult of thy mighty harmonies

Will take from both a deep, autumnal tone,   60
Sweet though in sadness. Be thou, Spirit fierce,
My spirit! Be thou me, impetuous one!

Drive my dead thoughts over the universe
Like withered leaves to quicken a new birth!
And, by the incantation of this verse,   65

Scatter, as from an unextinguished hearth
Ashes and sparks, my words among mankind!
Be through my lips to unawakened earth

The trumpet of a prophecy! O Wind,
If Winter comes, can Spring be far behind?   70

----

*Small, harplike instrument

As always, read the poem carefully. (Find a private place and read it aloud. You'll be carried away by the beauty of the sounds and imagery.) Now answer the following questions.

1. Look at the configuration of the poem. It is divided into five sections. What function might each section serve? _____

2. Count the lines in each section. How many? _____ Name the two stanza forms you encountered. _____

3. Check the rhyme scheme. Did you come up with *a b a b c b c d c d e d e e*? The first four tercets are written in a form called *terza rima*. Notice how this rhyme scheme interweaves the stanzas and creates unity throughout the poem. Did it cross your mind that each section might be a variation on the sonnet form? _____

4. Check the meter. You should notice that it is very irregular. (Freedom of form was a tenet of the Romantic Movement.)

5. Stanza one: Did you catch the *apostrophe*? The direct address to the wind places us in the poem's situation and provides the subject of the ode. Highlight the *alliteration* and trace the similes in line 3. _____

6. Stanza two: What are the "pestilence-stricken multitudes"? In addition to leaves, could they be the races of man? _____

7. Stanza three: See how the enjambment pulls you into this line. Find the simile. _____ Alliteration can be seen in "azure," "sister," "Spring," "shall."

8. Stanza four: What images are presented? _____ Locate the simile. _____ Find the contrast between life and death. _____ Highlight the personification.

9. Identify the essential paradox of the poem and life itself in the couplet.

We are not going to take you through the poem line by line. You may isolate those lines that speak to you. Here are a few of our favorites that are worth a second look:

- Lines 29–31
- Lines 35–42 for assonance
- Lines 53–54
- Lines 55–56
- Lines 57–70

You should be able to follow the development of ideas through the five sections. Were you aware of:

- The land imagery in section 1?
- The air imagery in section 2?
- The water imagery in section 3?
- The comparison of the poet to the wind in section 4?
- The appeal for the spirit of the wind to be the poet's spirit in section 5?

After you have read the poem, followed the organization, recognized the devices and images, you still have to interpret what you've read.

This ode has many possibilities. One interpretation linked it with the French Revolution and Shelley's understanding of the destructive regeneration associated with it. Another valid reading focuses on Shelley's loss of faith in the Romantic Movement. He asks for inspiration to breathe life into his work again. Try to propose other interpretations for this "Ode to the West Wind."

The Elegy

The *elegy* is a formal lyric poem written in honor of one who has died. *Elegiac* is the adjective that describes a work lamenting any serious loss.

One of the most famous elegies is by Percy Bysshe Shelley. It was written to mourn the loss of John Keats. Here is the first stanza of "Adonais." It contains all the elements of an elegy.

Adonais*

I weep for Adonais—he is dead!
O, weep for Adonais! Though our tears
Thaw not the frost which binds so dear a head!
And thou, sad Hour, selected from all years
To mourn our loss, rouse thy obscure compeers,   5

> And teach them thine own sorrow, say: "With me
> Died Adonais; till the Future dares
> Forget the Past, his fate and fame shall be
> An echo and a light unto eternity!"

————————

* An elegy on the death of John Keats, author of "Endymion," "Hyperion," etc.

Read this stanza several times. Try it aloud. Get carried away by the emotion. Respond to the imagery. Listen to the sounds; let the meter and rhyme guide you through. Consider the following:

1. Adonais, Shelley's name for Keats, is derived from Adonis. This is a mythological allusion to associate Keats with love and beauty. (The meter will tell you how to pronounce Adonais.)

2. Check the rhyme scheme. Did you come up with *a b a b b c b c*? See how the last two lines are rhymed to set this idea apart.

3. Line 1 contains a major *caesura* in the form of a dash. This forces the reader to pause and consider the depth of emotion and the finality of the event. The words that follow are also set off by the caesura and emphasized by the exclamation point. Notice that the meter is not interrupted by the caesura. (˘ ʹ ˘ ʹ ˘ ʹ ˘ ʹ ˘ ʹ is perfect iambic pentameter.) This line is a complete thought which is concluded by punctuation and is an example of an *end-stopped line*.

4. Line 2 utilizes repetition to intensify the sense of loss. Here the caesura is an exclamation point. Notice that the last three words of the line fulfill the meter of iambic pentameter but do not express a complete thought as did line 1. The thought continues into line 3. This is an example of *enjambment*.

5. Lines 2 and 3 contain *alliteration* ("Though," "tears," "Thaw," "the") and *consonance* ("not," "frost," continuing into line 4 with "thou").

6. Line 3 contains *imagery* and *metaphor*. What does the frost represent? _____

   _____

7. Line 4 contains an *apostrophe*, which is a direct address to the sad Hour, which is personified. To what event does the "sad Hour" refer? _____

   _____

8. Lines 4, 5, and 6 incorporate *assonance*. The vowel sounds provide a painful tone through "ow" sounds ("thou," "Hour," "our," "rouse," "sorrow").

9. Notice how the enjambment in lines 7–9 speeds the stanza to the final thought. This helps the pacing of the poem.

10. Reread the poem. Choose images and lines you respond to.

Have you read any elegies? List them here. Jot down the poet, title, and any images and lines you like. Add your own thoughts about the poem.

_____

_____

_____

_____

_____

Following is a list of some of the most beautiful elegies in the English language. Make it a point to read several. You won't be sorry.

"Elegy for Jane" by Theodore Roethke—a teacher's lament for his student.

"Elegy in a Country Church Yard" by Thomas Gray—a reflective look at what might have been.

"When Lilacs Last in the Dooryard Bloomed" and "O Captain, My Captain" by Walt Whitman—tributes to Abraham Lincoln.

"In Memory of W. B. Yeats" by W. H. Auden—a poet's homage to a great writer.

The Dramatic Monologue

The *dramatic monologue* relates an episode in a speaker's life through a conversational format that reveals the character of the speaker.

Robert Browning is the acknowledged master of the dramatic monologue. The following is an example of both the dramatic monologue and Browning's skill as a poet.

Porphyria's Lover

The rain set early in tonight,
    The sullen wind was soon awake,
It tore the elm-tops down for spite,
    And did its worst to vex the lake:
    I listened with heart fit to break.   5
When glided in Porphyria; straight
    She shut the cold out and the storm,
And kneeled and made the cheerless grate
    Blaze up, and all the cottage warm;
    Which done, she rose, and from her form   10
Withdrew the dripping cloak and shawl,
    And laid her soiled gloves by, untied
Her hat and let the damp hair fall,
    And, last, she sat down by my side
    And called me. When no voice replied,   15
She put my arm about her waist,
    And made her smooth white shoulder bare,
And all her yellow hair displaced,
    And, stooping, made my cheek lie there,
    And spread, o'er all, her yellow hair,   20

Murmuring how she loved me—she
   Too weak, for all her heart's endeavor,
To set its struggling passion free
   From pride, and vainer ties desever,
   And give herself to me forever.   25
But passion sometimes would prevail,
   Nor could tonight's gay feast restrain
A sudden thought of one so pale
   For love of her, and all in vain:
   So, she was come through wind and rain.   30
Be sure I looked up at her eyes
   Happy and proud; at last I knew
Porphyria worshipped me: surprise
   Made my heart swell, and still it grew
   While I debated what to do.   35
That moment she was mine, mine, fair,
   Perfectly pure and good: I found
A thing to do, and all her hair
   In one long yellow string I wound
   Three times her little throat around,   40
And strangled her. No pain felt she;
   I am quite sure she felt no pain.
As a shut bud that holds a bee,
   I warily oped her lids: again
   Laughed the blue eyes without a stain.   45
And I untightened next the tress
   About her neck; her cheek once more
Blushed bright beneath my burning kiss:
   I propped her head up as before,
   Only, this time my shoulder bore   50
Her head, which droops upon it still:
   The smiling rosy little head,
So glad it has its utmost will,
   That all it scorned at once is fled,
   And I, its love, am gained instead!   55
Porphyria's love: she guessed not how
   Her darling one wish would be heard.
And thus we sit together now,
   And all night long we have not stirred,
   And yet God has not said a word!   60

Read the poem aloud, or have someone read it to you. Try for a conversational tone.

1. Concentrate on following the storyline. (Were you surprised by the concluding events?)

2. Once you know the "story," look closely at the poem for all the clues concerning character and episode.

3. Automatically check for the relationship between form and content. Quickly scan for rhyme scheme and meter. You should notice a definite presence of rhyme in an unusual form *a b a b b c d c d d e f e f f*, etc. You should be able to recognize that the meter is iambic tetrameter. Rather than scan the entire poem, try lines throughout to see if a pattern exists.

4. *Lines 1–5:* What does the setting indicate or foreshadow? _____

_____

Lines 6–9: What diction and imagery is associated with Porphyria?

_____

Lines 10–12: Why are we told her gloves were soiled?

_____

Lines 20–25: Try to understand what the narrator is telling you here.

This reveals what is important to him. _____

Lines 30–37: Have you found the turning point? _____

Remember, literary analysis is like unraveling a mystery. Find motivational and psychological reasons for the narrator's behavior. _____

_____

Line 41: Notice how the caesura emphasizes the finality of the event. You are forced to confront the murder directly because of the starkness of the syntax. This is followed by the narrator's justification.

Line 43: Did you catch the simile? It's a little tricky to spot when "as" is the first word.

_____

Line 55: What character trait is revealed by the narrator? _____

_____

Lines 59–60: Notice how the rhyming couplet accentuates the final thought and sets it off from the previous lines. Interpret the last line. Did you see that the last two lines are end-stopped, whereas the majority of the poem utilizes enjambment to create a conversational tone? _____

_____

5. Did you enjoy this poem? Did you feel as if you were being spoken to directly? _____

_____

The AP often uses dramatic monologues because they can be very rich in narrative detail and characterization. This is a form you should become familiar with by read-ing several from different times and authors. Try one of these: Robert Browning —"My Last Duchess," "The Soliloquy of the Spanish Cloister," "Andrea Del Sarto"; Alfred Lord Tennyson —"Ulysses."

How many dramatic monologues have you read? List them here and add details and lines that were of interest and /or importance to you.

_____

_____

_____

_____

_____

The Sonnet

The *sonnet* is the most popular fixed form in poetry. It is usually written in iambic pentameter and is always made up of 14 lines. There are two basic sonnet forms: the *Italian* or *Petrarchan* sonnet, named after Petrarch, the poet who created it, and the *English* or *Shakespearean* sonnet, named after the poet who perfected it. Each adheres to a strict rhyme scheme and stanza form.

The subject matter of sonnets varies greatly, from expressions of love to philosophical considerations, religious declarations, or political criticisms. The sonnet is highly polished, and the strictness of its form complements the complexity of its subject matter. As you know by now, we like to explore the relationship between form and function. The sonnet effectively integrates these two concepts.

Let's compare the two forms more closely. The **Italian sonnet** is divided into an octave and a sestet. The rhyme scheme is:

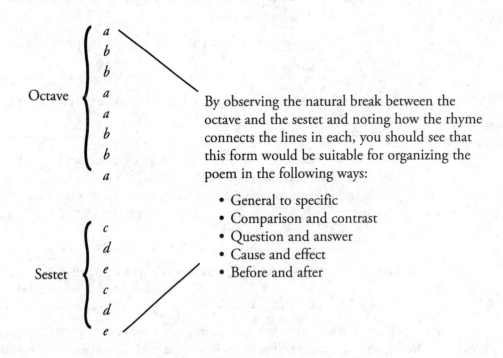

Octave
a
b
b
a
a
b
b
a

By observing the natural break between the octave and the sestet and noting how the rhyme connects the lines in each, you should see that this form would be suitable for organizing the poem in the following ways:

Sestet
c
d
e
c
d
e

- General to specific
- Comparison and contrast
- Question and answer
- Cause and effect
- Before and after

The **_Shakespearean sonnet_** has a different rhyme scheme and stanza form:

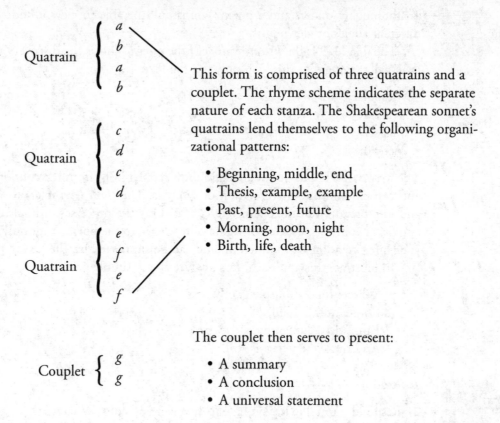

Quatrain
- *a*
- *b*
- *a*
- *b*

This form is comprised of three quatrains and a couplet. The rhyme scheme indicates the separate nature of each stanza. The Shakespearean sonnet's quatrains lend themselves to the following organizational patterns:

Quatrain
- *c*
- *d*
- *c*
- *d*

- Beginning, middle, end
- Thesis, example, example
- Past, present, future
- Morning, noon, night
- Birth, life, death

Quatrain
- *e*
- *f*
- *e*
- *f*

The couplet then serves to present:

Couplet
- *g*
- *g*

- A summary
- A conclusion
- A universal statement

Modern sonnets often vary rhyme and stanza form, but they will always have 14 lines.

For more practice with the sonnet, see Poems for Comparison and Contrast in this chapter. We recommend you read sonnets written by Shakespeare, Milton, Wordsworth, e e cummings, Edna St. Vincent Millay, and Keats.

The Villanelle

The **_villanelle_** is a fixed form in poetry. It has six stanzas: five tercets, and a final quatrain. It utilizes two refrains: The first and last lines of the first stanza alternate as the last line of the next four stanzas and then form a final couplet in the quatrain.

As an example, read: "Do Not Go Gentle Into That Good Night" by Dylan Thomas. Other villanelles that are worth a close reading include "The Art of Losing" by Elizabeth Bishop and "The Waking" by Theodore Roethke.

Interpretation of Poetry

KEY IDEA

Interpretation is not license for you to say just anything. Your comments/analysis/interpretation must be based on the given text.

How Do I Begin to Interpret Poetry?

To thoroughly understand a poem, you should be able to view it and read it from three different angles or viewpoints.

The first level is the *literal reading* of the poem. This is the discovery of what the poem is actually saying. For this, you only use the text:

- Vocabulary
- Structure
- Imagery
- Poetic devices

The *second level* builds on the first and draws conclusions from the connotation of the form and content and the interpretation of symbols. The *third level* refers to your own reading and interpretation of the poem. Here, you apply the processes of levels one and two, and you bring your own context or frame of reference to the poem. Your only restriction is that your interpretation is grounded in, and can be supported by, the text of the poem itself.

To illustrate this approach, let's analyze a very simple poem.

> Where ships of purple gently toss
> On seas of daffodil,
> Fantastic sailors mingle
> And then, the wharf is still.

1. Read it.

2. Respond. (You like it; you hate it. It leaves you cold. Whatever.)

3. Check rhyme and meter. We can see there is some rhyme, and the meter is iambic and predominantly trimeter. The first and third lines are irregular. (If this does not prove to be critical to your interpretation of the poem, move on.)

4. Check the vocabulary and syntax. Are there any words you are not familiar with?

5. Look for poetic devices and imagery.

6. Highlight, circle, connect key images and words.

7. Begin to draw inferences from the adjectives, phrases, verbs.

As an example, we have provided the following notes:

Movement

- Toss
- Mingle   } **Progression**
- Still

Images

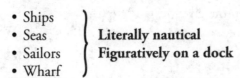

- Ships
- Seas   } **Literally nautical**
- Sailors } **Figuratively on a dock**
- Wharf

Syntax

- Ships of purple = purple ships (Where or when do you see purple ships?)
- Seas of daffodil = daffodil seas (When would seas be yellow?)
- Fantastic sailors = sailors of fantasy = clouds moving, birds flying (What might they be?)
- Wharf is still = place is quiet = ?

Put your observations together and formulate your interpretation. Write it below.

_____

_____

_____

Some students have said that they saw a field of flowers, bees and butterflies, a coronation, a celebration, and/or a royal event. These are all valid interpretations. Remember, this is only a simple exercise to acquaint you with the approaches you can use to analyze complex poetry. By the way, Emily Dickinson was writing about a sunset over Boston harbor.

Poetry for Analysis

This section will walk you through the analysis of several poems, presenting the poetry and a series of directed questions for you to consider. For maximum benefit, work with a highlighter and refer often to the poem. *Always* read the entire poem before you begin the analysis.

The Snake
by D. H. Lawrence

A snake came to my water-trough
On a hot, hot day, and I in pyjamas for the heat
To drink there.

In the deep, strange-scented shade of the great dark carobtree
I came down the steps with my pitcher   5
And must wait, must stand and wait, for there he was at the trough
    before me.

He reached down from a fissure in the earth-wall in the gloom
And trailed his yellow-brown slackness soft-bellied down, over the
    edge of the stone trough,   10
And rested his throat upon the stone bottom,
And where the water had dripped from the tap, in a small clearness,
He sipped with his straight mouth,
Softly drank through his straight gums, into his slack long body,
Silently.   15

Someone was before me at my water trough,
And I, like a second comer, waiting.
He lifted his head from his drinking, as cattle do,
And looked at me vaguely, as drinking cattle do,

And flickered his two-forked tongue from his lips, and mused a   20
    moment,
And stooped and drank a little more,
Being earth-brown, earth-golden from the burning bowels of the earth
On the day of Sicilian July, with Etna smoking.

The voice of my education said to me   25
He must be killed,
For in Sicily the black, black snakes are innocent, the gold are
    venomous.

The voice in me said, If you were a man
You would take a stick and break him now, and finish him off.   30

But must I confess how I liked him,
How glad I was he had come like a guest in quiet, to drink at my
    water-trough
And depart peaceful, pacified, and thankless,
Into the burning bowels of this earth?   35

Was it cowardice, that I dared not kill him?
Was it perversity, that I longed to talk to him?
Was it humility, to feel so honoured?
I felt so honoured.

And yet those voices: 40
If you were not afraid, you would kill him!
And truly I was afraid, I was most afraid,
But even so, honoured still more
That he should seek my hospitality
From out the dark door of the secret earth.   45

He drank enough
And lifted his head, dreamily, as one who has drunken,
And flickered his tongue like a forked night on the air, so black,
Seeming to lick his lips,
And looked around like a god, unseeing, into the air,   50
And slowly turned his head,
And slowly, very slowly, as if thrice a dream,
Proceeded to draw his slow length curving round
And climb again the broken bank of my wall-face.

And as he put his head into that dreadful hole,   55
And as he slowly drew up, snake-easing his shoulders, and entered
    farther,
A sort of horror, a sort of protest against his withdrawing into that
    horrid black hole,
Deliberately going into blackness, and slowly drawing himself   60
    after,
Overcame me now his back was turned.

I looked round, I put down my pitcher,
I picked up a clumsy log
And threw it at the water-trough with a clatter.   65

I think it did not hit him,
But suddenly that part of him that was left behind convulsed in
   undignified haste,
Writhed like lightning, and was gone
Into the black hole, the earth-lipped fissure in the wall-front,   70
At which, in the intense still noon, I stared with fascination.

And immediately I regretted it.
I thought how paltry, how vulgar, what a mean act!
I despised myself and the voices of my accursed human education.
And I thought of the albatross,   75
And I wished he would come back, my snake.

For he seemed to me again like a king,
Like a king in exile, uncrowned in the underworld,
Now due to be crowned again.
And so, I missed my chance with one of the lords   80
Of life.
And I have something to expiate:
A pettiness.

1. Since there is no regular rhyme scheme or length of lines or stanza form, we may conclude that this is *free verse*. _____ Yes _____ No

2. After reading the poem, you should be able to determine the situation, which is
   _____, and the speaker, who is
   _____.

3. The first stanza establishes the conflict, which is _____
   _____.

4. Find evidence of the developing conflict in lines 4–6. _____

5. Find examples of alliteration and assonance in lines 7–13. Notice how the sounds are appropriate for a snake rather than just random sounds.

6. Read line 12 aloud. Hear how slowly and "long" the sounds are, like the body of the snake itself.

7. Circle or highlight the imagery in lines 16–24. _____
   Notice how the scene is intensifying.

8. Restate the speaker's position in lines 25–28. _____

9. In lines 31–38, identify the conflict and the thematic ideas of the poem. Highlight them.

10. Identify the opposition facing the speaker in lines 36–39. State it. _____

_____

11. In lines 46–54, highlight the similes presented. Explore the nature of a snake and the connotation associated with one. _____

12. Interpret the setting as presented in lines 55–62. _____

13. The poem breaks at line 63. Highlight the change in the speaker at this point. Who is to blame for this action? _____

14. In line 75 there is a reference or allusion to the "Rime of the Ancient Mariner" by Coleridge, which is a poem in which a man learns remorse and the meaning of life as the result of a cruel, spontaneous act. Is this a suitable comparison for this poem's circumstances? Why? _____

15. Identify the similes and metaphor in lines 66–71. _____

16. Elaborate on the final confession of the speaker. May we conclude that the poem is a modern dramatic monologue? _____

> After you have considered these ideas, expand your own observations. Might the entire poem be a metaphor? Can it be symbolic of other pettinesses? Can you interpret this poem socially, religiously, politically, psychologically, sexually?

The following poem is particularly suitable for the interpretation of symbolism. Apply what you have learned and reviewed and respond to this sample.

The Sick Rose
by William Blake

O Rose, Thou Art Sick!
The Invisible Worm
That flies in the night
In the howling Storm,

Has found out thy bed
Of Crimson joy,
And his dark secret love
Does thy life destroy.

Try your hand at interpreting this poem:

1. Literally

2. Sexually

3. Philosophically

4. Religiously

5. Politically

Apply the following thematic concepts to the poem:

1. Passion

2. Deceit

3. Betrayal

4. Corruption

5. Disease

6. Madness

Interesting, isn't it, how much can be found or felt in a few lines. Read other poems by Blake, such as "Songs of Innocence" and "Songs of Experience."

Poems for Comparison and Contrast

Sometimes the AP exam requires you to compare and contrast two poems or prose selections in the essay section. Do not panic. The selections will usually be short and the points of comparison or contrast plentiful and accessible. This type of question can be interesting and provide you with a chance to really explore ideas.

Following are two poems suitable for this kind of analysis. Read each poem carefully. Take a minute to look at them and allow a few ideas to take shape in your mind. Then plan your approach logically. Remember, form and content are your guidelines.

She Walks in Beauty
by Lord Byron

She walks in Beauty, like the night
    Of cloudless climes and starry skies;
And all that's best of dark and bright
    Meet in her aspect and her eyes:
Thus mellowed to that tender light   5
    Which heaven to gaudy day denies.

One shade the more, one ray the less,
    Had half impaired the nameless grace
Which waves in every raven tress,
    Or softly lightens o'er her face;   10
Where thoughts serenely sweet express,
    How pure, how dear their dwelling-place.

And on that cheek, and o'er that brow,
   So soft, so calm, yet eloquent,
The smiles that win, the tints that glow,   15
   But tell of days in goodness spent,
A mind at peace with all below,
   A heart whose love is innocent!

Sonnet 130
by William Shakespeare

My mistress' eyes are nothing like the sun;
Coral is far more red than her lips' red;
If snow be white, why then her breasts are dun;
If hairs be wires, black wires grow on her head.
I have seen roses damasked red and white,   5
But no such roses see I in her cheeks;
And in some perfumes is there more delight
Than in the breath that from my mistress reeks.
I love to hear her speak, yet well I know
That music hath a far more pleasing sound;   10
I grant I never saw a goddess go:
My mistress, when she walks, treads on the ground.
And yet, by heaven, I think my love as rare
As any she belied with false compare.

It is essential that you read each poem again, marking, highlighting, connecting, etc. those points you will develop. List or chart your findings before you begin to write your essay.

Common Elements

- Both have the same topic—to a lover
- Both use similes: "She Walks"—"like the night"; "Sonnet 130"—"nothing like the sun"
- Both rely on nature imagery: "She Walks"—"starry skies"; "Sonnet 130"—"Coral, roses"
- Both deal with light or dark
- Both include references to lover's hair: "She Walks"—"raven tress"; "Sonnet 130"—"black wires"
- Both appeal to the senses: "She Walks"—"raven tress"; "Sonnet 130"—perfume, roses, music, garlic stink
- Both use alliteration: "She Walks"—"cloudless climes"; "Sonnet 130"—"goddess go"

Differences

- Form: "She Walks" lyric, has sestets; "Sonnet 130," 12 + 2 (3 quatrains and couplet)
- Kind of love: "She Walks" serious and adoring; "Sonnet 130"—critical and humorous
- Diction: "She Walks"—positive; "Sonnet 130"—negative
- Ending: "She Walks"—adoring; "Sonnet 130"—realistic
- Tone: "She Walks"—idyllic; "Sonnet 130"—realistic

*"Practice. Practice.
Practice."*
—Martha W.
  AP teacher

To recap: If you are given two selections, consider the following:

- What is the form or structure of the poems?
- What is the situation or subject of each?
- How are the poetic devices used?
- What imagery is developed?
- What thematic statements are made?
- What is the tone of each poem?
- What is the organization or progression of each poem?
- What attitudes are revealed?
- What symbols are developed?

Rapid Review

- Poetry has its own form.
- The foot, line, and stanza are the building blocks of poetry.
- Meter and rhyme are part of the sound of poetry.
- There are many types of rhyme forms.
- There are many types of poetic feet. They may be iambic, trochaic, anapestic, dactylic, or spondaic.
- There are several stanza forms.
- Narrative poetry tells stories.
- Ballads are simple narratives.
- Lyric poetry is subjective and emotional.
- Odes are formal lyrics that honor something or someone.
- Elegies are lyrics that mourn a loss.
- Dramatic monologues converse with the reader as they reveal events.
- The sonnet is a 14-line form of poetry.
- The villanelle is a fixed form that depends on refrains.
- Levels of interpretation depend on the literal and figurative meaning of poems.
- Symbols provide for many levels of interpretation.
- When comparing and contrasting poems, remember to consider speaker, subject, situation, devices, tone, and theme.

STEP **5**

Build Your Test-Taking Confidence

Practice Exam 1
Practice Exam 2

PRACTICE EXAM 1
ANSWER SHEET FOR MULTIPLE-CHOICE QUESTIONS

1. _____

2. _____

3. _____

4. _____

5. _____

6. _____

7. _____

8. _____

9. _____

10. _____

11. _____

12. _____

13. _____

14. _____

15. _____

16. _____

17. _____

18. _____

19. _____

20. _____

21. _____

22. _____

23. _____

24. _____

25. _____

26. _____

27. _____

28. _____

29. _____

30. _____

31. _____

32. _____

33. _____

34. _____

35. _____

36. _____

37. _____

38. _____

39. _____

40. _____

41. _____

42. _____

43. _____

44. _____

45. _____

46. _____

47. _____

48. _____

49. _____

50. _____

51. _____

"I need to honestly time myself on the practice exams, or else I don't really concentrate the way I should."
—Carol K.
 AP student

I _____ did _____ did not complete this part of the test in the allotted 1 hour.

I had _____ correct answers. I had _____ incorrect answers. I left _____ blank.

I have carefully reviewed the explanations of the answers, and I think I need to work on the following types of questions:

PRACTICE EXAM 1
ADVANCED PLACEMENT ENGLISH LITERATURE

Section I

Total time—1 hour

Carefully read the following passages and answer the questions that follow. Questions 1–14 are based on the following passage.

Bleak House
by Charles Dickens

Excerpt from Chapter 1—"In Chancery"

LONDON. Michaelmas Term lately over, and the Lord Chancellor sitting in Lincoln's Inn Hall. Implacable November weather. As much mud in the streets as if the waters had but newly retired from the face of the earth, and it would not be wonderful to meet a Megalosaurus, forty feet long or so, waddling like an elephantine lizard up Holborn Hill. Smoke lowering down from chimney-pots, making a soft black drizzle, with flakes of soot in it as big as full-grown   5
snowflakes—gone into mourning, one might imagine, for the death of the sun. Dogs, undistinguishable in mire. Horses, scarcely better; splashed to their very blinkers. Foot passengers, jostling one another's umbrellas in a general infection of ill-temper, and losing their foot-hold at street-corners, where tens of thousands of other foot passengers have been slipping and sliding since the day broke (if the day ever broke), adding new deposits to the crust upon   10
crust of mud, sticking at those points tenaciously to the pavement, and accumulating at compound interest.

Fog everywhere. Fog up the river, where it flows among green aits and meadows; fog down the river, where it rolls defiled among the tiers of shipping and the waterside pollutions of a great (and dirty) city. Fog on the Essex marshes, fog on the Kentish heights. Fog creeping into the   15
cabooses of collier-brigs; fog lying out on the yards, and hovering in the rigging of great ships; fog drooping on the gunwales of barges and small boats. Fog in the eyes and throats of ancient Greenwich pensioners, wheezing by the firesides of their wards; fog in the stem and bowl of the afternoon pipe of the wrathful skipper, down in his close cabin; fog cruelly pinching the toes and fingers of his shivering little 'prentice boy on deck. Chance people on the bridges peeping over   20
the parapets into a nether sky of fog, with fog all round them, as if they were up in a balloon, and hanging in the misty clouds.

Gas* looming through the fog in divers places in the streets, much as the sun may, from the spongey fields, be seen to loom by husbandman and ploughboy. Most of the shops lighted two hours before their time—as the gas seems to know, for it has a haggard and unwilling look.   25

The raw afternoon is rawest, and the dense fog is densest, and the muddy streets are muddiest near that leaden-headed old obstruction, appropriate ornament for the threshold of a leaden-headed old corporation, Temple Bar. And hard by Temple Bar, in Lincoln's Inn Hall, at the very heart of the fog, sits the Lord High Chancellor in his High Court of Chancery.

---

* (23) *gas*: gas lights

Never can there come fog too thick, never can there come mud and mire too deep, to assort   30
with the groping and floundering condition which this High Court of Chancery, most pestilent of
hoary sinners, holds this day in the sight of heaven and earth.

On such an afternoon, if ever, the Lord High Chancellor ought to be sitting here—as here he
is—with a foggy glory round his head, softly fenced in with crimson cloth and curtains,
addressed by a large advocate with great whiskers, a little voice, and an interminable brief, and   35
outwardly directing his contemplation to the lantern in the roof, where he can see nothing but
fog. On such an afternoon some score of members of the High Court of Chancery bar ought to be
—as here they are—mistily engaged in one of the ten thousand stages of an endless cause,
tripping one another up on slippery precedents, groping knee-deep in technicalities, running their
goat-hair and horse-hair* warded heads against walls of words and making a pretence of equity   40
with serious faces, as players might. On such an afternoon the various solicitors in the cause,
some two or three of whom have inherited it from their fathers, who made a fortune by it, ought
to be—as are they not?—ranged in a line, in a long matted well (but you might look in vain for
truth at the bottom of it) between the registrar's red table and the silk gowns, with bills, cross-bills,
answers, rejoinders, injunctions, affidavits, issues, references to masters, masters' reports,   45
mountains of costly nonsense, piled before them. Well may the court be dim, with wasting
candles here and there; well may the fog hang heavy in it, as if it would never get out; well may
the stained-glass windows lose their colour and admit no light of day into the place; well may the
uninitiated from the streets, who peep in through the glass panes in the door, be deterred from
entrance by its owlish aspect and by the drawl, languidly echoing to the roof from the padded   50
dais where the Lord High Chancellor looks into the lantern that has no light in it and where the
attendant wigs are all stuck in a fog-bank! This is the Court of Chancery, which has its decaying
houses and its blighted lands in every shire, which has its worn-out lunatic in every madhouse
and its dead in every churchyard, which has its ruined suitor with his slipshod heels and
threadbare dress borrowing and begging through the round of every man's acquaintance, which   55
gives to monied might the means abundantly of wearying out the right, which so exhausts
finances, patience, courage, hope, so overthrows the brain and breaks the heart, that there is not
an honourable man among its practitioners who would not give—who does not often give—the
warning, "Suffer any wrong that can be done you rather than come here!"

---

*(40) *goat-hair and horse-hair warded heads*: wigs worn by members of the court

1. In context, "Implacable November weather" [line 2] serves as
   A. the major theme of the passage
   B. the introduction to the extinction imagery
   C. a contrast to the tone of the passage
   D. the introduction to the controlling metaphor of the passage
   E. personification of "Michaelmas Term"

2. The juxtaposition of "Megalosaurus" [line 3] with London town has as its purpose
   A. indicating a natural disaster
   B. foreshadowing an outdated legal system
   C. reinforcing the animalistic nature of man
   D. indicating the magnitude of London's poverty
   E. revealing the onslaught of civil unrest

3. "Gone into mourning" in line 6 refers to
   A. snow-flakes
   B. smoke
   C. death of the sun
   D. flakes of soot
   E. drizzle

4. In the context of the passage, "death of the sun" [line 6] can be seen as parallel to the
   A. philandering of the Lord High Chancellor
   B. degradation of London
   C. indifference of the wealthy class
   D. blighted lands
   E. corruption of justice

5. "For it has a haggard and unwilling look"
   [line 25] refers to
   A. the fog
   B. the gas
   C. the shops
   D. the husbandman and ploughboy
   E. the sun

6. The purpose of lines 26–29 is to
   A. provide the major shift in the subject
   B. solidify the implacable nature of November
      weather
   C. reemphasize the nature of the fog
   D. proceed from setting to theme
   E. foreshadow a religious conversion

7. The attitude of the speaker in lines 26–29 can
   best be described as
   A. self-serving platitude
   B. vitriolic indictment
   C. disconsolate resignation
   D. unfounded aspiration
   E. pathetic desperation

8. Lines 37–41, beginning with "On such an
   afternoon" and ending with "as players might,"
   reinforce which of the following lines?
   A. 4–6
   B. 13–15
   C. 17–20
   D. 23–25
   E. 30–32

9. The imagery created in lines 46–52 serves to
   A. emphasize the poverty of London
   B. reinforce the crowded court condition
   C. characterize the role of lawyers in the court
   D. reveal the author's attitude toward his
      subject
   E. separate the exterior from the interior

10. One could best summarize lines 52–59 with
    which of the following statements?
    A. The court system is not just
    B. The court system needs to be revised
    C. The lawyers are corrupt
    D. The court system has the support of the
       attorneys
    E. The courts exist only to help the poor

11. The second and last paragraphs are primarily
    developed through the use of
    A. comparison and contrast
    B. simple sentences
    C. parallel structure
    D. rhetorical questions
    E. animal imagery

12. The organization of the passage moves from
    A. past to present
    B. positive to negative
    C. cause to effect
    D. general to specific
    E. literal to figurative

13. Within the passage, comparisons may be drawn
    about all of the following except
    A. actors and lawyers
    B. dinosaurs and the legal system
    C. fog and the court
    D. sinners and saints
    E. decay and justice

14. The overall tone of the passage can best be
    described as
    A. remorseful and resigned
    B. outraged and exhortative
    C. scathing and bitter
    D. victimized and vengeful
    E. dispassionate and objective

Questions 15–25 are based on the following poem.

The Writer
by Richard Wilbur

In her room at the prow of the house
Where light breaks, and the windows are tossed with linden,
My daughter is writing a story.

I pause in the stairwell, hearing
From her shut door a commotion of typewriter-keys   5
Like a chain hauled over a gunwale.

Young as she is, the stuff
Of her life is a great cargo, and some of it heavy:
I wish her a lucky passage.

But now it is she who pauses,   10
As if to reject my thought and its easy figure.
A stillness greatens, in which

The whole house seems to be thinking,
And then she is at it again with a bunched clamor
Of strokes, and again is silent.   15

I remember the dazed starling
Which was trapped in that very room, two years ago;
How we stole in, lifted a sash

And retreated, not to affright it;
And how for a helpless hour, through the crack in the door,   20
We watched this sleek, wild, dark

And iridescent creature
Batter against the brilliance, drop like a glove
To the hard floor, or the desk-top,

And wait then, humped and bloody,   25
For the wits to try it again; and how our spirits
Rose when, suddenly sure,

It lifted off from a chair-back,
Beating a smooth course for the right window
And clearing the sill of the world.   30

It is always a matter, my darling,
Of life or death, as I had forgotten. I wish
What I wished you before, but harder.

15. The last line of the poem "What I wished you before, but harder" implies that
   A. the speaker loves his daughter more than at the beginning of the poem
   B. the speaker realizes the intensity of life's challenges
   C. the speaker cannot be as creative as she
   D. the speaker feels he has failed her
   E. the daughter will never be a successful writer

16. Which of the following is used to develop the poem?
   A. cause and effect
   B. argument
   C. general to specific examples
   D. definition
   E. parallel analogy

17. Line 13 is an example of
   A. allusion
   B. alliteration
   C. personification
   D. simile
   E. apostrophe

18. "A smooth course for the right window" in line 29 parallels line(s)
   A. 1
   B. 5–6
   C. 8
   D. 9
   E. 11

19. The poem breaks after line
   A. 3
   B. 6
   C. 8
   D. 15
   E. 27

20. The final stanza serves all the following purposes *except*
   A. to restate the theme
   B. to reemphasize the father's love for his daughter
   C. to solidify the daughter's character
   D. to connect the two major sections of the poem
   E. to allow the father to be more sympathetic

21. Stanzas 1–3 include all the following analogies *except*
   A. the house as a ship
   B. the daughter's room as a ship's cabin
   C. life's problems as a ship's cargo
   D. writing as a safe harbor
   E. life as a sea journey

22. The father's sensitivity is supported by line(s)
   A. 3
   B. 4
   C. 11
   D. 19
   E. 21–22

23. Contrasts developed in the poem include all the following *except*
   A. stillness and clamor
   B. house and cargo
   C. bird and daughter
   D. life and/or death
   E. light and dark

24. According to the poem, the daughter, as young as she is, has
   A. endured hardships
   B. published her writing
   C. fought for her independence
   D. saved a starling
   E. left home and returned

25. The poet alludes to all the following as part of the process of a creative life *except*
   A. "Batter against the brilliance"
   B. "drop like a glove to the hard floor"
   C. "clearing the sill of the world"
   D. "the wits to try it again"
   E. "Beating a smooth course for the right window"

Questions 26–38 are based on the following passage.

Jane Eyre
by Charlotte Bronte

Miss Temple got up, took her hand and . . . returned to her own seat: as she resumed it, I heard her sigh low. She was pensive a few minutes, then rousing herself, she said cheerfully:—

"But you two are my visitors to-night; I must treat you as such." She rang her bell.

"Barbara," she said to the servant who answered it, "I have not yet had tea; bring the tray, and place cups for these two young ladies."   5

And a tray was soon brought. How pretty, to my eyes, did the china and bright teapot look, placed on the little round table near the fire! How fragrant was the steam of the beverage, and the scent of the toast! of which, however, I, to my dismay (for I was beginning to be hungry), discerned only a very small portion: Miss Temple discerned it   10
too:—

"Barbara," said she, "can you not bring a little more bread and butter? There is not enough for three."

Barbara went out: she returned soon:—

"Madam, Mrs. Harden says she has sent up the usual quantity."   15

Mrs. Harden, be it observed, was the housekeeper: a woman after Mr. Brocklehurst's own heart, made up of equal parts of whalebone and iron.

"Oh, very well!" returned Miss Temple; "we must make it do, Barbara, I suppose." And as the girl withdrew, she added, smiling, "Fortunately, I have it in my power to supply deficiencies for this once."   20

Having invited Helen and me to approach the table, and placed before each of us a cup of tea with one delicious but thin morsel of toast; she got up, unlocked a drawer, and taking from it a parcel wrapped in paper, disclosed presently to our eyes a good-sized seed-cake.

"I meant to give each of you some of this to take with you," said she; "but as there   25
is so little toast, you must have it now," and she proceeded to cut slices with a generous hand.

We feasted that evening as on nectar and ambrosia; and not the least delight of the entertainment was the smile of gratification with which our hostess regarded us, as we satisfied our famished appetites on the delicate fare she liberally supplied. Tea over and the   30
tray removed, she again summoned us to the fire; we sat one on each side of her, and now a conversation followed between her and Helen, which it was indeed a privilege to be admitted to hear.

Miss Temple had always something of serenity in her air, of state in her mien, of refined propriety in her language, which precluded deviation into the ardent, the excited, the   35
eager: something which chastened the pleasure of those who looked on her and listened to her, by a controlling sense of awe; and such was my feeling now: but as to Helen Burns, I was struck with wonder.

The refreshing meal, the brilliant fire, the presence and kindness of her beloved instructress, or, perhaps, more than all these, something in her own unique mind, had   40
roused her powers within her. They woke, they kindled: first, they glowed in the bright tint of her cheek, which till this hour I had never seen but pale and bloodless; then they shone in

the liquid lustre of her eyes, which had suddenly acquired a beauty more singular than that
of Miss Temple's—a beauty neither of fine colour nor long eyelash, nor pencilled brow,
but of meaning, of movement, of radiance. Then her soul sat on her lips, and language   45
flowed, from what source I cannot tell: has a girl of fourteen a heart large enough, vigorous
enough to hold the swelling spring of pure, full, fervid eloquence? Such was the
characteristic of Helen's discourse on that, to me, memorable evening; her spirit seemed
hastening to live within a very brief span as much as many live during a protracted
existence.   50

    They conversed of things I had never heard of! Of nations and times past; of
countries far away: of secrets of nature discovered or guessed at: they spoke of books: how
many they had read! What stores of knowledge they possessed! They seemed so
familiar with French names and French authors: but my amazement reached its climax
when Miss Temple asked Helen if she sometimes snatched a moment to recall the Latin her   55
father had taught her, and taking a book from a shelf, bade her read and construe a page of
"Virgil"; and Helen obeyed, my organ of Veneration expanding at every sounding line.
She had scarcely finished ere the bell announced bedtime: no delay could be admitted;
Miss Temple embraced us both, saying, as she drew us to her heart:—
    "God bless you, my children!"   60
    Well has Solomon said—"Better is a dinner of herbs where love is, than a stalled ox
and hatred therewith."

26. From the passage, it can be concluded that
Mrs. Harden is
A. in love with Mr. Brocklehurst
B. generous with the girls
C. a confidante of Miss Temple's
D. strong-willed and inflexible
E. Miss Temple's superior

27. Religious imagery in this passage is developed
by all the following *except*
A. Miss Temple's name
B. feasting on nectar and ambrosia
C. the taking of tea and toast
D. Miss Temple's benediction
E. being summoned to sit by the fire

28. The "smile of gratification with which our
hostess regarded us" (line 29) indicates that
Miss Temple derives pleasure from
A. having power over the girls
B. being a role model for the girls
C. keeping secrets
D. outsmarting the girls
E. providing for the girls

29. For the speaker, the most nourishing part of
the evening was
A. the seed cake
B. the tea and toast
C. the company of an adult
D. the conversation
E. the brilliant fire

30. The speaker is amazed by
A. Miss Temple's beauty
B. the breadth of Helen's knowledge
C. Miss Temple's generosity
D. her own knowledge
E. her envy of the attention Helen receives

31. ". . . her spirit seemed hastening to live within
a very brief span as much as many live during
a protracted existence" (lines 48–49) is an
example of
A. circular reasoning
B. satire
C. foreshadowing
D. denouement
E. digression

32. The reader can infer from lines 45– 47 ("Then her soul sat on her lips . . . eloquence") that
   A. Helen has traveled the world
   B. Helen likes to show off intellectually
   C. Miss Temple has been tutoring Helen
   D. the speaker is afraid of Helen
   E. Helen is an instrument of divine inspiration

33. The last sentence of the passage may be best interpreted to mean
   A. It is better to be rich than poor
   B. Everything in moderation
   C. The greatest of all riches is love
   D. Denial of riches leads to love
   F. Riches lead to hatred

34. The pronoun "they" in lines 41–42 refers to
   A. her powers
   B. her unique mind
   C. the meal and the fire
   D. Helen and Miss Temple
   E. Helen's eyes

35. The tone developed in the passage is best described as
   A. amused indifference
   B. subdued admiration
   C. pedantic
   D. reverent wonder
   E. remorseful

36. The reader may infer all the following *except* that
   A. the evening has transformed Helen
   B. the speaker is observant of and sensitive to human nature
   C. the evening is in contrast to their daily lives
   D. Miss Temple will save the two children
   E. love of learning is important to the speaker

37. The description of Miss Temple in lines 34–38 reveals her to be a woman of
   A. religious fervor
   B. restraint and reservation
   C. passionate beliefs
   D. submissive inclinations
   E. dominating sensibilities

38. Based on the passage, all the following can be inferred about Jane's character *except that* she is
   A. cognizant of her limitations
   B. a great observer
   C. of an inquisitive nature
   D. highly impressionable
   E. religious

Questions 39–51 are based on the following poem.

The Pulley
by George Herbert

When God at first made man,
Having a glass of blessings standing by,
Let us, said He, pour on him all we can.
Let the world's riches, which dispersed lie,
Contract into a span.   5

So Strength first made a way,
Then Beauty flowed, then Wisdom, Honor, Pleasure.
When almost all was out, God made a stay,
Perceiving that alone of all his treasure
Rest in the bottom lay.   10

For if I should, said He,
Bestow this jewel also on my creature,
He would adore my gifts instead of me,
And rest in Nature, not the God of Nature:
So both should losers be.   15

Yet let him keep the rest,
But keep them with repining restlessness.
Let him be rich and weary, that at least
If goodness lead him not, yet weariness
May toss him to my breast.   20

(Note: Poem reprinted in its original form.)

39. The "pulley" of the title refers to
   A. the balance between God and nature
   B. the conflict between beauty and riches
   C. the conflict between blessings and curses
   D. God's method of controlling mankind
   E. the conflict between winners and losers

40. In line 9, "alone of all his treasure" refers to
   A. wisdom
   B. honor
   C. pleasure
   D. strength
   E. rest

41. According to the first stanza, God is
   A. totally generous
   B. suspicious of humankind
   C. drunk with power
   D. planning to test humanity
   E. forgiving of human weakness

42. In line 16, "Yet let him keep the rest" refers to
   A. all the gifts, *except* "rest"
   B. the Sabbath
   C. nature
   D. a glass of blessings
   E. "this jewel"

43. God will control humans by keeping them
   A. away from evil
   B. poor
   C. alone
   D. weak
   E. fatigued

44. The pun in this poem depends upon the reading of which word?
   A. pour
   B. alone
   C. rest
   D. losers
   E. least

45. The dominant imagery concerns
   A. wealth
   B. goodness
   C. God
   D. nature
   E. contracts

46. In line 12, "this jewel" refers to
   A. wisdom
   B. my creature
   C. glass of blessings
   D. rest
   E. nature

47. The first and last lines of each stanza are written in
   A. iambic pentameter
   B. iambic trimeter
   C. trochaic trimeter
   D. spondaic tetrameter
   E. dactylic trimeter

48. The conflict of the poem is best expressed in line
   A. 3
   B. 8
   C. 13
   D. 15
   E. 17

49. For George Herbert, the God of all mankind is
A. all-forgiving and generous
B. disappointed and jealous
C. judgmental and punitive
D. regretful and plaintive
E. speculative and manipulative

50. The organization of the first two stanzas depends upon
A. contrast and comparison
B. paradox
C. chronological order
D. specific to general
E. description

51. We can infer that the speaker is
A. heretical
B. non-materialistic
C. scientific
D. skeptical
E. materialistic

END OF SECTION I

Section II

Total time—2 hours

Question 1

(Suggested time 40 minutes. This question counts as one-third of the total score for Section II.)

In a well-organized essay, discuss how Alice Walker conveys the complex meaning of "The Flowers" and how she prepares the reader for the ending of this short story. Consider at least two elements of the writer's craft such as imagery, symbol, setting, narrative pace, diction, and style.

The Flowers
by Alice Walker

It seemed to Myop as she skipped lightly from her house to pigpen to smokehouse that the days had never been as beautiful as these. The air held a keenness that made her nose twitch. The harvesting of the corn and cotton, peanuts and squash, made each day a golden surprise that caused excited little tremors to run up her jaws.

Myop carried a short, knobby stick. She struck out at random at chickens she liked,   5
and worked out the beat of a song on the fence around the pigpen. She felt light and good in the warm sun. She was ten, and nothing existed for her but her song, the stick clutched in her dark brown hand, and the tat-de-ta-ta-ta of accompaniment.

Turning her back on the rusty boards of her family's sharecropper cabin, Myop walked along the fence till it ran into the stream made by the spring. Around the spring,   10
where the family got drinking water, silver ferns and wildflowers grew. Along the shallow banks pigs rooted. Myop watched the tiny white bubbles disrupt the thin black scale of soil and the water that silently rose and slid away down the stream.

She had explored the woods behind the house many times. Often, in late autumn, her mother took her to gather nuts among the fallen leaves. Today she made her own path,   15
bouncing this way and that way, vaguely keeping an eye out for snakes. She found, in addition to various common but pretty ferns and leaves, an armful of strange blue flowers with velvety ridges and a sweetsuds bush full of the brown, fragrant buds.

By twelve o'clock, her arms laden with sprigs of her findings, she was a mile or more from home. She had often been as far before, but the strangeness of the land made it not as   20
pleasant as her usual haunts. It seemed gloomy in the little cove in which she found herself. The air was damp, the silence close and deep.

Myop began to circle back to the house, back to the peacefulness of the morning.

It was then she stepped smack into his eyes. Her heel became lodged in the broken ridge between brow and nose, and she reached down quickly, unafraid, to free herself. It was   25
only when she saw his naked grin that she gave a little yelp of surprise. He had been a tall man. From feet to neck covered a long space. His head lay beside him. When she pushed back the leaves and layers of earth and debris Myop saw that he'd had large white teeth, all of them cracked or broken, long fingers, and very big bones. All his clothes had rotted away except some threads of blue denim from his overalls. The buckles of the overalls had turned   30
green.

Myop gazed around the spot with interest. Very near where she'd stepped into the head was a wild pink rose. As she picked it to add to her bundle she noticed a raised mound, a ring, around the rose's root. It was the rotted remains of a noose, a bit of shredding plow-line,

now blending benignly into the soil. Around the overhanging limb of a great spreading   35
oak clung another piece, frayed, rotted, bleached, and frazzled—barely there—but spinning
restlessly in the breeze. Myop laid down her flowers.

    And the summer was over.

Question 2

(Suggested time 40 minutes. This question counts as one-third of the total score for Section II.)

In a well-organized essay, discuss the distinguishing differences between the complex connotations of the two main words in the title of the poem "The Naked and the Nude" as they are developed by Robert Graves. Refer to such literary techniques as tone, style, poetic devices, structure, and imagery.

The Naked and the Nude
by Robert Graves

> For me, the naked and the nude
> (By lexicographers construed
> As synonyms that should express
> The same deficiency of dress
> Or shelter) stand as wide apart   5
> As love from lies, or truth from art.
>
> Lovers without reproach will gaze
> On bodies naked and ablaze;
> The Hippocratic eye will see
> In nakedness, anatomy;   10
> And naked shines the Goddess when
> She mounts her lion among men.
>
> The nude are bold; the nude are sly
> To hold each treasonable eye.
> While draping by a showman's trick   15
> Their dishabille in rhetoric,
> They grin a mock-religious grin
> Of scorn at those of naked skin.
>
> The naked, therefore, who compete
> Against the nude may know defeat;   20
> Yet when they both together tread
> The briary pastures of the dead,
> By Gorgons with long whips pursued,
> How naked go the sometime nude!

Question 3

(Suggested time 40 minutes. This question counts as one-third of the total score for Section II.)

From your study of full-length works, choose one in which a character or group intentionally dissembles in order to advance a specific agenda. Be sure to discuss the complex nature of the deceit or misrepresentation and how it contributes to the development of that character or the meaning of the work. You may choose a work from the list below or another novel or play of literary merit.

The Stranger	*Hamlet*
Oedipus	*Twelfth Night*
Jane Eyre	*King Lear*
Desire Under the Elms	*The Great Gatsby*
Heart of Darkness	*The Importance of Being Earnest*
The Secret Sharer	*Hedda Gabler*
Beloved	*A Doll's House*
A Streetcar Named Desire	*Catch-22*
Major Barbara	*The Kite Runner*

END OF SECTION II

ANSWERS TO MULTIPLE-CHOICE QUESTIONS

Answer Key

1. D	18. D	35. D
2. B	19. D	36. D
3. A	20. C	37. B
4. E	21. D	38. E
5. B	22. D	39. D
6. A	23. B	40. E
7. B	24. A	41. A
8. E	25. B	42. A
9. D	26. D	43. E
10. A	27. E	44. C
11. C	28. E	45. A
12. E	29. D	46. D
13. D	30. B	47. B
14. C	31. C	48. C
15. B	32. E	49. E
16. E	33. C	50. C
17. C	34. A	51. B

Answers and Explanations

1. **D.** All of the weather images illustrate and reinforce the conditions that exist within the legal system.

2. **B.** The image of an extinct, gigantic, lumbering creature in the midst of London is as out of place as the efficacy of the court system that Dickens describes in the passage.

3. **A.** This is another basic reference question. The image is one of smoke-flakes wearing black for mourning.

4. **E.** The key here is "In the context of the passage." The death of the sun symbolizes the end of enlightenment, warmth, hope, and nurturing—all of which are characteristic of the High Court of Chancery.

5. **B.** This is a basic antecedent question. You need to trace "it" back to "gas."

6. **A.** The author takes the two major images and combines them (fog:court).

7. **B.** The deliberate repetition and diction (for example: "leaden-headed," "obstruction") is evidence of the bitter accusation.

8. **E.** "Mud," "mire," "groping," and "floundering" are echoed by "endless cause," "tripping," "slippery," and "knee-deep."

9. **D.** Phrases such as "court be dim," "wasting candles," "admit no light of day," "lantern that has no light" all reveal the author's attitude toward the court.

10. **A.** The listing of the effects of the court on the people specifically indicate how justice is not being served. There is no direct call for revision of the court in this passage.

11. **C.** In paragraph 2 the repetition of "fog," and the repetition of "On such," "Well may," and "which has" in the last paragraph, all serve to tightly structure both the description and the indictment presented in the excerpt.

12. **E.** The excerpt begins with a specific description of London in November and progresses to a symbolic depiction of the Court of Chancery.

13. **D.** Although there is an allusion to the court being a sinner, there is no reference to redemption anywhere in the passage.

14. **C.** The previous questions should have pointed you toward this answer. There is no resignation in the author. He rails against the system (A). While it is obvious the writer is outraged, he does not call for action on the part of the reader (B). We may infer that he has been victimized, but there is no evidence of that in this excerpt (D). His sarcasm, diction, and imagery reveal a subjective point of view (E).

15. **B.** The entire poem hinges on the speaker's epiphany about life and creativity, which occurs in the last stanza. It is this realization that points to choice B. Choice A is silly and should be eliminated immediately. There is no discussion of the daughter's talent, which eliminates choice E. Although C and D sound plausible and may even be insights raised by the reader, once again there is no concrete evidence in the poem to support these choices.

16. **E.** The careful reader should recognize that the poem introduces a new idea in lines 16–30, and he or she should question the reason for this. It is obvious that the episode of the starling is meant to parallel the intensity of the creative process the daughter is experiencing.

17. **C.** The house is personified as "thinking." This is a question that is really a freebie if you've done your preparation. The answer depends on your knowledge of simple terms and your ability to identify examples of them in a work.

18. **D.** A question of this type demands that you actually refer to the passage. (You might try highlighting or underlining to emphasize line 29 and the various choices. This will prevent you from losing your place or focus.) Use the process of elimination until you find an "echo" word or phrase. In line 9, "passage" parallels "course" and points to choice D. It is a good idea to follow the choices in order for clarity and continuity because each rereading may give you help with another question.

19. **D.** Question 2 may help you with this answer. Skim the poem from line 1 until you strike a new idea—the dazed bird. The answer has to be D. A, B, and C all describe the daughter and are on topic, while line 27 refers to the previous idea, in this case, the starling introduced earlier.

20. **C.** The perceptive reader will understand that the stanza is not about the daughter at all, whereas each of the other ideas is valid and can be supported in the context of the stanza.

21. **D.** The use of nautical terms dominates the first section of the poem, establishing the concept of life as a sea journey or passage. The words, "prow" (line 1), "gunwale" (line 6), and "great cargo" (line 8) all support choices A, B, C, and E. The only image not stated concerns writing as a safe harbor.

22. **D.** This is essentially a reading question and one you should find easy to answer. Start with the first choice and work your way through each of the others. Highlight or underline lines, look for concrete evidence, and eliminate unsupported choices. Line 19 indicates the sensitivity shown by the father's consideration for the trapped bird.

23. **B.** This type of question is more complicated than the others because there are many steps involved in finding the answer. Don't just rely on memory. Actually circle or highlight the contrasts as you skim the poem. You may have a quick flash. If so, look immediately to prove it. If you can't, you have your answer. In this case, B. To illustrate the process, here are the images that prove that the other choices are contained in the poem.
    A. Line 5: commotion; line 12: stillness
    C. Lines 22–23: the implied analogy of child and bird
    D. Line 32: life and death
    E. Line 2: light breaks; line 21: dark

24. **A.** This simple reading question is a giveaway. Stanza three tells the reader that "the stuff of her life is a great cargo, and some of it heavy." You should be able to interpret the metaphor as life's difficulties.

25. **B.** All the choices, with the exception of B, reflect the need to persist in order to achieve a goal—freedom and creation. Only B is grounded to the hard floor.

26. **D.** The answer is obvious if you carefully read lines 15–17. A heart made up of whalebones and iron is synonymous with strong-willed and inflexible.

27. **E.** Temple, feasting, food of the gods, and benediction can all imply religious connotations. Tea and toast can be a direct allusion to taking communion. Being asked to "come sit by the fire" is simply a request, nothing more.

28. **E.** "Gratification" involves thankfulness. And, in this case, Miss Temple is pleased that she is able to give the girls some special foods during their visit.

29. **D.** This is a metaphorical construction. With it, Jane lets the reader know that having the opportunity to be part of engaging and exciting conversation was like food for her mind and soul.

30. **B.** Lines 39–59 of this excerpt are devoted to Helen's mind, knowledge, and eloquence.

31. **C.** This is one of those questions that assumes the student is familiar with the definitions of specific terms. "Seemed hastening" is almost a literal flag waving in front of the reader's eyes signaling that something will happen in the future.

32. **E.** Helen's "soul sitting on her lips," her "secret sources of language," and her "purity and radiance" all relate to the realm of the divine.

33. **C.** Herbs are simple and of small quantity. An ox, on the other hand, is overwhelmingly large and overabundant. Love is better than hate. This analogy is straightforward and obvious.

34. **A.** This is the frequently used antecedent question. All you have to do is substitute each of the choices for the word "they," and it will be obvious that your only viable choice is "her powers."

35. **D.** If you read the passage carefully, Jane's wonder and deference are apparent. Look at lines 39–50 to see her sense of awe. Look at line 38. It clearly states Jane's wonder at Helen.

36. **D.** There is nothing in this passage that indicates either of the two girls needs to be saved.

37. **B.** "Serenity," "state in her mien," "refined propriety" in lines 34–35 are synonymous with one who is restrained. The remainder of the lines illustrates and supports this characterization.

38. E. Although there is considerable religious diction and imagery in the passage, none of it directly relates to Jane's character and her being a religious person.

39. D. A pulley is a device used to bring something to a particular destination. In this case, man to God.

40. E. If you recast lines 9 and 10 into a sentence, you can easily see that "treasure" is the antecedent of "Rest." This is an example of poetic inversion.

41. A. Lines 3 and 4 are the indicators. Look carefully at what God is doing—giving all the world's riches away.

42. A. Use the process of substitution to help you find the answer. If you place each of the choices in place of "Rest," you will see that the only appropriate choice is A.

43. E. Lines 17 and 18 clearly indicate that God intends for man to be without rest.

44. C. The pun depends on your knowing that a play on words and their meanings is essential to the understanding of this poem. Choice C refers to both renewal and the remains of the blessings.

45. A. Each stanza presents an image to support choice A. "Riches" (line 4), "treasure" (line 9), "jewel" (line 12), and "rich" (line 18) sustain the concept of wealth.

46. D. This is another question that benefits from using the process of substitution to locate an antecedent. This procedure will lead you to lines 9 and 10 and choice D.

47. B. You should notice immediately that the first and last lines of each stanza are shorter than the other lines. It is a good idea to briefly check to see if the form is iambic (˘ ´) because the iambic foot is the most common one in the English language. Count the number of iambs, and you will come up with three (tri). (*Note*: If meter presents a problem to you, this may be a question you should choose to skip.)

48. C. God is wary of man's potential goodness and loyalty and devises another method of ensuring mankind's adoration and reliance on Him.

49. E. A, B, C, and D are all partially supported in the poem. But, only E has *both* characteristics evident in the poem's context.

50. C. The words "when," "first," "then," and "when" are all indicative of the chronological pattern of the first two stanzas.

51. B. The text of the poem, especially in the choice of blessings the speaker presents, indicates that he is interested in the world of the spirit rather than the world of material possessions and investigations. The diction proves he considers these nonmaterial concepts to be the real "riches," "treasure," "jewel," and "gifts."

Rating the Essay Section

Rubrics for "The Flowers" by Alice Walker

A high-range score (5, 6):

- Indicates complete understanding and support of the prompt.
- Uses appropriate literary techniques to illustrate how Walker prepares the reader for the ending of the story.
- Thoroughly explores the contrasts inherent in the story.
- Fully presents Myop's character.
- Recognizes the underlying theme related to prejudice and innocence.
- Responds insightfully to image, diction, and setting.
- Presents suitable and unique interpretations of the text.
- Demonstrates a mature, sophisticated writing style.

A midrange score (3, 4):

- Refers accurately to the prompt.
- Utilizes appropriate devices in the analysis of Walker's preparation for the surprise ending.
- Adequately supports the thesis.
- Uses obvious references and details.
- May miss the subtleties of the story.
- Inferences are based on an acceptable reading of the text.
- Demonstrates writing that is adequate to convey the writer's intent.
- May exhibit a few errors in syntax and/or diction.

Sample Student Essays

Student Essay A

". . . the days had never been as beautiful as these . . . each day a golden surprise." Surprise is the element Alice Walker presents in her story "The Flowers." It is at the heart of the meaning of this story which is driven forward by imagery, setting, and diction.

In the beginning of the story, Walker utilizes diction that creates an atmosphere of euphoric childhood innocence. Myop, the main character, "skipped lightly." Walker describes the harvests, which evince "excited little tremors" in Myop as she anticipates the new day.

This jocund diction continues into the second paragraph. Specifically, Myop feels "light and good" in the heat of the warm sun. In addition, ten year old Myop creates her own world in which nothing exists "but her song." In line 8, the use of onomatopaeia, "tat-de-ta-ta-ta" reinforces the idea of a happy, carefree youth.

Paragraph three, however, marks a small yet significant shift in the passage. Walker begins the paragraph with "Turning her back on the rusty boards of her family's sharecropper cabin, Myop . . . " Myop's world is not behind her, but moves forward to the familiar woods.

As the story progresses, there is a significant shift in paragraphs four and five. Walker begins to prepare the reader for her profound conclusion. While Myop has often explored the woods behind the house with her mother, today she sets out alone and "made her own path." As she walks through the woods, she cautiously keeps an eye out for snakes. The solitude of her journey, and the possibility of danger, builds suspense and prepares the reader for the dark surprise of the ending.

The diction of paragraphs four and five also contributes to the sudden shift in the passage. While the diction in the beginning was blithe, describing "beautiful," the language in paragraph five is negative, foreshadowing the conclusion. Specifically, Myop is disoriented by the, "strangeness of the land."

It was "not as pleasant" as her usual expeditions. Furthermore, words such as "gloomy" and "damp" reiterate the dark setting and prepare the reader for the grotesque conclusion of the story. 30

Paragraph six, which is only one sentence long, marks a brief transition into the ending of the passage. Myop wants to return to her house, to the "peacefulness of the morning." But, while she was able to turn her back on the reality of her poverty, she will not be able to ignore the next truth that hits her. 35

"Stepping smack into his eyes," Myop encounters death, but is unafraid as she "frees herself." She is filled with innocent curiosity and gazes "around the spot with interest." Ironically, as she picks her "wild pink rose," a symbol of beauty, she spots the noose and has her epiphany.

The transition in image, setting, and diction all propel Walker's theme— 40 the coming of age. In the last paragraph Myop picks up the flowers and places her bouquet in front of the lynched man. It is as if she is at a funeral, as if she has sobered from her carefree state to one of realization. For, in the last line, the images of the beginning are finally crushed. Myop can no longer return to the world of flower-gathering or sun-lit skipping. For Myop, the "summer is over." 45

This is a high-ranking essay for the following reasons:

- Indicates complete understanding of the prompt (lines 3–4).
- Cites appropriate details to support the thesis:
  - Imagery (lines 15, 25–30, 36)
  - Diction (lines 5–6, 10, 30)
  - Setting (lines 1, 15–16)
- Thoroughly explores contrasts (lines 12, 16–17, 45).
- Presents unique insights into the underlying theme (lines 16–17, 22–23, 41–43).
- Adheres well to topic; exhibits transitions and connective tissue.
- Has a definite, clear progression of thought and a strong writer's voice.

This high-ranking essay presents a solid, mature, and insightful discussion and analysis of Myop's "epiphany" and how Walker prepares the reader for it.

Student Essay B

In the short story "The Flowers" by Alice Walker, the author conveys the meaning of the story and prepares the reader for the ending by using various literary techniques. Some of these are symbol, narrative pace, and style.

The narrative pace starts out as slow and relaxed as Myop explores the land around her family's sharecropper cabin. Every little detail is described creating 5 an image of the blissful summer day. Myop's exuberance is portrayed through diction such as "skipped lightly," "she felt light and good," "bouncing," and "she was singing." Her innocence is shown by the way she is able to block out everything but her happiness and her song. The colors used in the beginning of the story further form the image that is being set up because they are earthy yet 10 shiny colors such as "golden," "silver," and "dark brown."

The fifth paragraph is a transition of narrative pace. The diction and tone change from peaceful and relaxed to tense and dark. Diction such as "strangeness" and "gloomy" take over. When describing the new atmosphere, Walker uses syntax like "the air was damp, the silence close and deep." 15

From here, the story continues to darken and reaches a climax when Myop steps on a dead man's face. She then discovers his body—in parts and decaying. Walker's use of colors suddenly changes too. Now, "blue," "green," and "wild pink" are used. Although these colors can be seen as positive, in this story, they represent "rotting." Myop finds the noose as she picks up a flower. Such irony. 20

The last paragraph/sentence is brief and compact. It simply reads, "And the summer was over." The summer can be seen as a symbol of Myop's innocence. With the end of her summer, when she lays down her flowers, her innocence is gone forever. She can no longer exist "for nothing but her song." She had seen death in the midst of her paradise. 25

This is a midrange essay (3, 4) for the following reasons:

- Makes adequate, expedient presentation of the details in developing the thesis.
- Illustrates an understanding of the selected literary devices used in the story, but does not fully link or expand them with regard to the thesis (lines 9–10, 14–15).
- Has unsupported interpretation in lines 18–19.
- In many places, the syntax resembles a list because ideas are not fully developed (lines 16–20).

This midrange essay addresses the prompt and provides details to support the thesis. While the writer obviously understood both the story and the author's process, the subtleties are not fully explored and the syntax lacks fluidity.

Rubrics for "The Naked and the Nude" by Robert Graves

A high-range score (5, 6):

- Indicates complete understanding of the requirements for discussing the differences in connotation between "naked" and "nude."
- Recognizes and identifies the many differences between the two words.
- Utilizes appropriate literary techniques to present a coherent distinction between the two words.
- Responds to the irony in the final stanza.
- Perceives Graves's tone and preference for one of the words.
- Interprets allusions, images, symbols, etc.
- Uses smooth transitions and clear connective tissue.
- Demonstrates a mature writing style.

A midrange score (3, 4):

- Refers accurately to the thesis involving the contrast in meanings between two words.
- Adequately supports the thesis with appropriate details.
- Is less adept at interpreting the poem.
- May not be sensitive to the complex allusions and images or vocabulary.
- Demonstrates writing that is adequate to convey the writer's intent.

Sample Student Essays

Student Essay A

Many people tend to use the words "naked" and "nude" interchangeably. Yet Robert Graves objects to this misconception in his poem "The Naked and the Nude." Although both words mean "without clothes," Graves interprets them differently with regard to their connotations. He points out that "naked" refers to the body itself, whereas, "nude" refers to a personality or state of mind. Through   5 his use of various allusions and imagery, Graves contrasts the two synonyms.

Graves dedicates one stanza apiece to explain his perception of each word. When describing the "naked," Graves uses several classical allusions. He points out that "the Hippocratic eye will see in nakedness, anatomy." Likewise, "naked shines the Goddess when she mounts her lion among men." It's clear that   10 nakedness only refers to the naked body. However, Graves uses allusions to deception and trickery to explain his concept of the nude. He says, "the nude are bold, the nude are sly . . . they grin a mock-religious grin of scorn at those of naked skin." The concept of nude seems to be more of a cunning state of mind—"being naked with attitude."   15

The poet uses these details to create a certain imagery that clearly explains this discrepancy. His use of classical allusions creates images of peace, beauty, and spirituality which imply the inherent beauty of the human body on a physical level. Yet, the imagery created by the second set of details does not deal with the physical body. Graves explains that the nude have a cunning state of mind, "while draping   20 by a showman's trick their dishabille in rhetoric."

The contrast described in the poem, body versus mind, is reinforced when Graves tells us that the naked are physical bodies that are admired by "Lovers without reproach" and men of medicine. The nude, however, are more than that; they "are sly" and "hold each treasonable eye." The writer concludes that the naked, therefore, who   25 compete against the nude may know defeat because the nude are more complex and cynical.

Graves's final stanza transfers the vulnerability of the naked to the nude. When treading "the briary patches of the dead," the nude will not have artifice to protect them from the Gorgons' whips—they will be the naked as well as the nude.   30

This is a high-ranking essay for the following reasons:

- Shows complete understanding of the prompt.
- Immediately presents an accurate distinction between "naked" and "nude" (lines 4–5).
- Utilizes allusion and imagery correctly and links examples to meaning (lines 8–11, 12–15, 17–18).
- Reinforces the contrast throughout the essay (lines 16, 22, 29–30).
- Indicates perceptive, subtle analysis (lines 20–21, 29).
- Is well organized.
- Demonstrates a mature writing style.

This high-ranking essay is indicative of a confident writer and thinker. The paper is well focused, and it exhibits the writer's facility with literary terminology and analysis.

Student Essay B

The poem "The Naked and the Nude" written by Robert Graves explicitly shows how connotations can change the meaning of a thought or statement through images and other poetic devices. Those who are "naked" and those who are "nude" are not, according to the poem, in the same state of undress.

The speaker of the poem describes the differences between the naked and the nude using a variety of images and descriptions. He feels that one who is naked is hiding nothing while one who is nude is a picture of deception and art. The images of "Lovers without reproach will gaze on bodies naked and ablaze" depicts the honesty and truth that is given with love. Also the "Hippocratic eye will see in nakedness, anatomy." When this "eye" sees a naked person it is seeing what is really there and not what could be held in the deception of a person who is nude.

Although the naked are personified as "love" and "truth," when they "compete against the nude they may know defeat." This statement shows how those who are naked can sometimes be deceived and beaten by those who are artful liars. However, when it comes to the life after death, those who have been nude will also be naked, meaning that no matter what they were in life, when they die there will be no hiding behind the art of the body. Also, the facade that was built in life to hide from the truth will not work when it comes to the end.

Tone is another device that is used to convey the different connotations of naked and nude. When those who are naked are being discussed, the tone is not only positive, it presents an image of those who are happy with their position in life. For example, nakedness is linked with words such as "love," "truth," "shines," and "Goddess." However, when the speaker directs his attention on the nude, the tone is just the opposite. Nude is associated with "scorn," "showman," and "mock-religious." The speaker's tone in the descriptions of the two states of undress presents a clear difference in the connotations of the two words in the title of the poem.

The style and structure of the poem also contribute to conveying the two different connotations of naked and nude. The simple rhyme scheme shows how simplistic those who are naked can be as opposed to the deception and intricacies of those who are nude. The four stanza's each have a theme that it conveys. The first stanza exhibits the differences between the naked and the nude. The second stanza has the theme of the freedom of the naked, while the third shows the deception of the nude. The fourth and final stanza reinforces the theme that everyone will be naked after death.

This is a midrange essay for the following reasons:

- Accurately addresses the prompt.
- Understands deception and artifice (lines 6–7).
- Refers to suitable textual material to support the thesis (lines 8–9, 22–24).

- Demonstrates an ability to handle literary analysis (19–25, 27–29).
- Stays on topic.
- Has several awkward sentences and punctuation and agreement errors (lines 10–11, 13–29, and 30).
- Uses transitions and connective tissue.

It's obvious that the writer of this mid-range essay understands both the prompt and process of literary analysis. The second half of the paper is not as strong as the first. Perhaps, this writer was feeling the time pressure.

Rubrics for the Free-Response Essay

A high-range score (5, 6):

- Effectively and coherently addresses the intentional dissembling of a character or group.
- Effectively and coherently analyzes how the dissembling contributes to character development.
- Effectively and coherently discusses how the dissembling contributes to the meaning of the work.
- Chooses an appropriate novel or play.
- Uses references insightfully to support and illustrate the dissembling.
- Thoroughly discusses the character's nature and its relation to the theme.
- Strongly adheres to topic.
- Substantiates development of the thesis.
- Exhibits mature writing style.

A midrange score (3, 4):

- Identifies the intentional dissembling of a character or group.
- Chooses an acceptable novel or play.
- Adequately addresses the prompt with respect to intentional dissembling and how it contributes to both character development and meaning.
- Uses obvious references to support the prompt.
- Discussion of the character's nature and its relation to the theme is less developed.
- Adheres to topic, but may have lapses in coherence.
- Discussion of the theme is less developed.
- Writing style is acceptable but may show lapses in syntax and/or diction.

Sample Student Essays

Student Essay A

"To thine own self be true," advises Polonius in Shakespeare's *Hamlet*. Too bad he doesn't follow his own counsel when he continually dissembles to advance his own position in Claudius's court. This deceitfulness is the cause of the destruction of the lives of his children, himself, and ultimately the kingdom. His seemingly minor deceits reinforce the theme of betrayal and deception in the play.

5

Our first impression of Polonius is a positive one when we see him supporting Laertes's desire to return to his studies in Paris. However, his fatherly advice, "to not be false to any man" is ironic because he has already hired Reynaldo to spy on his son. He tells Reynaldo to use a "bait of falsehood" to see if Laertes's friends will be faithful and true. Polonius plans for this to include starting rumors and even malicious lies. Later in the play, Shakespeare has Rosencrantz and Guildenstern play out a parallel scene with Hamlet. 10

As with his son, Polonius seems to be genuinely concerned with the well-being of his daughter Ophelia. He tells her to reject the "love" letters and tokens from Hamlet 15 because he fears Hamlet only wants to take advantage of her and will not and cannot marry her. But soon we see the other side of this paternal scheme when Polonius willingly uses his daughter's emotional connections to Hamlet for his own purpose of furthering his service to Claudius. Hoping to prove that Hamlet's madness is caused by love sickness, he permits himself to advance his own agenda even though he has to 20 know that it will cause pain and distress for both Ophelia and Hamlet.

Inevitably, Polonius's dissembling leads to his own destruction. Ever the deceitful sycophant, he suggests to Claudius that he hide behind the arras in Gertrude's chamber in order to spy on both her and Hamlet. While eavesdropping, he cries out when he believes that Hamlet is attacking the Queen. Believing the voice to be that of 25 Claudius, Hamlet thrusts his sword through the curtain, fatally wounding Polonius. Here, the irony lies in his death resulting from an attempt to protect Gertrude.

It is this act that is the catalyst for the subsequent tragic events: Ophelia's madness and death, Laertes's desire for revenge, and Hamlet's fleeing Denmark. The final tragedies of the play—the deaths of Ophelia, Laertes, Gertrude, Claudius, and 30 Hamlet—are all the results of further dissembling which is foreshadowed by Polonius's deceit.

Although Polonius dies in Act III, he sets the foundation for the theme of deceit and murder throughout the remainder of the drama. Truly, something was rotten in the state of Denmark, and it was Polonius. 35

This is a high-range essay for the following reasons:

- Demonstrates a clear and focused understanding of the prompt and its demands.
- Exhibits solid evidence of the writer's knowledge of the chosen work.
- Demonstrates the ability to garner insights from the work.
- Uses appropriate illustrations and details (lines 8–9, paragraphs 3 and 4).
- Uses strong connective tissue.
- Demonstrates thorough development of ideas that are linked to the meaning of the work (lines 3–6, 11–13, 19–21).
- Strongly adheres to topic and organization.
- Uses mature vocabulary and syntax (lines 22–23, 28).

This high-range essay is strong because of its clear voice and strong organization. The introductory paragraph establishes the premise, which is fully supported in the body paragraphs. Rather than a summary, the concluding paragraph makes an insightful final comment connecting the topic and student interpretation.

Student Essay B

Often, in literature, there is a gap between the appearance of a situation and the meaning of the truth behind it. In Shakespeare's *Hamlet*, the protagonist assumes the antic disposition as a means of investigating the veracity of the ghost's admonition, "The serpent that did sting thy father's life, now wears his crown." In addition to contributing to the psychological development of Hamlet's character, this deceit augments many of the important themes in the play. In a work whose main topic is the search for truth, Hamlet's misrepresentation acts as a warning to sift through the surface appearance of things to discover purpose in this world.

Throughout the play, nothing is really as it seems. Hamlet's feigned madness is perhaps the most egregious example of this pattern. The melancholy Dane becomes a different man behind the mask of insanity. He is free to taunt Polonius regarding his lack of intelligence, or to scold his mother for her sexual improprieties, or to chastise Ophelia for her attempt to trick him. He is free to express himself without the fear of being held responsible for his insolence. This is a psychological coping method for Hamlet to deal with the trauma of a father's death and a mother's betrayal. Hamlet represses his anger and is paralyzed by it. The course of the play is a struggle for Hamlet to overcome his repression and to deal with the problems before him. Pretending to be mad is symbolic of this inner struggle and Hamlet's shield from the world.

Many of the major themes in *Hamlet* are also embodied in Hamlet's misrepresentation. The pervading irony in the play is that the "madman" is really thinking rationally. He sees what others do not and recognizes that his father was killed at Claudius's hands. Hamlet is a man who can and does make plans to seek the truth, and he carries these plans out. Another major theme is that of appearance versus reality. Connected to and with Hamlet's situation is a king who is a murderer, a mystery involving a ghost, a play within a play, a royal request which will turn into an invasion of Denmark, spying for proof of madness, fatherly advice to his children, and friends who are enemies. Each of these separately and all of them together enhance this theme of the play.

Hamlet is a search for truth. Through the protagonist's discovery of self and the revelation of Claudius's guilt, he embodies everyman's striving for understanding. Dissembling as a madman, Hamlet is able to work toward his goal of gaining authentic knowledge of past events and future battles.

This is a solid midrange essay for the following reasons:

- Writer has an obvious voice that engages the reader.
- Uses strong vocabulary.
- Decisively identifies theme and character.
- References are appropriate.

5

10

15

20

25

30

- Uses parallel structure well.
- Indicates cause and effect with supporting details.
- Uses inferences rather than plot.
- Good use of connective tissue.

Here is a paper that shows great promise and strength in the first half, but it loses continuity and lacks development in the second half. It seems that the writer has run out of time and is anxious to complete the essay. This student is a real thinker, but is trapped by time constraints.

PRACTICE EXAM 2
ANSWER SHEET FOR MULTIPLE-CHOICE QUESTIONS

1. _____

2. _____

3. _____

4. _____

5. _____

6. _____

7. _____

8. _____

9. _____

10. _____

11. _____

12. _____

13. _____

14. _____

15. _____

16. _____

17. _____

18. _____

19. _____

20. _____

21. _____

22. _____

23. _____

24. _____

25. _____

26. _____

27. _____

28. _____

29. _____

30. _____

31. _____

32. _____

33. _____

34. _____

35. _____

36. _____

37. _____

38. _____

39. _____

40. _____

41. _____

42. _____

43. _____

44. _____

45. _____

46. _____

47. _____

48. _____

49. _____

50. _____

51. _____

52. _____

53. _____

54. _____

55. _____

I _____ did _____ did not complete this part of the test in the allotted 1 hour.

I had _____ correct answers. I had _____ incorrect answers. I left _____ blank.

I have carefully reviewed the explanations of the answers, and I think I need to work on the following types of questions:

PRACTICE EXAM 2
ADVANCED PLACEMENT ENGLISH LITERATURE

Section I

Total time —1 hour

Carefully read the following passages and answer the questions that follow.
Questions 1–12 are based on the following passage from William Shakespeare's *Richard II*.

Act 5—Scene 5   Pomfret Castle
King Richard II:

I have been studying how I may compare
This prison where I live unto the world:
And for because the world is populous
And here is not a creature but myself,
I cannot do it; yet I'll hammer it out.   5
My brain I'll prove the female to my soul,
My soul the father; and these two beget
A generation of still-breeding thoughts,
And these same thoughts people this little world,
In humours like the people of this world,   10
For no thought is contented. The better sort,
As thoughts of things divine, are intermix'd
With scruples and do set the word itself
Against the word:
As thus, 'Come, little ones,' and then again,   15
'It is as hard to come as for a camel
To thread the postern of a small needle's eye.'
Thoughts tending to ambition, they do plot
Unlikely wonders; how these vain weak nails
May tear a passage through the flinty ribs   20
Of this hard world, my ragged prison walls,
And, for they cannot, die in their own pride.
Thoughts tending to content flatter themselves
That they are not the first of fortune's slaves,
Nor shall not be the last; like silly beggars   25
Who sitting in the stocks refuge their shame,
That many have and others must sit there;
And in this thought they find a kind of ease,
Bearing their own misfortunes on the back
Of such as have before endured the like.   30
Thus play I in one person many people,
And none contented: sometimes am I king;
Then treasons make me wish myself a beggar,
And so I am: then crushing penury
Persuades me I was better when a king;   35

> Then am I king'd again: and by and by
> Think that I am unking'd by Bolingbroke,
> And straight am nothing: but whate'er I be,
> Nor I nor any man that but man is
> With nothing shall be pleased, till he be eased   40
> With being nothing.

1. This passage is an example of
   A. an elegy
   B. a villanelle
   C. an ode
   D. free verse
   E. a soliloquy

2. The extended metaphor in this passage develops around
   A. royalty
   B. poverty
   C. fortune
   D. prison
   E. treason

3. In line 5, "yet I'll hammer it out" refers to Richard's
   A. aggression
   B. thought processes
   C. anger at his circumstances
   D. arrogance
   E. self-loathing

4. The conceit in lines 6–11 is based on
   A. sexuality
   B. psychology
   C. genealogy
   D. religion
   E. human nature

5. In line 10, "the people of this world" refers to Richard's
   A. still breeding thoughts
   B. brain and soul
   C. "humours"
   D. children
   E. royal subjects

6. Lines 10–22 are developed using each of the following *except*
   A. personification
   B. direct address
   C. simile
   D. hyperbole
   E. synecdoche

7. Richard attempts to comfort himself with the idea that
   A. others have and are enduring comparable hardships
   B. it is possible to escape his prison
   C. prayer will redeem him
   D. his offspring will carry on his legacy
   E. fortune or fate will intervene

8. The organization of this passage moves from
   A. past to present
   B. definition to an example
   C. specific circumstances to universal conclusion
   D. general principle to specific instances
   E. positive attitude to negative one

9. Lines 38–41 conclude the passage with an example of
   A. couplet
   B. spondee
   C. epitaph
   D. paradox
   E. understatement

10. Richard's major epiphany occurs within lines
  A. 1–5
  B. 11–14
  C. 38–41
  D. 18–22
  E. 23–27

11. Contrasts developed in the passage include all of the following *except*
  A. freedom and imprisonment
  B. men and women
  C. wealth and poverty
  D. power and powerlessness
  E. past and present

12. The theme of isolation (lines 3–4) is reinforced by which of the following lines?
  A. 24–25
  B. 36–38
  C. 25–27
  D. 11–14
  E. 31–32

Questions 13–25 are based on the following passage.

The Solitude of Self
by Elizabeth Cady Stanton

The point I wish plainly to bring before you on this occasion is the individuality of each human soul; the right of individual conscience and judgment; our republican idea, the individual citizenship. In discussing the right of woman we are to consider, first, what belongs to her as an individual in a world of her own, the arbiter of her own destiny, an imaginary Robinson Crusoe, with her woman Friday, on a solitary island. Her rights   5
under such circumstances are to use all her faculties for her own safety and happiness.

Secondly, if we consider her as a citizen, as a member of a great nation, she must have the same rights as all members, according to the fundamental principles of our government.

The strongest reason for giving woman all the opportunities for higher education,   10
for the full development of her faculties, her forces of mind and body; for giving her the most enlarged freedom of thought and action; a complete emancipation from all forms of bondage, of custom, dependence, superstition; from all the crippling influences of fear—is the solitude and personal responsibility of her own individual life. The strongest reason why we ask for woman a voice in the government under which she lives; in the religion   15
she is asked to believe; a quality in social life, where she is the chief factor; a place in the trades and professions, where she may earn her bread, is because of her birth right to self-sovereignty; because, as an individual, she must rely on herself. No matter how much women prefer to lean, to be protected and supported, nor how much men desire to have them do so, they must make the voyage of life alone, and for safety in an emergency, they   20
must know something of the laws of navigation. To guide our own craft, we must be captain, pilot, engineer, with chart and compass to stand at the wheel; to watch the winds and waves, and know when to take in the sail, and to read the signs in the firmament over all. It matters not whether the solitary voyager is a man or woman; nature, having endowed them equally, leaves them to their own skill and judgment in the hour of danger, and, if not   25
equal to the occasion, alike they perish.

We come into the world alone, unlike all who have gone before us, we leave it alone, under circumstances peculiar to ourselves. No mortal ever has been, no mortal ever will be just like the soul just launched on the sea of life. No one has ever found two blades of ribbon grass alike, and no one will ever find two human beings alike. Seeing, then, that what must 30 be the infinite diversity of human character, we can appreciate the loss to a nation when any class of the people is uneducated and unrepresented in the government.

We ask for the complete development of every individual, first, for his own benefit and happiness. In fitting out an army, we give each soldier his own knapsack, arms, powder, blanket, and utensils. We provide alike for all their individual necessities; then each man bears 35 his own burden. We ask complete individual development for the general good. The great lesson that nature seems to teach us is self-dependence, self-protection, self-support.

Amid the greatest triumphs and darkest tragedies of life, we walk alone. On the divine heights of human attainment, we stand alone. Alone we starve or steal . . . Seeing, then, that life must ever be a march and a battle, that each soldier must be equipped for his own protection, 40 it is the height of cruelty to rob the individual of a single natural right.

Whatever may be said of man's protecting power in ordinary conditions, amid all the terrible disasters by land and sea, in the supreme moments of danger, alone woman must ever meet the horrors of the situation. In that solemn solitude of self that links us with the immeasurable and the eternal, each soul lives alone forever . . . 45

And yet, there is a solitude which each and every one of us has always carried with him, more inaccessible than the ice cold mountains, more profound than the midnight sea; our inner being which we call ourself.

Such is individual life. Who, I ask you, can take, dare take on himself the rights, the duties, the responsibilities of another human soul? 50

13. The attitude of the author toward the education of women is
A. denigrating
B. ambivalent
C. imperious
D. indifferent
E. imperative

14. In the passage, the author uses each of the following *except*
A. metaphor
B. complex sentence structure
C. satire
D. allusion
E. parallel structure

15. For the author, the primary purpose of the education of women is
A. self-sufficiency
B. control of others
C. to be equal with men
D. to meet the demand of society
E. to teach others

16. Paragraph three is developed using all the following *except*
A. ironic contrast
B. examples
C. cause and effect
D. extended metaphor
E. parallel structure

17. The concept that all people have diversity in common is an example of
A. paradox
B. cause and effect
C. analogy
D. understatement
E. parody

18. The "laws of navigation" (line 21) refer to
A. military laws
B. celestial navigation
C. laws of nature
D. tools needed for survival
E. God's commandments

19. "Our own craft" (line 21) is a metaphor for our
   A. soul
   B. skills
   C. bodies
   D. navy
   E. place in government

20. The twentieth-century civil rights movement could most easily embrace which of the following paragraphs?
   A. 1
   B. 3
   C. 4
   D. 6
   E. 7

21. According to the passage, man and woman are alike in all the following ways *except*
   A. Nature made them equal.
   B. They are both solitary voyagers.
   C. If unprepared, both will die.
   D. Each has an inner being.
   E. They are interdependent.

22. Paragraph 7 contains examples of
   A. allusion
   B. hyperbole
   C. rhetorical questions
   D. simile
   E. apostrophe

23. In exhorting the public to work for equal rights for women, the author stresses
   A. the military needs of the nation
   B. the physical strength of women
   C. women's conflict with the universe
   D. the eternal nature of the soul
   E. the individuality and solitude of each person

24. The last sentence of the passage is an example of
   A. oxymoron
   B. irony
   C. rhetorical question
   D. a question dependent upon a logical fallacy
   E. paradox

25. Which of the following lines is not a thematic statement of the passage?
   A. 1–3 ("The point . . . citizenship")
   B. 5–6 ("Her . . . happiness")
   C. 30–32 ("Seeing . . . government")
   D. 34–35 ("In . . . utensils")
   E. 49–50 ("Such is . . . soul")

Questions 26–40 are based on the following poem.

Love Poem
by John Frederick Nims

My clumsiest dear, whose hands shipwreck vases,
At whose quick touch all glasses chip and ring,
Whose palms are bulls in china, burs in linen,
And have no cunning with any soft thing

Except all ill-at-ease fidgeting people: 5
The refugee uncertain at the door
You make at home; deftly you steady
The drunk clambering on his undulant floor.

> Unpredictable dear, the taxi drivers' terror,
> Shrinking from far headlights pale as a dime   10
> Yet leaping before red apoplectic streetcars—
> Misfit in any space. And never on time.
>
> A wrench in clocks and the solar system. Only
> With words and people and love you move at ease.
> In traffic of wit expertly manoeuvre   15
> And keep us, all devotion, at your knees.
>
> Forgetting your coffee spreading on our flannel,
> Your lipstick grinning on our coat,
> So gayly in love's unbreakable heaven
> Our souls on glory of spilt bourbon float.   20
>
> Be with me, darling, early and late. Smash glasses—
> I will study wry music for your sake.
> For should your hands drop white and empty
> All the toys of the world would break.

26. As used in the second stanza, "undulant" most closely means
A. polished
B. inebriated
C. wavy
D. dirty
E. cluttered

27. With reference to the title, the irony lies in the
A. reversal of the speaker's thoughts
B. absence of the beloved
C. kindness of the lover
D. enumeration of the lover's weaknesses
E. wit of the lover

28. The image of "hands drop white and empty" (line 23) implies the
A. breaking of vases
B. death of the lover
C. lover's clumsy nature
D. spilt bourbon
E. smashed glasses

29. The word "only" in line 13 serves to
A. introduce a contrasting thought
B. indicate isolation
C. make the rhyme effective
D. indicate cause and effect
E. indicate passage of time

30. According to the poem, the lover is all the following *except*
A. clever
B. clumsy
C. playful
D. selfish
E. gracious

31. "Be with me, darling" (line 21) is an example of
A. hyperbole
B. personification
C. allusion
D. invective
E. apostrophe

32. The poem is essentially a
A. caricature
B. satire
C. narrative
D. character study
E. parable

33. Lines 5 and 6 illustrate an example of
A. enjambment
B. oxymoron
C. jargon
D. connotation
E. ambiguity

34. The tone of the poem is
A. effusive
B. elegiac
C. benevolent
D. didactic
E. adoring

35. The speaker's attitude toward his love is
A. critical
B. embarrassed
C. enthralled
D. impatient
E. ill-at-ease

36. "Toys of the world" in the last line of the poem may be best understood as a metaphor for
A. life's pleasures
B. youthful infatuations
C. shattered dreams
D. material objects
E. lovers of the world

37. "A wrench in clocks and the solar system" (line 13) can be best interpreted to mean
A. the speaker is uncomfortable
B. star-crossed lovers
C. being obsessive about time
D. the inability to face the future
E. being out of synch with established conventions

38. The poem is written in
A. iambic pentameter
B. free verse
C. quatrains
D. blank verse
E. epigrams

39. Line 3 includes an example of
A. metaphor
B. synecdoche
C. metonymy
D. simile
E. onomatopoeia

40. Line 20 employs
A. internal rhyme
B. cacophony
C. apostrophe
D. literary conceit
E. assonance

Questions 41–55 are based on the following passage.

Excerpt from *As I Lay Dying*, "Addie," by William Faulkner

In the afternoon when school was out and the last one had left with his little dirty snuffling nose, instead of going home I would go down the hill to the spring where I could be quiet and hate them. It would be quiet there then, with the water bubbling up and away and the sun slanting quiet in the trees and the quiet smelling of damp and rotting leaves and new earth, especially in the early spring, for it was worst then.   5

I could just remember how my father used to say that the reason for living was to get ready to stay dead for a long time. And when I would have to look at them day after day, each with his and her secret and selfish thought, and blood strange to each other blood and strange to mine, and think that this seemed to be the   10 only way I could get ready to stay dead, I would hate my father for having planted me. I would look forward to the times when they faulted, so I could whip them. When the switch fell I could feel it upon my flesh; when it welted and ridged it was my blood that ran, and I would think with each blow of the switch: Now you are aware of me! Now I am something in your secret and selfish life, who have marked your blood with my own for ever and ever.   15

And so I took Anse. I saw him pass the school house three or four times before I learned that he was driving four miles out of his way to do it. I noticed then how he was beginning to hump—a tall man and young—so that he looked already like a tall bird hunched in the cold weather, on the wagon seat.   20

In early spring it was worst. Sometimes I thought that I could not bear it, lying in bed at night, with the wild geese going north and their honking coming faint and high and wild out of the wild darkness, and during the day it would seem as though I couldn't wait for the last one to go so I could go down to the spring. And so when I looked up that day and saw Anse standing there in his Sunday clothes, turning his hat   25 round and round in his hands, I said:

"If you've got any womenfolks, why in the world dont they make you get your hair cut?"

"I aint got none," he said. Then he said suddenly, driving his eyes at me like two hounds in a strange yard: "That's what I come to see you about."   30

"And make you hold your shoulders up," I said. "You haven't got any? But you've got a house. They tell me you've got a house and a good farm. And you live there alone, doing for yourself, do you?" He just looked at me, turning the hat in his hands. "A new house," I said. "Are you going to get married?"

And he said again, holding his eyes to mine: "That's what I come to see you   35 about."

Later he told me, "I aint got no people. So that wont be no worry to you. I dont reckon you can say the same."

"No. I have people. In Jefferson."

His face fell a little. "Well, I got a little property. I'm forehanded; I got a   40 good honest name. I know how town folks are, but maybe when they talk to me . . ."

"They might listen," I said. "But they'll be hard to talk to." He was watching my face. "They're in the cemetery."

"But your living kin," he said. "They'll be different."

"Will they?" I said. "I dont know. I never had any other kind."   45

So I took Anse.

41. The "geese" (line 22) are a symbolic representation of
A. Addie's desire to be part of a family
B. Addie's desire to be connected to nature
C. Addie's desire to be free
D. the children Addie teaches
E. the people in Jefferson

42. In the first paragraph, the reader learns all the following *except*
A. the point of view of the piece
B. the speaker's tone
C. the conflicts
D. the setting
E. the central event of the narration

43. In lines 29–44, the character of Anse is revealed by which of the following literary techniques?
  A. colloquial diction
  B. rhetorical questions
  C. a shift in tense
  D. omniscient point of view
  E. humor

44. Figurative language is found in lines
  A. 4 and 8
  B. 23 and 25–26
  C. 1 and 2
  D. 19–20 and 29–30
  E. 7–8 and 35

45. The concept of alienation is supported by all of the following *except*
  A. "each with his and her secret and selfish thought"
  B. "blood strange to each other blood and strange to mine"
  C. "When the switch fell I could feel it upon my flesh"
  D. "They're in the cemetery"
  E. "I aint got no people"

46. Addie marries because
  A. she is in love with Anse
  B. it was expected of women
  C. she thinks he will take her north
  D. Anse presents himself at that particular time
  E. she wants children

47. The reader can infer that Addie's role in the marriage will be
  A. supportive
  B. controlling
  C. submissive
  D. grateful
  E. erotic

48. The repetition of the phrase "so I took Anse" serves to
  A. further develop the setting
  B. establish an ironic situation
  C. highlight the importance of the event
  D. support Addie's ambivalence
  E. establish a matter-of-fact explanation of the relationship

49. In line 21, "In early spring it was worst," "it" refers to Addie's
  A. restless nature
  B. longing for Anse
  C. sadistic tendencies
  D. students' behavior
  E. desire to be married

50. Addie whips the children primarily because
  A. they talk back to her
  B. she hates her job
  C. she believes corporal punishment will make the children learn better
  D. she wants them to know she is there
  E. she sees no other way to control them

51. *ALL* of the following ideas are presented and supported in the passage *EXCEPT*
  A. the relationship between life and death
  B. isolation and alienation
  C. freedom and commitment
  D. frustration and resignation
  E. hope and liberation

52. Addie's philosophy and behavior most likely come from
  A. her religious beliefs
  B. her father
  C. her childhood experiences
  D. her people in Jefferson
  E. her education

53. Which of the following images are contrasted in the passage?
    A. the hill . . . the spring (lines 2–3)
    B. water bubbling up . . . sun slanting (line 4)
    C. rotting leaves . . . new earth (line 5)
    D. welted . . . ridged (line 13)
    E. secret . . . selfish (line 15)

54. On an interpretive level, Addie associates quiet with all of the following *except*
    A. hatred
    B. innermost feelings
    C. escape
    D. nature
    E. death

55. Symbolically, "early spring" may represent
    A. bubbling water
    B. the blood
    C. "womenfolks"
    D. Addie's life force
    E. secret and selfish lives

END OF SECTION I

Section II

Total time—2 hours

Question 1

(Suggested time 40 minutes. This question counts as one-third of the total score for Section II.)

In the short story "Reginald's Choir Treat," Saki contrasts two complex philosophies of life. In a well-organized essay, identify and discuss these two views and which of them the reader can infer is preferred by the narrator. Develop your discussion referring to at least two elements of the writer's craft such as irony, contrast, narration, dialogue, allusion, and tone.

Reginald's Choir Treat
by Saki

"Never," wrote Reginald to his most darling friend, "be a pioneer. It's the Early Christian that gets the fattest lion."

Reginald, in his way, was a pioneer.

None of the rest of his family had anything approaching Titian hair or a sense of humour, and they used primroses as a table decoration.   5

It follows that they never understood Reginald, who came down late to breakfast, and nibbled toast, and said disrespectful things about the universe. The family ate porridge, and believed in everything, even the weather forecast.

Therefore the family was relieved when the vicar's daughter undertook the reformation of Reginald. Her name was Anabel; it was the vicar's one extravagance. Anabel was   10
accounted a beauty and intellectually gifted: she never played tennis, and was reputed to have read Maeterlinck's "Life of a Bee." If you abstain from tennis and read Maeterlinck in a small country village, you are of necessity intellectual. Also she had been twice to Fecamp to pick up a good French accent from the Americans staying there; consequently she had a knowledge of the world which might be considered useful in dealings with a worldling.   15

Hence the congratulations in the family when Anabel undertook the reformation of the wayward member.

Anabel commenced operations by asking her unsuspecting pupil to tea in the vicarage garden; she believed in the healthy influence of natural surroundings, never having been in Sicily, where things are different.   20

And like every woman who has ever preached repentance to unregenerate youth, she dwelt on the sin of an empty life, which always seems so much more scandalous in the country, where people rise early to see if a new strawberry has happened during the night.

Reginald recalled the lilies of the field, "which simply sat and looked beautiful, and defied competition."   25

"But that is not an example for us to follow," gasped Anabel.

"Unfortunately, we can't afford to. You don't know what a world of trouble I take in trying to rival the lilies in their artistic simplicity."

"You are really indecently vain in your appearance. A good life is infinitely preferable to good looks."   30

"You agree with me that the two are incompatible. I always say beauty is only skin deep."

Anabel began to realize that the battle is not always to the strong-minded. With the immemorial resource of her sex, she abandoned the frontal attack and laid stress on her unassisted labours in parish work, her mental loneliness, her discouragements—and at the   35
right moment she produced strawberries and cream. Reginald was obviously affected by the

latter, and when his preceptress suggested that he might begin the strenuous life by helping
her to supervise the annual outing of the bucolic infants who composed the local choir, his
eyes shone with the dangerous enthusiasm of a convert.

Reginald entered on the strenuous life alone, as far as Anabel was concerned. The   40
most virtuous women are not proof against damp grass, and Anabel kept to her bed with a
cold. Reginald called it a dispensation; it had been the dream of his life to stage-manage a
choir outing. With strategic insight, he led his shy, bullet-headed charges to the nearest
woodland stream and allowed them to bathe; then he seated himself on the discarded
garments and discoursed on their immediate future, which, he decreed, was to embrace a   45
Bacchanalian procession through the village. Forethought had provided the occasion with
a supply of tin whistles, but the introduction of a he-goat from a neighbouring orchard was a
brilliant afterthought. Properly, Reginald explained, there should have been an outfit of
panther skins; as it was, those who had spotted handkerchiefs were allowed to wear them,
which they did with thankfulness. Reginald recognized the impossibility in the time at his   50
disposal, of teaching his shivering neophytes a chant in honour of Bacchus, so he started
them off with a more familiar, if less appropriate, temperance hymn. After all, he said, it
is the spirit of the thing that counts. Following the etiquette of dramatic authors on first
nights, he remained discreetly in the background while the procession, with extreme
diffidence and the goat, wound its way lugubriously towards the village. The singing had   55
died down long before the main street was reached, but the miserable wailing of pipes
brought the inhabitants to their doors. Reginald said he had seen something like it in pictures;
the villagers had seen nothing like it in their lives, and remarked as much freely.

Reginald's family never forgave him. They had no sense of humour.

Question 2

(Suggested time 40 minutes. This question counts as one-third of the total score for Section II.)

In "The Tables Turned," by William Wordsworth and "To David, About His Education" by Howard Nemerov,
the poets reveal their complex attitudes toward education. In a well-organized essay, discuss their similarities
and differences. You may wish to consider style, tone, poetic devices, structure, and imagery.

The Tables Turned
by William Wordsworth

Up! up! my friend, and quit your books;
Or surely you'll grow double:
Up! up! my friend, and clear your looks;
Why all this toil and trouble?   4

The sun, above the mountain's head,
A freshening lustre mellow
Through all the long, green fields has spread,
His first sweet evening yellow.   8

Books! 'tis a dull and endless strife:
Come, hear the woodland linnet,
How sweet his music! on my life,
There's more of wisdom in it.   12

And hark! how blithe the throstle sings!
He, too, is no mean preacher:
Come forth into the light of things,
Let Nature be your teacher.   16

She has a world of ready wealth,
Our minds and hearts to bless,—
Spontaneous wisdom breathed by health,
Truth breathed by cheerfulness.   20

One impulse from a vernal wood
May teach you more of man,
Of moral evil and of good,
Than all the sages can.   24

Sweet is the lore which Nature brings;
Our meddling intellect
Misshapes the beauteous forms of things,—
We murder to dissect.   28

Enough of Science and of Art;
Close up those barren leaves;
Come forth, and bring with you a heart
That watches and receives.   32

To David, About His Education
by Howard Nemerov

The world is full of mostly invisible things,
And there is no way but putting the mind's eye,
Or its nose, in a book, to find them out,
Things like the square root of Everest
Or how many times Byron goes into Texas,   5
Or whether the law of the excluded middle
Applies west of the Rockies. For these
And the like reasons, you have to go to school
And study books and listen to what you are told,
And sometimes try to remember. Though I don't know   10
What you will do with the mean annual rainfall
On Plato's Republic, or the calorie content
Of the Diet of Worms, such things are said to be
Good for you, and you will have to learn them
In order to become one of the grown-ups   15
Who sees invisible things neither steadily nor whole,
But keeps gravely the grand confusion of the world
Under his hat, which is where it belongs,
And teaches small children to do this in their turn.

Question 3

(Suggested time 40 minutes. This question counts as one-third of the total score for Section II.)

Frequently a work of literature will concern itself with a major transformation in a character. This transformation could be actual or symbolic. Choose a full-length work and write a well-organized essay in which you discuss the complex nature of the transformation and its relationship to character and theme. You may choose from the list below or another novel or play of literary merit.

Frankenstein	*Othello*
Hamlet	*I Know Why the Caged Bird Sings*
Metamorphosis	*Gulliver's Travels*
Native Son	*Sula*
Dr. Jekyll and Mr. Hyde	*The Importance of Being Earnest*
A Doll's House	*The Color Purple*
The Poisonwood Bible	*The Awakening*
Twelfth Night	*Things Fall Apart*
Invisible Man	*King Lear*
The Joy Luck Club	*The Stranger*
Madame Bovary	*The Scarlet Letter*
Pygmalion	

END OF SECTION II

ANSWERS TO MULTIPLE-CHOICE QUESTIONS

Answer Key

1. E	**20.** C	**39.** A
2. D	**21.** E	**40.** E
3. B	**22.** B	**41.** C
4. C	**23.** E	**42.** E
5. A	**24.** C	**43.** A
6. E	**25.** D	**44.** D
7. A	**26.** C	**45.** C
8. C	**27.** D	**46.** D
9. D	**28.** B	**47.** B
10. C	**29.** A	**48.** E
11. B	**30.** D	**49.** A
12. E	**31.** E	**50.** D
13. E	**32.** D	**51.** E
14. C	**33.** A	**52.** B
15. A	**34.** E	**53.** C
16. A	**35.** C	**54.** A
17. A	**36.** A	**55.** D
18. D	**37.** E	
19. C	**38.** C	

Answers and Explanations

1. E. This is a terminology question. This is a soliloquy that reveals Richard's thoughts to the audience through his internal monologue that is stated audibly.

2. D. References to kingship are part of Richard's real world, and therefore not part of the metaphor. Images of poverty, fortune, and beggars' penury support and develop the thoughts he has in his state of deprivation. Treason also refers to his thoughts, which he hopes will enable him to deal with his imprisonment.

3. B. Again, this is basically a vocabulary question. To "hammer" something out is to analyze a problem thoroughly.

4. C. The image is one of conception, but Richard's thoughts are going to reproduce and people the world that is in his mind.

5. A. Building on the information in the previous question, the only reliable answer is A.

6. E. This is a terminology question that requires an understanding of how the term can be used in a work. An example of personification is found in lines 23–24. You can locate direct address in line 15; hyperbole is used in lines 16–17. Lines 25–26 contain an example of simile. Synecdoche is a literary device that has the part representing the whole, and it is not used in this passage.

7. A. Lines 23–30 provide the evidence that thinking of others helps to ease one's personal hardship.

8. C. The opening two lines establish Richard's imprisonment, and the concluding lines state, "Nor I nor any man," which expands the concept from a specific situation to a universal concept.

9. D. Richard realizes that to be truly at ease, he must accept that he has lost everything that previously seemed to bring him contentment. This contradictory concept is an example of paradox.

10. C. All of Richard's thoughts about religion, ambition, and contentment lead to the concluding statement beginning in line 38 that he accepts being nothing and is thereby content.

11. B. Although "female" and "father" are mentioned, there is no inherent contrast between them.

12. E. Lines 3–4 express the literal solitude. Lines 31–32 describe his figurative coping with this solitude.

13. E. This is one of those questions that assumes you have a working AP-level vocabulary. You can immediately eliminate A and D because of their negative associations. "Ambivalent" relates to being undecided, and "imperious" refers to a controlling attitude. Therefore, E is the appropriate choice, since Stanton is stressing the need to ensure equal rights to women.

14. C. Metaphor can be spotted in paragraphs 3 and 5. Complex sentence structure is part of the author's style. Just look at the first sentence of paragraph 3. Allusions are part of paragraph 1, and parallel structure is incorporated into paragraphs 3 and 5. You will find no examples of satire in this passage.

15. A. The idea of self-sufficiency as the key to personal safety and happiness is stressed in almost every paragraph. Close reading reveals that none of the other choices is developed.

16. A. Ironic contrast is absent from the entire passage. You can locate examples of each of the other choices. Examples are found in paragraph 5; cause and effect are part and parcel of paragraph 3; an extended metaphor is developed in paragraph 3; and parallel structure is used in paragraph 4.

17. A. "Diversity" and "common" are mutually exclusive terms. If you know the definition of paradox, this will lead you to paradox as the only appropriate choice.

18. D. The answer to this question depends on a clear understanding of the extended metaphor developed around sailing. A sailor needs to use the laws of navigation to safely sail the seas, just as a human being needs self-sufficiency to survive the world at large.

19. C. Following the structure of the extended sea/sailor metaphor, you should recognize that self-sufficiency refers to the "craft as body" being independent.

20. **C.** Paragraph 4 stresses the need for a strong nation to accept differences and to understand that any diminished class diminishes the entire country.

21. **E.** The focus of the entire passage is on the solitary nature of human beings and the need for self-sufficiency. Although men and women must interact, ultimately each is responsible for himself or herself.

22. **B.** If you know the definition of hyperbole, you will recognize the examples in paragraph 7: "each and every one . . . ," "always . . . ," "more inaccessible than the ice cold mountains . . . ," and "more profound than the midnight sea."

23. **E.** The answer comes from a careful reading and understanding of the complete passage and its organization. The concept of equality and human rights was basic for Stanton, as it is for anyone involved in civil rights.

24. **C.** Here, again, a working familiarity with literary terminology is required. Since Stanton asks a question that does not require a direct response, C is the appropriate choice.

25. **D.** These lines are part of the metaphor Stanton develops to support the other four choices cited.

26. **C.** You should use the context of lines 7–8 to help you. "Steady" implies a lack of movement and leads you to the best choice, "wavy," which implies motions.

27. **D.** The entire poem lists the beloved's faults, yet the speaker adores her for them. This contradiction is the essence of the ironic title. Choice A is close, but it refers to the situation of the entire poem, not just the title.

28. **B.** It is easy to jump to the conclusion that the lover has broken yet another object. However, A, C, D, and E all support that idea; therefore, they cancel one another out.

29. **A.** You are required to reread the lines prior to the word "only" in order to realize that it provides a contrast. B and C are readily eliminated with a glance, and D and E are not supported by the poem.

30. **D.** Pay careful attention to the word "except." Then use substitution to find the one quality she does not exhibit. The answer is supported in line 15 with "wit," line 1 with "clumsiest," line 14 with "at ease," and line 19 with "gayly."

31. **E.** By definition, an apostrophe is an example of direct address.

32. **D.** Even though there is some exaggeration and humor, they are used to develop the character of the beloved, and a narrative requires elements of a story.

33. **A.** As you can see, it is imperative that you know terminology. To make sense, lines 5 and 6 must be read smoothly to the punctuation rather than to the end of the line.

34. **E.** The tone is revealed clearly in lines 16, 19, 23, and 24. The speaker adores his beloved.

35. **C.** This is a question that is almost too easy. Use your information from questions 30, 31, and 34 to help you recognize that all the other choices are negative.

36. **A.** As toys bring joy and delight, so, too, does the lover bring pleasure to the speaker's life. She holds toys and the speaker in her hands.

37. **E.** The clocks and solar system represent time and space. (See metonymy in Chapter 8.) "Wrench" indicates a breakdown of a system (e.g., "throwing a wrench into the system").

38. **C.** A straightforward, factual question. Again, you need to know your terms.

39. **A.** This is a poetic term and example question. The two metaphors are that palms are "bulls" and "burs in linen."

40. **E.** This is a subtle question which asks you to hear the sound of the line. All the open "O" sounds reinforce the idea of floating. None of the other given devices is present in this line.

41. **C.** One of the universal symbols of freedom is flight. To refer to "wild geese going north" is to reinforce Addie's desire to be free.

42. **E.** "I" indicates a first person narrator point of view. The phrases "little dirty snuffling nose," "damp and rotting leaves," and "it was worst then" are indicative of conflict, setting, and tone. What is *not* mentioned in this first paragraph is a central event.

43. **A.** These lines are primarily composed of dialogue, so it is here that you should look for your answer. Vocabulary, similes, and syntax all point to colloquial (informal, conversational) diction.

44. D. The similes found in these two sets of lines are examples of figurative language. The other lines are factual and reportorial.

45. C. The concepts and images associated with alienation are found in phrases containing "secret," "blood strange," "cemetery," and "got no people." C, on the other hand, is cause and effect.

46. D. There is no evidence of any of the other choices in the passage. The very last line begins with the word "so." It is indicative of a matter-of-fact result of Anse being in the right place at the right time.

47. B. In this passage, Addie's conversation and interaction with Anse always place him in a subservient, uncomfortable position. See lines 27–28 and 31–33 to support the idea of her dominance.

48. E. Lines 17 and 46 indicate a straightforward cause and effect that just so happens to lead to Addie marrying Anse. Ambivalence, irony, setting, and highlighting an event are *not* references of the given phrase.

49. A. The "it" in this question is used the second time in the same way. See lines 4–6: The early spring, longing, potential, and desire to be free as wild geese lead to the conclusion that Addie has a restless nature.

50. D. Lines 1–15 give you the direct answer. ". . . and I would think with each blow of the switch: Now you are aware of me!"

51. E. A careful reading of the passage will lead you through Addie's experiences and thoughts about living and dying, about being alone, about being in a relationship, and about being free. Therefore, you need to recognize that, for Addie, hope and liberation is not in her future.

52. B. The second paragraph gives you the correct answer. It directly refers to the father.

53. C. Contrast demands difference. The only appropriate choice, therefore, is "rotting leaves . . . new earth." Rotting and new are the contrast here.

54. A. Paragraphs 1, 2, and 4 allow the reader into Addie's psyche. The one characteristic *not* associated with her seeking quiet is hatred.

55. D. This is another universal symbol. The associations with spring, especially early spring, center around renewal, regeneration, hope, fertility, and the continuance of life.

Rating the Essay Section

Rubrics for "Reginald's Choir Treat" by Saki

A high-range score (5, 6):

- Indicates complete understanding of the prompt.
- Identifies the two views of life presented in the story.
- Recognizes which view is preferred by the author.
- Effectively and coherently analyzes Saki's craft.
- Is cognizant of satire.
- Recognizes the humor in the allusions.
- Understands the irony and tone of the essay.
- Delineates Reginald's character.
- Cites appropriate textual references.
- Presents advanced insight.
- Strongly adheres to topic and uses connective tissue.
- Demonstrates an ability to manipulate language in a mature style.

A midrange score (3, 4):

- Refers accurately to the prompt.
- Presents the two philosophies.
- Refers accurately to Saki's craft.

- Infers the narrator's preference of lifestyle.
- Presents less developed discussion of the two views of life.
- Adequately links elements of the discussion.
- May miss the satire of the story.
- Concentrates on the obvious rather than on the inferences and implications.
- Organization is adequate.
- May exhibit a few errors in syntax and/or diction.

Sample Student Essays

Student Essay A

In the short story "Reginald's Choir Treat" Saki contrasts two philosophies of life. One is a daring, cynical, and whimsical approach to life, like Reginald's. The other is a conservative, intellectual, religious, reforming approach to life like Anabel's. The author's sarcastic tone with a hint of diffidence indicates that he agrees with Reginald's cause, but he pities the fact that few people can relate to or understand "pioneers." Saki contrasts and 5 shows the irony of both Anabel and Reginald's actions and perspectives about life to help the reader understand the two philosophies. However, even Anabel's philosophy shares some similarities to Reginald's and is more appealing to Saki's story than that of Reginald's family, which lives a modest, pedestrian, and uncompromising life, with no tolerance for the whims of Reginald. 10

Reginald does not fit in with his family's lifestyle. He questioned the universe and pleased himself with unconventional fantasies. Anabel is a gifted vicar's daughter who leads a charitable life and tries to be worldly at the same time. She attempts to make Reginald more religious and to coax him with her womanly charms but is unsuccessful. Saki ironically has her traveling to a French resort to pick up a good French accent from 15 the Americans living there. She also persuades Reginald to lead a more virtuous life like herself and then ironically leaves Reginald to complete one of her charitable obligations without her. In a dialogue between the two main characters, Saki uses conversation to contrast Reginald with Anabel's perspectives. She speaks against the "sin of an empty life," and Reginald recalls the artistic "simplicity of the lilies" that simply sit and look beautiful. 20 The greatest humorous irony of the story is Reginald turning religious charity work in the form of a choir outing into a whimsical pagan festival which is an allusion to the mythological Bacchus, the god of wine and pleasure. He shows his carefree and sarcastic approach to life by giving choirboys "tin whistles" and parading them through the streets with symbols of Bacchus. Another irony is that he has children honor Bacchus (god of wine) with a 25 temperance hymn familiar to them, and that the parade which was intended to be gay turns out to be a lugubrious procession with the "miserable wailing of pipes."

A sign that Saki sides with Reginald's unappreciated actions over those of Anabel, or especially those of his family, is in the story's conclusion. Reginald's family never forgives him, and Saki adds that they felt this way because "they had no sense of humour." 30

This makes it clear that the unfortunate and almost bitter ending is their flaw and not Reginald's because they should have appreciated the humor of the situation.

Saki shows that he shares some of Reginald's philosophy with his frequent use of irony and sarcasm. He shows that people who share Anabel's philosophy will not be able to reform those whimsical pioneers like Reginald. But, they should be amiable and attempt to appreciate the sense of humor in the actions of those like Reginald. If not, they will be doomed to live an ill-humored, mundane life like that of Reginald's family.

This is a high-ranking essay for the following reasons:

- Contains a clear opening, which sets up the organization of the essay.
- Is direct and accurate.
- Establishes Saki's attitude.
- Introduces sarcasm and defends it (lines 3–5).
- Clarifies distinction between the two views and the characters (lines 5–10, 11–14).
- Contains strong textual references.
- Addresses the writer's craft.
- Juxtaposes the two characters and their opposing views (lines 18–20).
- Provides a perceptive interpretation of a grammatical detail (lines 29–31).
- Strongly adheres to topic.
- Uses echo words well.
- Draws appropriate conclusions based on the evidence presented (lines 34–37).
- Writes good transitions.
- Organization, syntax, and diction are adequate.

This is an essay that can be categorized as high. Its strong textual references and understanding of the subtleties allow it to be in the high range even though there are some lapses in syntax.

Student Essay B

Saki's short story "Reginald's Choir Treat" contrasts two different philosophies of life. Each philosophy is represented by different characters. Conformity is represented by Anabel and nonconformity is represented by Reginald. In this story, Anabel and Reginald's parents try to make Reginald conform to the rest of society. Yet, his choir treat demonstrates that their goal failed. Through his use of tone, dialogue, and contrast, Saki indirectly shows his support of Reginald's nonconformity.

Saki uses a sarcastic tone, particularly towards Anabel and the other conformists. The first line of the story has an adage from Reginald: "never be a pioneer. It's the Early Christian that gets the fattest lion." This saying sets the sarcastic tone for the rest of the story. Later on, in his description of Anabel, Saki notes that, "if you abstain from tennis and read Maeterlinck in a small country village, you are of necessity intellectual." Likewise, in his description of Reginald's family, Saki points out that the rest of his family used "primroses as a table decoration." Saki is mocking all the conformists because of their desire to conform to society. He uses this sarcastic tone to demonstrate his partiality towards Reginald's free nature.

35

5

10

15

Saki also uses a contrast between Reginald and Anabel. The only direct
description of Reginald is that "[He], in his way, is a pioneer." On the other hand, the
author describes many details about Anabel. He calls Anabel, "the vicar's one extravagance."
Yet, in this case, Saki uses the pronoun "it" to refer to Anabel's fanciful name,
demonstrating his distaste for her. He sarcastically relates that "Anabel was accounted   20
a beauty and intellectually gifted" because "she had been twice to Fecamp to pick up a good
French accent from the Americans staying there." Saki presents the notion that many
believe the conformists are better than the nonconformists and uses Anabel to refute that
notion. Despite these accolades Saki has attributed to her, he mocks her and her philosophy.

Similarly, Saki uses dialogue to demonstrate his favoring nonconformity. The   25
conversation between Reginald and Anabel revolves around trying to convince Reginald to
abandon his nonconformity. She tries to do so by insulting him. Anabel tells him that
"[He is] really indecently vain in [his] appearance." For a woman who is supposed to be
smart and sweet, she does not display any of those qualities here. Her nasty nature
towards Reginald in this dialogue further emphasizes Saki's distaste for her and   30
her philosophy.

Obviously, Saki views individual expression as important and nonthreatening.
He recognizes that the best weapon to fight conformity is humor.

This is a midrange essay for the following reasons:

- Clearly sets up the prompt and the organization of the essay (lines 1–6).
- Establishes the characters of Reginald and Anabel.
- Recognizes and discusses sarcasm (lines 10–11).
- Presents dialogue as indicative of character (lines 25–30).
- Makes inferences and understands satire.
- Presents author's preference and defends it (lines 7, 13–15).
- Draws threads of essay together and synthesizes technique with interpretation (lines 32–33).

What does not allow this essay to be rated in the high range is its syntax and diction.

Rubrics for the Poetry Essay

A high-range score (5, 6):

- Effectively and coherently discusses each poet's attitude toward education.
- Effectively and coherently discusses the similarities and differences between the two poems.
- Indicates a fluency with poetic analysis.
- Identifies and analyzes appropriate references to support an interpretation.
- Exhibits strong topic adherence and connective tissue.
- Draws mature inferences.
- Responds to subtleties in both poems.
- Writer's syntax and diction demonstrate a mature style.

A midrange score (3, 4):

- Adequately addresses the prompt.
- Identifies and discusses the writers' techniques.
- Adequately discusses similarities and differences between the two poems.

- Presents an adequate discussion of each poet's attitude.
- Displays acceptable writing skills.
- May not be sensitive to inference and tone.
- Focuses on the obvious and may not recognize the subtleties in both poems.
- Writing may have a few errors in syntax and/or diction.

Student Essay A

"The Tables Turned" by William Wordsworth and "To David, About His Education" by Howard Nemerov promulgate two different views of education. While they both agree that being taught and learning are important and necessary, there is a disagreement about where the lessons should come from, the purpose and direction of education, and the value which education possesses. Not only are the ideas of each selection dissimilar, but the structure, tone, and imagery are as well, which facilitates each poet's argument. 5

"The Tables Turned" espouses learning through experience and living in nature. The speaker wants students to "quit their books" (1) and "Let Nature be your teacher" (16). He believes that there is a great deal more to be learned from experience than can ever be found in a book. The education suggested in this poem is a practical one. Learning about the environment and how the world works from experiencing it will allow a person to make his own conclusions and proceed as he sees fit. Wordsworth believes that his brand of education through nature will provide "spontaneous wisdom breathed by health/truth breathed by cheerfulness" (19–20). This education does not merely cultivate the mind, but also the soul and spirit. 10 15

On the other hand, "To David, About His Education" suggests that the important parts of life are learned through books. Where the Wordsworth poem calls books "dull and endless strife" (9), it calls for putting the mind's eye / or its nose, in a book (2–3) to receive a proper education. Nemerov's poem suggests that studying from books is a more effective way to learn but cannot procure a benefit to the method. He merely states, "You will have to learn them/ in order to become one of the grown-ups" (14–15), not to become any kind of an enlightened, educated person. The images in the poem by Nemerov are of ridiculous facts and esoteric information, such as "the square root of Everest" (4) or the "calorie content of the Diet of Worms" (13). The images are hyperbolic examples of the need for an education through books. Only this kind of an education will produce the answers to such questions. 20 25

In contrast, Wordsworth used natural images to explain the merit of education through experience. He notes that there is more wisdom in the songs of birds than in the world's books. 30

The tone that Wordsworth uses is accusatory and somewhat didactic. In lines 17–18 he says that time is being wasted on books when nature has so much more to offer. He urges the student to "Let Nature be your teacher" (16). Yet, Nemerov uses 35 the tone of an all-knowing sage to suggest that there is a plethora of knowledge available in texts. The facts stated in his poem are obviously false, like "how many times Byron goes to Texas" (5), but their inclusion reinforces the tone of great wisdom and knowledge.

Likewise, the diction that Wordsworth uses, such as "intellect," "wisdom," and 40
"truth" convey a more complete education than words like "learn," "remember," or "find out" which appear in Nemerov's poem.

Although both poems advocate a form of education, the means to their ends are quite different.

This is a high-ranking essay for the following reasons:

- Contains a sophisticated and complex introduction to the task at hand (lines 1–8).
- Clearly and concisely identifies the attitude of both poets toward education and supports it with references to the text (lines 10–11, 23–25).
- Perceives implications arising from the poems (lines 12–13).
- Uses connective tissue well.
- Contrast discussed with support (lines 26–33).
- Pulls together the similarities and differences with respect to imagery (lines 28–29), tone (lines 35–37), and diction (lines 40–42).

This spare essay falls into the high range because it is packed with appropriate detail and effective and coherent analyses and interpretation.

Student Essay B

William Wordsworth and Howard Nemerov disagree about how one should be educated. Their differences in style, structure, and most importantly, tone are quite obvious from the very opening line of each poem.

Although most people would tend to agree with Nemerov's viewpoint that a
proper education is achieved through schooling, Wordsworth makes an interesting 5
opposition in his poem, "The Tables Turned," which questions the concept of an education through school, favoring a more "hands on" approach. By opening his poem with the exclamation "Up! Up!," he immediately attracts attention to the page. His instructions to quit studying, however, are quite ironic considering his allusion to
Shakespeare's Macbeth. While he attempts to prove that studying is worthless, he 10
is illustrating through his references that he is a learned man. Additionally, Wordsworth glorifies Nature by pointing out the "freshening lustre" and "sweet music," which also makes studying seem dull and boring in comparison. The imagery Wordsworth uses clearly illustrates his bias that nature is better than school. Nature is
always referred to as "light," and "sweet," whereas studies are thought of as "toil and 15
trouble," "a dull and endless strife," and "barren leaves." By continuing to use exclamation points and "exciting" words including "hark" throughout the poem, Wordsworth continues in his upbeat state when referring to Nature. In fact, Wordsworth is so reverent toward nature that he personifies her. The most glaring

point illustrated in the poem comes in the last verse. Wordsworth basically sums up   20
his entire poem in those four lines, which exclaim that studying nature is a more
fulfilling education than constantly reading books of Science and Art.

Throughout the poem "To David, About His Education," Nemerov illustrates
just as Wordsworth did through his reference to Shakespeare, that he is very educated.
At times, it seems as if Nemerov has a sarcastic, almost cynical approach toward   25
school, with his mocking of things taught in school, such as "the square root of Everest."
Yet, he realizes the underlying benefits of a proper education, as he points out that "such
things are said to be good for you." Nemerov uses a very unusual structure in this poem,
as he applies two or more academic subjects which may have nothing in common except
that they are both taught in school, and he is able to tie them together to make sense,   30
almost in joking manner. Statements such as "the law of the excluded middle applies
west of the Rockies" illustrate this method, as does the "calorie content of the Diet of
Worms." Although Diet of Worms has nothing to do with eating, Nemerov connects the
two almost as if his brain has been overloaded with useless information, similar to the
way a student might accidentally confuse the material of multiple subjects he is   35
studying. Nemerov fully understands the value of an education "in order to become
one of the grown-ups."

Wordsworth and Nemerov have blatantly opposing opinions about the best method
of education. While Wordsworth illustrates through his poem that an education through
Nature is more valuable than spending hours reading books, Nemerov understands that   40
in order to be accepted by society, a knowledge of academic subjects is vital.

This is a midrange essay for the following reasons:

- Adequately illustrates a facility with analysis with respect to imagery (lines 13–16) and tone (lines 18–19, 25–26, 31–32).
- Is clearly on topic with good use of connective tissue.
- Provides adequate evidence to defend interpretations (lines 31–36).

This is a strong midrange essay with clear analysis, topic adherence, and support. Details chosen are obvious, and the presentation has a few lapses in syntax and diction.

Rubrics for the Free-Response Essay

A high-range score (5, 6):

- Effectively and coherently addresses the nature of the transformation.
- Effectively and coherently discusses the effects of the transformation on character and meaning.
- Insightful choice of details from an appropriate novel or play.
- Differentiates between actual and symbolic transformations.
- Focuses on the results of the transformation with regard to character and theme.
- Thoroughly discusses a specific character in context.
- Strongly adheres to topic.
- Demonstrates mature writing style.

A midrange score (3, 4):

- Adequately identifies and discusses the transformation.
- Adequately addresses the transformation's effect on the character and theme.
- Results of transformation are presented with less developed discussion and/or analysis.
- Relies on obvious details to support the prompt or discussion.
- Adequately adheres to topic and uses connective tissue.
- Demonstrates some errors in syntax and diction.

Sample Student Essays

Student Essay A

In the novel <u>The Color Purple</u> by Alice Walker, the heroine, Celie, grows and develops tremendously as an individual. Throughout the course of the story, Celie undergoes major spiritual and psychological transformations. In essence, Celie is reborn. The novel's themes of the power of faith, a united sisterhood, and rebirth are all emphasized by Celie's dramatic character evolution.   5

The novel begins with Celie writing a letter to God, telling him how her father has been raping her. Only fourteen years old, Celie is naive and still somewhat immature. She doesn't understand what her father is doing to her, and even more unfortunately, she doesn't have anyone to confide in. Thus, the reader senses Celie's immense isolation as she shares her confusion with, and only with, God.   10

Celie's life takes on a turn for the worse when she is sent to live with her arranged husband, Mr.—, who beats her and doesn't appreciate her. She does all of his work for him and his children, and again she has not a friend to turn to. However, when Mr.—'s son, Harpo, marries Sophia, Celie comes into contact with another woman. Celie doesn't really understand Sophia because she is a   15
strong-willed, independent person who actually stands up to men. Thus, the reader senses the weakness in Celie's character when she advised Harpo to beat Sophia. Celie has been abused her whole life, and to her, being beaten is part of being a woman. She is totally numb to abuse; she even imagines herself to be a tree when being abused. This is her way to escape and void all feelings, to be   20
indifferent to the pain.

Naturally, she is envious of Sophia's strength and character, and so she feels a beating would do Sophia good. When Sophia discovers that it was Celie who told Harpo to beat her, she is both furious and hurt. Sophia confronts Celie, and this a pivotal point in the novel. Celie realizes that she meant enough to   25
Sophia for her to be upset, which means that Celie has actually affected another person. The two women quickly mend their relationship and begin a quilt to symbolize their friendship. This ties into the theme of sisterhood because now Celie has a friend, and the unity that the two share becomes an amazing force throughout the novel.   30

Celie's character undergoes the strongest transformation after meeting another "sister," Shug Avery. The circumstances under which Shug and Celie become friends are incredible, for Shug is Mr.—'s mistress. However, their unlikely bond is the main cause of Celie's rebirth. It was Shug who first expressed appreciation to Celie for helping her get better after a serious illness. No 35 one had ever thanked Celie before, but Shug was so gratified for her care that she wrote a song for Celie. This small act of appreciation becomes the turning point in Celie's life. She now feels she is no longer as numb as a lifeless tree.

Shug's influence leads Celie to go from being a passive victim to becoming an assertive, vibrant, independent woman. Shug was the one who makes Mr.— stop 40 beating Celie, as well as the one who found Celie's lost sister Nettie's letters which Mr.— had been hiding. Shug even inspires Celie to begin her own pants-making business, giving Celie total economic independence and creative freedom. Thus, the theme of rebirth is emphasized. Walker stresses how the human soul is an unbelievably powerful force, and how it contains the strength to emerge victorious despite adversity. 45

Shug Avery is also responsible for giving Celie a new spiritual outlook on life. She explains to Celie that God isn't necessarily an old, white-bearded man. Shug's view is that God is everything and is everywhere. The title becomes significant when Shug tells Celie that God becomes angry if you walk past the color purple in a field and don't notice it. This is a significant step in Celie's spiritual life because she now doesn't 50 feel that God is a man who is indifferent and deaf to her prayers. She has renewed her belief, and the theme of the power of faith is reinforced, for Celie's faith has remained strong.

The Color Purple is a perfect example of a work of literature where the character undergoes a dramatic transformation. Celie changes from a numb, unassertive victim to 55 being an aggressive, creative, vibrant, and independent woman. The unity of her female confidants and her unending faith allowed her to undergo such a deep transformation.

This essay is within the high-range parameters for the following reasons:

- Presents a clear, strong statement of the essay's purpose and indication of the organization of the essay.
- Presents clear, appropriate information.
- Incorporates connected meaning with every point made.
- Thoroughly presents Celie's character.
- Provides pivotal moments and details to illustrate the prompt.
- Strongly adheres to topic.
- Uses good connective tissue.
- Organization allows presentation to build chronologically and from the merely physical to the metaphysical.
- Indicates both a perceptive reading of the novel and an understanding of some of its complexities.
- Demonstrates mature manipulation of language.

This is a solid high-range essay which clearly indicates a reader who not only "got" the novel but also "got" the tasks demanded of the prompt.

Student Essay B

Set in the malevolent, shadowy era of the Cold War, Ian
McEwan's <u>The Innocent</u> centers on a fervent young Brit working for
a covert anti-Soviet intelligence agency. His youthful good nature,
manners, and naiveté are what make Leonard Marnham "the
innocent." The new threat constantly slithering around the corner is   5
the dreaded red snake of Communism, ensnaring and asphyxiating
the world with its wicked omnipotence. Leonard travails scrupulously
and surreptitiously for its willful opposition and relies on his innocence
throughout his occupation and life. When suddenly thrust into a
spiral of new and exciting, but vaguely frightening experiences exploring   10
the life he never lived, something immense in Leonard changes. This
flagrant transformation is momentous and permanent.

The most vital characterization of the protagonist is his underlying
innocence, which is repeatedly and implicitly emphasized throughout the
novel. The reader and revolving characters are drawn into Leonard's   15
ingenuousness until he chooses to walk a path unknown to him which
results in his surrendering his innocence. This transformation begins
when Leonard becomes enraptured by the discovery of his own sexuality.
He is an innocent in the purest sense of the word. Maria, his young,
German lover, uncorks a surge of forceful new sensations and emotions   20
in Leonard. This unleashing of unbridled passion allows him to give in to
urges that ultimately push him over the edge. His exploration of sexuality
brings new found masculinity and confidence. Leonard officially enters
manhood and undergoes a tremendous transformation of temperament.
His behavior is increasingly unrestrained. At a crucial turning point,   25
Leonard willfully imposes himself on Maria, ignoring all cries of distress
of his lover. It is then that the reader becomes fully aware of Leonard's
grave potential to give rein to his basest nature.

Following this traumatic incident with Maria, Leonard distinctly
apologizes and makes a conscious effort to reform himself. The two scarred   30
companions reconcile only superficially and suffer perceptible losses of
intimacy. The plot is complicated by the appearance of Maria's inebriated
and disgruntled husband who attacks Leonard. After a crushing blow to
his genitals, Leonard unleashes a shocking display of malice and murders
and mutilates his assailant.   35

When Leonard callously forces himself onto Maria, we see his
capability for harsh insensitivity, resulting in severe damage. But when
Leonard slaughters Otto, and severs all his limbs, in order to fit the body
into a suitcase, with the intent of eschewing penalty, it is all but too clear
that Leonard Marnham is no longer the shy, unripe innocent the author   40
introduced us to.

In reference to Leonard's inhumanity the author uses irony to convey the idea that human actions during this time period were largely inhumane. McEwan's assessment of humanity and essentially his thesis by writing <u>The Innocent</u> is that man is inherently evil, requiring only the slightest corruption (such as Leonard's entrance into manhood and the decadence exemplified by society) to unveil his intrinsic iniquity.

45

This essay is within the midrange parameters for the following reasons:

- Clearly understands the prompt and has a clear voice.
- Uses specifics from the text to illustrate points (paragraphs 2 and 3).
- Organization builds to a strong conclusion.
- Adheres to topic well.
- Demonstrates a willingness to stretch with regard to syntax and diction.
- Exhibits instances of awkward word choice (lines 7, 12, 37).
- Exhibits instances of awkward sentences (lines 9–11, 25–27).
- Does not provide a balanced characterization of Leonard.
- Does not provide proof of Leonard's innocence other than his sexuality.
- Veers dangerously close to plot summary.

It is obvious that this is an eager, intelligent, and thoughtful reader and writer. However, the results of the transformation on Leonard are not as fully developed as the prompt demands. It is only at the end of the essay that the transformation is connected to theme.

Appendixes

Suggesting Reading Guide
General Bibliography
Glossary
Websites

SUGGESTED READING GUIDE

As you probably know, a standard curriculum for AP Lit does not exist. Instead, teachers are urged to present material that will be appropriately challenging and enlightening while providing the opportunity for literary analysis. There are several ways of organizing the literature you study in an AP Literature and Composition course. Regardless of specifics, a broad selection of literature, covering many centuries and many styles, should be offered. Be confident that your teacher and course will meet the needs of the AP requirements.

We've developed several ways for you to reflect upon your own background. Once you have a clear overview of what you do know, you will be able to assess your particular strengths and weaknesses. You will also see the interrelationships of the literature you've studied and the commonalities and differences you will draw on to write your essays.

One approach to organizing your studies is chronological. This is the traditional survey of literature from "Beowulf to Virginia Woolf to Thomas Wolfe." This broad-based study provides you with many samples from different time periods and offers a context grounded in history. Another approach is the thematic one. Works are grouped by common ideas and are variations on a theme through time and genre. Often, it is obvious that certain works share a common sensibility. Generally, these characteristics are classified together as a literary movement. By connecting form and function, this type of reflection will broaden your understanding and analysis.

What follows is a bibliographic overview of literary movements.

Classicism

The classical writer generally exhibits or is concerned with the following:

- Universality
- Noble ideas
- Dignified language
- Restraint
- Clarity
- Objectivity
- The importance of structure
- An edifying purpose

Suggested classical works and authors:

Homer	*The Iliad, The Odyssey*
The Bible	"Genesis," "Exodus," "Matthew"
Sophocles	*Antigone, Oedipus Rex*
Euripides	*Medea*
Aristotle	"On the Nature of Tragedy"
Plato	"The Apology," "The Allegory of the Cave"

Molière	*Tartuffe, The Misanthrope*
Racine	*Phaedra*
John Milton	"L'Allegro," "Il Penseroso," "On His Blindness," *Paradise Lost* (excerpts)
Alexander Pope	"An Essay on Man," "An Essay on Criticism," "The Rape of the Lock"
Jonathan Swift	*Gulliver's Travels*
Voltaire	*Candide*

Make a list of classical works you have read: Cite title, author, and major thoughts about each.

_____

_____

_____

_____

_____

Realism

KEY IDEA

The realistic writer generally exhibits or is concerned with the following:

- Truth and actuality
- Detail
- Character portrayal
- Psychology
- Objectivity
- Lack of sentimentality

Suggested realistic works and authors:

Chaucer	*The Canterbury Tales*
Fyodor Dostoyevsky	*Crime and Punishment*
Leo Tolstoy	*Anna Karenina*
Anton Chekhov	*The Cherry Orchard*
Ernest Hemingway	*The Sun Also Rises*
Henrik Ibsen	*Hedda Gabler, A Doll's House*

Make a list of realistic works you have read: Cite title, author, and major thoughts about each.

_____

_____

_____

_____

_____

Romanticism

The romantic writer generally exhibits or is concerned with the following:

- Emotions and passion
- Imagination and wonder
- The variety and power of Nature
- The individual
- Freedom and revolution
- Dreams and idealism
- Mystery and the supernatural
- Experimentation with form
- Spontaneity

Suggested romantic prose works and authors:

Anonymous	*Beowulf*
Bocaccio	*The Decameron*
Rabelais	*Gargantua*
Cervantes	*Don Quixote*
Shakespeare	*Hamlet, King Lear*
Goethe	*Faust*
Hawthorne	*The Scarlet Letter*
Bronte	*Jane Eyre*
Hugo	*Les Miserables*

Suggested romantic poetic works and authors:

Multiple authors	The Ballads—Scottish and British
Shakespeare	Sonnets
Robert Burns	"To a Mouse," "John Anderson, My Jo," "A Red, Red, Rose"
William Blake	"A Poison Tree," "The Sick Rose," "London," "The Chimney Sweep"
William Wordsworth	"Tintern Abbey," "My Heart Leaps Up," "London, 1802," "The World Is Too Much With Us," "I Wandered Lonely as a Cloud," "Ode on Intimations of Immortality," Preface to the Lyrical Ballads
Samuel Taylor Coleridge	"Kubla Khan," "The Frost at Midnight," "The Rime of the Ancient Mariner"
Lord Byron	"Sonnet on Chillon," "When We Two Parted," "Maid of Athens," "The Isles of Greece," "She Walks in Beauty"
Percy Bysshe Shelley	"Ode to the West Wind," "To a Skylark," "Ozymandias"
John Keats	"On First Looking Into Chapman's Homer," "Ode to a Nightingale," "Ode on a Grecian Urn," "When I Have Fears That I May Cease to Be"
Alfred, Lord Tennyson	"Ulysses"
Robert Browning	"My Last Duchess," "Pippa's Song," "Soliloquy of the Spanish Cloister"

Make a list of romantic works you have read: Cite title, author, and major thoughts about each.

_____

_____

_____

_____

_____

Impressionism

The impressionist writer generally exhibits or is concerned with the following:

- Appeals to the senses
- Mood and effects
- Vagueness and ambiguity
- Momentary insights
- Impressions of setting, plot, and character
- Emphasis on color and light
- Emotions and feelings
- Sensations into words

Suggested impressionistic works and authors:

Henry James	*The American*
Joseph Conrad	*Heart of Darkness*, *The Secret Sharer*, "The Lagoon"
Katherine Mansfield	"Bliss"
Kate Chopin	"Story of an Hour," *The Awakening*

Make a list of impressionistic works you have read: Cite title, author, and major thoughts about each.

_____

_____

_____

_____

_____

Expressionism

The expressionist writer generally exhibits or is concerned with the following:

- Subjective responses
- Inner reality
- Abstract and mystical ideas

- Symbols and masks
- Man and society in chaos
- Creation of new worlds

Suggested expressionistic works and authors:

James Joyce	*Dubliners*
Eugene O'Neill	*Desire Under the Elms, The Hairy Ape, The Iceman Cometh*
T. S. Eliot	"The Hollow Men," "The Love Song of J. Alfred Prufrock"
Franz Kafka	*Metamorphosis, The Trial*

Make a list of expressionistic works you have read: Cite title, author, and major thoughts about each.

_____

_____

_____

_____

_____

_____

Naturalism

The naturalist writer generally exhibits or is concerned with the following:

- Realism to its extreme
- Fact and detail
- Social awareness and reform
- A broad spectrum of subjects, both positive and negative
- Man as animal in society
- Scientific impartiality

Suggested naturalistic works and authors:

Tennessee Williams	*A Streetcar Named Desire, Cat on a Hot Tin Roof*
Frank Norris	*The Octopus*
Stephen Crane	*Maggie, A Girl of the Streets*
Upton Sinclair	*The Jungle*

Make a list of naturalistic works you have read: Cite title, author, and major thoughts about each.

_____

_____

_____

_____

_____

A note about literary movements: These are the movements you will find emphasized in the Western canon of literature. However, be aware that there are other literary movements that are currently recognized. Among them are the:

- Symbolist—an outgrowth of romanticism
- Existentialist—concern with man's alienation
- Absurdist—takes existentialism one step further into the realm of fractured reality
- Magical realism—modern genre that moves between the objective world and the world of fantasy

GENERAL BIBLIOGRAPHY

Recommended Poets

In addition to those referred to throughout this book, the following poets are representative of the poets you will encounter on the exam.

Matthew Arnold

W. H. Auden

Elizabeth Bishop

Gwendolyn Brooks

Billy Collins

e. e. cummings

T. S. Eliot

Lawrence Ferlinghetti

Robert Francis

Robert Graves

Donald Hall

Seamus Heaney

Galway Kinnell

Maxine Kumin

Pablo Neruda

Sharon Olds

Wilfred Owen

Linda Pastan

Edna St. Vincent Millay

May Swenson

Dylan Thomas

Recommended Authors

Chinua Achebe: *Things Fall Apart*

Aeschylus: *Oresteia*

Margaret Atwood: *The Handmaid's Tale*

Jane Austen: *Pride and Prejudice, Sense and Sensibility*

James Baldwin: *Go Tell It on the Mountain*

Saul Bellow: *The Adventures of Augie March*

Charlotte Bronte: *Jane Eyre*

Emily Bronte: *Wuthering Heights*

Albert Camus: *The Stranger*

Willa Cather: *My Antonia, One of Ours, Death Comes to the Archbishop*

Anton Chekhov: *The Cherry Orchard*

Kate Chopin: *The Awakening*

Sandra Cisneros: *The House on Mango Street*

Joseph Conrad: *Heart of Darkness, Lord Jim, The Secret Sharer*

Stephen Crane: *The Red Badge of Courage*

Don Delillo: *White Noise*

Charles Dickens: *Great Expectations, A Tale of Two Cities*

Isak Dinesen: *Out of Africa*

Fyodor Dostoyevsky: *Crime and Punishment*

Theodore Dreiser: *An American Tragedy, Sister Carrie*

George Eliot: *Silas Marner, Middlemarch*
Ralph Ellison: *Invisible Man*
Euripides: *Medea*
William Faulkner: *As I Lay Dying, The Sound and the Fury*
Henry Fielding: *Tom Jones*
F. Scott Fitzgerald: *The Great Gatsby*
Gustave Flaubert: *Madame Bovary*
E. M. Forster: *A Passage to India*
Thomas Hardy: *Jude the Obscure, Tess of the D'Urbervilles*
Nathaniel Hawthorne: *The Scarlet Letter*
Joseph Heller: *Catch-22*
Ernest Hemingway: *The Sun Also Rises*
Homer: *The Iliad, The Odyssey*
Khaled Hosseini: *The Kite Runner*
Zora Neale Hurston: *Their Eyes Were Watching God*
Aldous Huxley: *Brave New World*
Henrik Ibsen: *A Doll's House, Ghosts, Hedda Gabler*
Kazuo Ishiguro: *The Remains of the Day*
Henry James: *The Turn of the Screw, The American*
James Joyce: *A Portrait of the Artist as a Young Man, Dubliners*
Franz Kafka: *Metamorphosis, The Trial*
Ken Kesey: *One Flew Over the Cuckoo's Nest*
Maxine Hong Kingston: *The Woman Warrior*
D. H. Lawrence: *Sons and Lovers*
Gabriel García Márquez: *One Hundred Years of Solitude*
Herman Melville: *Moby-Dick, Billy Budd*
Arthur Miller: *Death of a Salesman, The Crucible*
Toni Morrison: *Beloved, Song of Solomon*
V. S. Naipaul: *A Bend in the River*
Tim O'Brien: *The Things They Carried*
Eugene O'Neill: *Desire Under the Elms, Long Day's Journey into Night*
George Orwell: *1984*
Alan Paton: *Cry, the Beloved Country*
Jean Rhys: *Wide Sargasso Sea*
Jean Paul Sartre: *No Exit, Nausea*
William Shakespeare: *Hamlet, King Lear, Macbeth, Othello, Twelfth Night*
George Bernard Shaw: *Major Barbara, Man and Superman, Pygmalion*
Mary Shelley: *Frankenstein*
Sophocles: *Antigone, Oedipus Rex*
John Steinbeck: *The Grapes of Wrath, Of Mice and Men, Cannery Row*
Tom Stoppard: *Rosencrantz and Guildenstern Are Dead*
Jonathan Swift: *Gulliver's Travels*
Amy Tan: *The Kitchen God's Wife*
Leo Tolstoy: *Anna Karenina*
Mark Twain: *Adventures of Huckleberry Finn*
John Updike: *Rabbit Run*
Voltaire: *Candide*
Kurt Vonnegut: *Slaughterhouse-Five*
Alice Walker: *The Color Purple*

Edith Wharton: *Ethan Frome, The House of Mirth*
Oscar Wilde: *The Importance of Being Earnest*
Thornton Wilder: *Our Town*
Tennessee Williams: *A Streetcar Named Desire, The Glass Menagerie*
Virginia Woolf: *To the Lighthouse*
Richard Wright: *Native Son*

allegory A work that functions on a symbolic level.

alliteration The repetition of initial consonant sounds, such as "Peter Piper picked a peck of pickled peppers."

allusion A reference contained in a work.

anapest A metrical pattern of two unaccented syllables followed by an accented syllable (˘ ˘ ´).

antagonist The force or character that opposes the main character, the protagonist.

annotation To make personal notes on a text in order to get a better understanding of the material. These notes can include questions, an argument with the author acknowledging a good point, a clarification of an idea, theme, etc.

apostrophe Direct address in poetry. Yeats's line "Be with me Beauty, for the fire is dying" is a good example.

aside Words spoken by an actor intended to be heard by the audience but not by other characters on stage.

aubade A love poem set at dawn which bids farewell to the beloved.

ballad A simple narrative poem, often incorporating dialogue that is written in quatrains, generally with a rhyme scheme of *a b c d*.

blank verse Unrhymed iambic pentameter. Most of Shakespeare's plays are in this form.

cacophony Harsh and discordant sounds in a line or passage of a literary work.

caesura A break or pause within a line of poetry indicated by punctuation and used to emphasize meaning.

catharsis According to Aristotle, the release of emotion that the audience of a tragedy experiences.

character One who carries out the action of the plot in literature. Major, minor, static, and dynamic are types of characters.

climax The turning point of action or character in a literary work, usually the highest moment of tension.

comic relief The inclusion of a humorous character or scene to contrast with the tragic elements of a work, thereby intensifying the next tragic event.

conflict A clash between opposing forces in a literary work, such as man vs. man; man vs. nature; man vs. God; man vs. self.

connotation The interpretive level of a word based on its associated images rather than its literal meaning.

convention A traditional aspect of a literary work, such as a soliloquy in a Shakespearean play or a tragic hero in a Greek tragedy.

couplet Two lines of rhyming poetry; often used by Shakespeare to conclude a scene or an important passage.

dactyl A foot of poetry consisting of a stressed syllable followed by two unstressed syllables, (´ ˘ ˘).

denotation The literal or dictionary meaning of a word.

denouement The conclusion or tying up of loose ends in a literary work; the resolution of the conflict and plot.

deus ex machina A Greek invention, literally "the god from the machine" who appears at the last moment and resolves the loose ends of a play. Today, the term refers to anyone, usually of some stature, who untangles, resolves, or reveals the key to the plot of a work. See the conclusion of Euripides's *Medea* for an example or the sheriff at the end of *Desire Under the Elms* by O'Neill.

diction The author's choice of words.

dramatic monologue A type of poem that presents a conversation between a speaker and an implied listener. Browning's "My Last Duchess" is a perfect example.

elegy A poem that laments the dead or a loss. "Elegy for Jane" by Roethke is a specific example. Gray's "Elegy in a Country Church Yard" is a general example.

enjambment A technique in poetry that involves the running on of a line or stanza. It enables the poem to move and to develop coherence as well as directing the reader with regard to form and meaning. Walt Whitman uses this continually.

epic A lengthy, elevated poem that celebrates the exploits of a hero. *Beowulf* is a prime example.

epigram A brief witty poem. Pope often utilizes this form for satiric commentary.

euphony The pleasant, mellifluous presentation of sounds in a literary work.

exposition Background information presented in a literary work.

fable A simple, symbolic story, usually employing animals as characters. Aesop and La Fontaine are authors who excel at this form.

figurative language The body of devices that enables the writer to operate on levels other than the literal one. It includes metaphor, simile, symbol, motif, hyperbole, and others discussed in Chapter 8.

flashback A device that enables a writer to refer to past thoughts, events, episodes.

foot A metrical unit in poetry; a syllabic measure of a line: iamb, trochee, anapest, dactyl, and spondee.

foreshadowing Hints of future events in a literary work.

form The shape or structure of a literary work.

free verse Poetry without a defined form, meter, or rhyme scheme.

hyperbole Extreme exaggeration. In "My Love is Like a Red, Red Rose," Burns speaks of loving "until all the seas run dry."

iamb A metrical foot consisting of an unaccented syllable followed by an accented one; the most common poetic foot in the English language, (˘ ´).

idyll A type of lyric poem which extols the virtues of an ideal place or time.

image A verbal approximation of a sensory impression, concept, or emotion.

imagery The total effect of related sensory images in a work of literature.

impressionism Writing that reflects a personal image of a character, event, or concept. *The Secret Sharer* is a fine example.

irony An unexpected twist or contrast between what happens and what was intended or expected to happen. It involves dialogue and situation, and it can be intentional or unplanned. Dramatic irony centers around the ignorance of those involved while the audience is aware of the circumstance.

lyric poetry A type of poetry characterized by emotion, personal feelings, and brevity; a large and inclusive category of poetry that exhibits rhyme, meter, and reflective thought.

magical realism A type of literature that explores narratives by and about characters who inhabit and experience their reality differently from what we term the objective world. Writers who are frequently placed in this category include Gabriel García Márquez, Günter Grass, and Isabel A llende.

metaphor A direct comparison between dissimilar things. "Your eyes are stars" is an example.

metaphysical poetry Refers to the work of poets like John Donne who explore highly complex, philosophical ideas through extended metaphors and paradox.

meter A pattern of beats in poetry. (Answers to questions in poetry review: 5, 3, 2, 2, 4)

metonymy A figure of speech in which a representative term is used for a larger idea. ("The pen is mightier than the sword.")

monologue A speech given by one character. (Hamlet's "To be or not to be . . . ")

motif The repetition or variations of an image or idea in a work which is used to develop theme or characters.

narrative poem A poem that tells a story.

narrator The speaker of a literary work.

octave An eight-line stanza, usually combined with a sestet in a Petrarchan sonnet.

ode A formal, lengthy poem that celebrates a particular subject.

onomatopoeia Words that sound like the sound they represent (hiss, gurgle, bang).

oxymoron An image of contradictory terms (bittersweet, pretty ugly, giant economy size).

parable A story that operates on more than one level and usually teaches a moral lesson. (*The Pearl* by John Steinbeck is a fine example. See *Allegory*.)

paradox A set of seemingly contradictory elements which nevertheless reflects an underlying truth. For example, in Shakespeare's *Much Ado About Nothing*, the Friar says to Hero, "Come, Lady, die to live."

parallel plot A secondary story line that mimics and reinforces the main plot. (Hamlet loses his father, as does Ophelia.)

parody A comic imitation of a work that ridicules the original.

pathos The aspects of a literary work that elicit pity from the audience.

personification The assigning of human qualities to inanimate objects or concepts. (Wordsworth personifies "the sea that bares her bosom to the moon" in the poem "London, 1802.")

plot A sequence of events in a literary work.

point of view The method of narration in a work.

protagonist The hero or main character of a literary work, the character the audience sympathizes with.

quatrain A four-line stanza.

resolution The denouement of a literary work.

rhetorical question A question that does not expect an explicit answer. It is used to pose an idea to be considered by the speaker or audience.

rhyme/rime The duplication of final syllable sounds in two or more lines.

rhyme scheme The annotation of the pattern of the rhyme.

rhythm The repetitive pattern of beats in poetry.

romanticism A style or movement of literature that has as its foundation an interest in freedom, adventure, idealism, and escape.

satire A mode of writing based on ridicule, which criticizes the foibles and follies of society without necessarily offering a solution. (Jonathan Swift's *Gulliver's Travels* is a great satire that exposes mankind's condition.)

scansion Analysis of a poem's rhyme and meter.

sestet A six-line stanza, usually paired with an octave to form a Petrarchan sonnet.

sestina A highly structured poetic form of 39 lines, written in iambic pentameter. It depends upon the repetition of six words from the first stanza in each of six stanzas.

setting The time and place of a literary work.

simile An indirect comparison that uses the word, "like" or "as" to link the differing items in the comparison. ("Your eyes are like stars.")

soliloquy A speech in a play which is used to reveal the character's inner thoughts to the audience. (Hamlet's "To be or not to be . . . " is one of the most famous soliloquies in literature.)

sonnet A 14-line poem with a prescribed rhyme scheme in iambic pentameter. (See Chapter 9 for a comparison between Shakespearean and Petrarchan sonnets.)

spondee A poetic foot consisting of two accented syllables (´ ´).

stage directions The specific instructions a playwright includes concerning sets, characterization, delivery, etc. (*See Hedda Gabler* by Ibsen.)

stanza A unit of a poem, similar in rhyme, meter, and length to other units in the poem.

structure The organization and form of a work.

style The unique way an author presents his ideas. Diction, syntax, imagery, structure, and content all contribute to a particular style.

subplot A secondary plot that explores ideas different from the main storyline. (In *Hamlet*, the main storyline has Hamlet avenging the death of his father. The subplot has Hamlet dealing with his love for Ophelia.)

subtext Implied meaning of a work or section of a work.

symbol Something in a literary work that stands for something else. (Plato has the light of the sun symbolize truth in "The Allegory of the Cave.")

synecdoche A figure of speech that utilizes a part as representative of the whole. ("All hands on deck" is an example.)

syntax The grammatical structure of prose and poetry.

tercet A three-line stanza.

theme The underlying ideas that the author illustrates through characterization, motifs, language, plot, etc.

tone The author's attitude toward his subject.

tragic hero According to Aristotle, a basically good person of noble birth or exalted position who has a fatal flaw or commits an error in judgment which leads to his downfall. The tragic hero must have a moment of realization and live and suffer.

trochee A single metrical foot consisting of one accented (stressed/long) syllable followed by one unaccented (unstressed/short) syllable (´ ˘).

understatement The opposite of exaggeration. It is a technique for developing irony and/or humor where one writes or says less than intended.

villanelle A highly structured poetic form that comprises six stanzas: five tercets and a quatrain. The poem repeats the first and third lines throughout.

WEBSITES

There are literally thousands of sites on the Internet that are in some way related to the study of college-level English. We are not attempting to give you a comprehensive list of all of these websites. What we are going to do is to provide you with a list that is most relevant to your preparation and review for the AP Literature and Composition exam. It is up to you to log on to a site that may be of interest to you and to see for yourself just what it can offer and whether or not it will be of specific benefit to you. Don't forget that you have a dedicated AP website from McGraw-Hill that can be of great help to you as you work your way through the AP English Literature course and as you prepare for the exam in May. Go to The Cross-Platform Prep Course: www.xplatform.mhprofessional.com and enter your access code printed on the back cover.

> *Note:* These websites were available and online at the time this book was revised. Please be aware that we cannot guarantee that a site you choose to explore will be operating when you go to that URL.

Because this is an Advanced Placement exam for which you are preparing, why not go to the source as your first choice? The College Board's AP site is called AP Central:

- **http://www.collegeboard.com/apc**

Related to British Literature:

- Romanticism: **http://www.uh.edu/engines/romanticism/poets.html**
- British history: **http://www.bbc.co.uk/history**
- Study guide: **http://www.studyguide.org/brit_lit_timeline.htm**
- Ultimate Shakespeare site: **http://playshakespeare.com**

Related to American Literature:

- Authors, timelines, literary movements: **http://public.wsu.edu/~campbelld/amlit/sites.htm**
- Literature: Voice of the Shuttle: **http://vos.ucsb.edu**

Of General Interest:

- Purdue Online Writing Lab: **http://owl.english.purdue.edu**
- For links to other websites for English literature: **http://www.kn.att.com/wired/fil/pages/listaplitma.html**
- For terms, exercises, tips, and rules from a primate with attitude, go to Grammar Bytes: **http://chompchomp.com**
- For help with rhetorical and literary terms, there are three useful sites: **http://mcl.as.uky.edu/glossary-rhetorical-terms**, **http://andromeda.rutgers.edu/~jlynch/Terms/**, and **http://humanities.byu.edu/rhetoric/**

- For access to the world of arts and letters, including newspapers, literary magazines, and blogs: **http://artsandlettersdaily.com**
- To download free e-books: **www.bartleby.com**
- For a directory to free downloadable e-books as well as articles, reviews, and comments: **www.e-booksdirectory.com**
- For WebNotes, a useful tool that allows you to compile and organize information from multiple Web pages and share findings: **www.webnotes.net**

Each of these websites will lead you to many more. You will have to take the time to explore the various sites and to make your own evaluation as to their value to you and your expectations.

We suggest you use your favorite Web server or search engine and type in ADVANCED PLACEMENT ENGLISH (AP), or ADVANCED PLACEMENT (AP) LITER ATURE. (Our favorite search engine is www.google.com.) From that point on, you can "surf the net" for those sites that suit your particular needs. You will have to take the time to explore these various domains and to make your own evaluation of their value to you and your expectations. Perhaps, you might even decide to set up your own AP Lit website or chat room.

NOTES

NOTES

NOTES

NOTES

NOTES

The Cross-Platform Prep Course

McGraw-Hill Education's multi-platform course gives you a variety of tools to help you raise your test scores. Whether you're studying at home, in the library, or on-the-go, you can find practice content in the format you need—print, online, or mobile.

Print Book

This print book gives you the tools you need to ace the test. In its pages you'll find smart test-taking strategies, in-depth reviews of key topics, and ample practice questions and tests. See the Welcome section of your book for a step-by-step guide to its features.

Online Platform

The Cross-Platform Prep Course gives you additional study and practice content that you can access *anytime, anywhere*. You can create a personalized study plan based on your test date that sets daily goals to keep you on track. Integrated lessons provide important review of key topics. Practice questions, exams, and flashcards give you the practice you need to build test-taking confidence. The game center is filled with challenging games that allow you to practice your new skills in a fun and engaging way. And, you can even interact with other test-takers in the discussion section and gain valuable peer support.

Getting Started

To get started, open your account on the online platform:

Go to www.xplatform.mhprofessional.com

↓

Enter your access code, which you can find on the inside back cover of your book

↓

Provide your name and e-mail address to open your account and create a password

↓

Click "Start Studying" to enter the platform

It's as simple as that. You're ready to start studying online.

Your Personalized Study Plan

First, select your test date on the calendar, and you'll be on your way to creating your personalized study plan. Your study plan will help you stay organized and on track and will guide you through the course in the most efficient way. It is tailored to *your* schedule and features daily tasks that are broken down into manageable goals. You can adjust your test date at any time and your daily tasks will be reorganized into an updated plan.

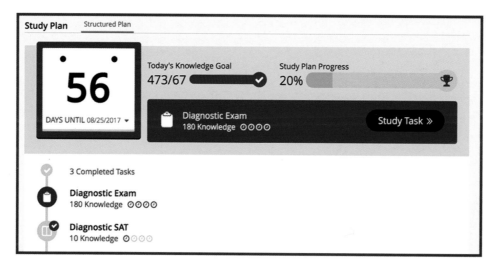

You can track your progress in real time on the Study Plan Dashboard. The "Today's Knowledge Goal" progress bar gives you up-to-the minute feedback on your daily goal. Fulfilling this every time you log on is the most efficient way to work through the entire course. You always get an instant view of where you stand in the entire course with the Study Plan Progress bar.

If you need to exit the program before completing a task, you can return to the Study Plan Dashboard at any time. Just click the Study Task icon and you can automatically pick up where you left off.

Practice Tests

One of the first tasks in your personalized study plan is to take the Diagnostic Test. At the end of the test, a detailed evaluation of your strengths and weaknesses shows the areas where you need the most focus. You can review your practice test results either by the question category to see broad trends or question-by-question for a more in-depth look.

The full-length tests are designed to simulate the real thing. Try to simulate actual testing conditions and be sure you set aside enough time to complete the full-length test. You'll learn to pace yourself so that you can work toward the best possible score on test day.

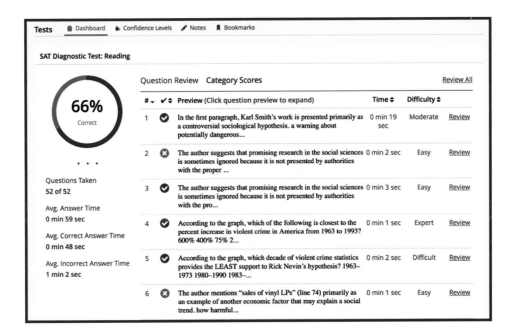

Lessons

The lessons in the online platform are divided into manageable pieces that let you build knowledge and confidence in a progressive way. They cover the full range of topics that you're likely to see on your test.

After you complete a lesson, mark your confidence level. (You must indicate a confidence level in order to count your progress and move on to the next task.) You can also filter the lessons by confidence levels to see the areas you have mastered and those that you might need to revisit.

> *Use the bookmark feature to easily refer back to a concept or leave a note to remember your thoughts or questions about a particular topic.*

Practice Questions

All of the practice questions are reflective of actual exams and simulate the test-taking experience. The "Review Answer" button gives you immediate feedback on your answer. Each question includes a rationale that explains why the correct answer is right and the others are wrong. To explore any topic further, you can find detailed explanations by clicking the "Help me learn about this topic" link.

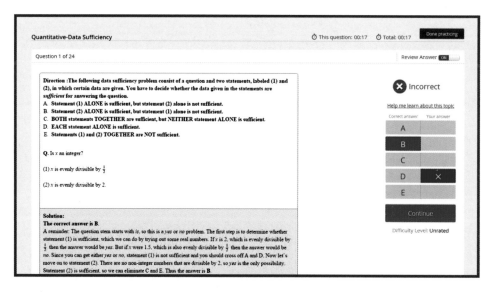

You can go to the Practice Dashboard to find an overview of your performance in the different categories and sub-categories.

Dashboard

The dashboard is constantly updating to reflect your progress and performance. The Percentile Rank icon shows your position relative to all the other students enrolled in the course. You can also find information on your average scores in practice questions and exams.

A detailed overview of your strengths and weaknesses shows your proficiency in a category based on your answers and difficulty of the questions. By viewing your strengths and weaknesses, you can focus your study on areas where you need the most help.

Flashcards

The hundreds of flashcards are perfect for learning key terms quickly, and the interactive format gives you immediate feedback. You can filter the cards by category and confidence level for a more organized approach. Or, you can shuffle them up for a more general challenge.

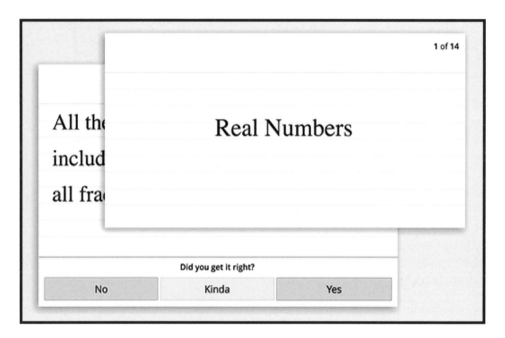

Another way to customize the flashcards is to create your own sets. You can either keep these private or share or them with the public. Subscribe to Community Sets to access sets from other students preparing for the same exam.

Game Center

Play a game in the Game Center to test your knowledge of key concepts in a challenging but fun environment. Increase the difficulty level and complete the games quickly to build your highest score. Be sure to check the leaderboard to see who's on top!

Social Community

Interact with other students who are preparing for the same test. Start a discussion, reply to a post, or even upload files to share. You can search the archives for common topics or start your own private discussion with friends.

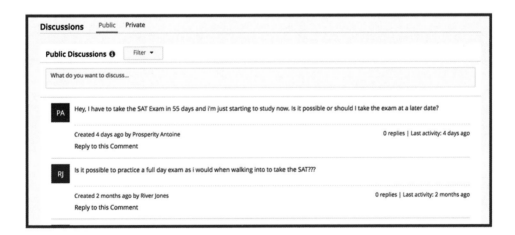

Mobile App

The companion mobile app lets you toggle between the online platform and your mobile device without missing a beat. Whether you access the course online or from your smartphone or tablet, you'll pick up exactly where you left off.

Go to the iTunes or Google Play stores and search "McGraw-Hill Education Cross-Platform App" to download the companion iOS or Android app. Enter your e-mail address and the same password you created for the online platform to open your account.

Now, let's get started!